Voluntary Associations

Perspectives on the Literature

Voluntary Associations

Perspectives on the Literature

by Constance Smith and Anne Freedman

Harvard University Press   Cambridge, Massachusetts   1972

Preface

Americans of all ages, all conditions, and all dispositions constantly form associations. They have not only commercial and manufacturing companies, in which all take part, but associations of a thousand other kinds, religious, moral, serious, futile, general or restricted, enormous or diminutive. The Americans make associations to give entertainments, to found seminaries, to build inns, to construct churches, to diffuse books, to send missionaries to the antipodes; in this manner they found hospitals, prisons, and schools. If it is proposed to inculcate some truth or to foster some feeling by the encouragement of a great example, they form a society. Wherever at the head of some new undertaking you see the government in France, or a man of rank in England, in the United States you will be sure to find an association.

Alexis de Tocqueville, *Democracy in America*, II, 106

Voluntary associations have been part of the American scene from the founding of the nation to the present. The American penchant for turning to voluntary action as a solution to social, political, and personal problems has, if anything, probably intensified since Tocqueville made his observations in the first part of the nineteenth century. There even appears to have been something of a resurgence of interest in voluntarism in the few years since we began our research in the early 1960s. At that time the image of the volunteer was somewhat tarnished and "voluntary association" frequently suggested lodges with outdated rituals, complacent businessmen at Rotary luncheons, and women in fussy hats at garden club meetings. Indeed, lodges and luncheon clubs were experiencing a decline, from which some of them only now seem to be recovering, and many women were turning from their volunteer work to paid jobs, with a resulting decrease in the strength of women's clubs.

However, even in the Kennedy years, voluntarism was taking on new life in the initial success of the Peace Corps, which was the first of a growing number of government sponsored organizations employing volunteers. Under Nixon, an Office of Voluntary Action has been established within the Department of Housing, along with a privately sponsored but closely related National Center for Voluntary Action, to encourage this trend.

The government was, however, far from alone in rediscovering the values of voluntary group action. Social scientists and social philosophers advocated the formation of voluntary groups, while students, blacks, conservationists, feminists, and welfare mothers all employed the voluntary association as a tool in their various struggles. Their goals and rhetoric may at times have been radical, but their weapon — the voluntary organization — was very much within the American tradition.

This report on what we know about voluntary associations and their functions in the lives of individuals and social systems grew out of Constance Smith's lifetime concerns as a political scientist with the viability of democratic institutions and as a professional woman with the role of educated women in the modern social system. She became interested in voluntary organizations because they appeared to her to be important components of the democratic polity as well as a major outlet for the talent and energies of women. Under her direction, the Radcliffe Institute sponsored a variety of projects dealing with the voluntary association. Studies were made of the Institute's scholars and of other groups of educated women which included analysis of the subjects' volunteer activities. *The Next Step*, the Institute's publication on part-time opportunities for women, deals at length with the volunteer career. When I arrived in Cambridge as a new PhD in political science, Connie, who had been one of my professors when I was an undergraduate at Douglass College, put me to work in the libraries of Harvard University on an extensive search of the existing literature on voluntarism.

It very quickly became obvious that the field was in great disarray and that scholars were proceeding in ignorance of each other's efforts. We decided that we could perform a service for the Institute and for other scholars by providing a guide to the literature. The present bibliographic essay resulted from that decision. It was to have been followed by a more theoretical piece in which we would attempt to develop a theory, or at least a frame of reference, to give focus to our own anticipated field research. However, the progress of this book was considerably slowed, and plans for future collaborative theory building and data gathering efforts laid aside, when Connie became ill. She continued to work on the manuscript as much as her ebbing strength allowed and retained her active interest in the project until her death from cancer at the age of forty-eight in November 1970.

For the most part, we have dealt with the scholarly literature produced by academicians rather than the journalistic accounts of organizational activities or the voluminous material printed by organizations for their memberships. Gathering and reviewing this latter type of material would have been an overwhelming task. Almost every organization has at least one regular publication which is sent to the members, and many also issue reports and studies of various types. Some associations have even commissioned organization histories, usually having them published privately.

Since studies of voluntary associations are widely scattered in the literature of several disciplines, we cannot be certain that we have examined all of the available material; but our search has been thorough, and we believe that this bibliography is an accurate guide to the existing literature. It is intended to serve others as a tool and a foundation for further research. We have tried to organize the material into major sub-areas of interest, but we have not provided a conceptual framework of our own. We had originally intended to organize the findings of other students of voluntary associations into a theoretically oriented propositional inventory, but abandoned this goal as premature when we became aware of the state of the research. For the most part, the field is still undeveloped and the available information is scanty. Much of the data have been gathered unsystematically, and are in too crude a state for careful secondary analysis. We believe it would be misleading to place inexact and sometimes unreliable information into exact pigeonholes, or to use language and concepts which would give a greater aura of validity to the data than we felt was warranted. In fact, we found it was even impossible to strictly adhere to our definition of a voluntary organization, since to do so would have resulted in omitting some important studies and data which were based on slightly different concepts of the voluntary organization. In particular, a number of studies lump voluntary associations into a single category with other kinds of organizations, especially churches and unions. We therefore included these studies, but for clarity have indicated which works employ concepts at variance from our own.

In order to facilitate comparability with the bulk of the work in the field, we adopted the definition of voluntary associations as "organizations that people belong to part time and without pay, such as clubs, lodges, good-works agencies and the like" which appears in Berelson and Steiner's widely known inventory of social science findings, *Human Behavior* (p. 364). A similar definition of voluntary associations as "spare-time, participatory associations" can be found in David Sills' authoritative article on "Voluntary Associations" in the 1968 edition of the *International Encyclopedia of the Social Sciences* (16:363).

The voluntary organization then is a nonprofit, nongovernment, private group which an individual joins by choice. Members are not born into such associations as they are into the family or the church, nor drafted into them as in the case with the military, nor are they required to join in order to make a living as is frequently true of unions and professional groups. Business and trade associations, adjuncts to profit making institutions, do not precisely qualify as voluntary associations either, although they do at times have some of the features of voluntary organizations. Political parties and related political clubs, which differ in both function and legal status from voluntary associations, are also excluded. Finally, it should be noted that our interest is in structured, formally organized, relatively permanent, secondary groupings as opposed to less structured, informal, ephemeral, or primary groupings. A formal organization is identified by the presence of offices which are filled through some established procedure; periodic, scheduled meetings; qualifying criteria for membership; and some formalized division and specialization of labor, although the organizations do not necessarily exhibit all of these characteristics to the same degree. Secondary associations may include informal, primary groups within them; but they are not themselves intimate, personal "face-to-face" groups.

We believe that our conception as outlined above is in accord with the dominant usage in the social sciences. Raymond Morris, in a 1965 review of British and American research on voluntary associations, also defines them as "groups in which membership is in no sense obligatory, which have a formal constitution," but do not have paid officials at the local level. Moreover, Morris excludes churches, labor unions, small primary or laboratory groups, and political pressure groups operating at the national level, in order to conform to general usage (pp. 186–187). Similarly, David Sills specifically excludes from consideration in his Encyclopedia essay on "Voluntary Associations" organizations whose major activity is related to the "business of making a living" and those in which the volunteer members are in a minority compared to employees or other participants (16:363).

Our discussion of the literature on voluntary associations is divided into eight chapters, each of which concludes with a bibliography listing both the works cited in the chapter and other works not specifically dealt with in the text, but related to the subject matter of the chapter. Some of the entries are annotated, and some are listed in more than one chapter bibliography although we tried to avoid duplication as much as possible.

The first chapter of the essay deals with the classificatory schemes which have been suggested by students of voluntary associations; with general discussions of voluntarism including those of historical character; and with the theories which have been advanced concerning the origins, growth, and functions of voluntary associations. The second and third chapters are devoted to theoretical works related to the political role of voluntary associations. The second chapter is largely focused on the writings of pluralists and the third on recent critics of pluralism and the response of pluralists to their attacks. The fourth chapter deals with empirical studies of the political relevance of voluntary organizations. Chapters five and six are both concerned with sociological studies of voluntarism. The fifth chapter deals with general discussions of voluntary associations and with the variety of survey material available including those of national and cross-cultural scope as well as more limited efforts. In the sixth chapter, studies which focus on the variables of social class, race, and ethnicity in relation to voluntary organizations are discussed. Community studies and a number of other works dealing with miscellaneous sociological and psychological factors are also considered. The seventh chapter covers material focusing on traditional voluntary associations. The eighth deals with volunteer work within such institutional settings as government agencies and social welfare organizations.

The authors are, of course, responsible for the contents of this book, but there are a number of people who helped at various stages in its production. The staff of the Radcliffe Institute, particularly the present Dean, Alice Smith, and Doris Lorentzen, Administrative Assistant, have been involved in this project from its beginning and have been most helpful, as has the President of Radcliffe, Mary I. Bunting. I would also like to thank Clifford Mitchell, Randy Wisener, and Richard

Fritz, who served as my research assistants at various points; James Luther Adams, David Horton Smith, Nicholas Babchuk, and Violet Seider, who provided me with materials from their files; and finally, my extremely patient and understanding husband, Philip Freedman.

Anne Freedman
Roosevelt University
Chicago, December 1971

Contents

Voluntary Associations

Perspectives on the Literature

Chapter One   A Theoretical Overview

The term "theory" has to be applied to the study of voluntary associations with care, since very little theory, in any strict sense of the word, has yet been developed in the field. There is no grand, all encompassing, and generally accepted theory of voluntarism, or even a respectable middle-range theory. For the most part, one finds a series of largely unrelated hypotheses dealing with various aspects of voluntary associations and with participation in them. This state of affairs seems to reflect the general feeling among scholars that the study of associations does not comprise a separate field with its own distinguishing concepts and orientation. Instead, the psychologist uses the tools and concepts of his discipline to explain the psychological dimensions of associational functioning through his distinctive frame of reference, and so on. Nicholas Babchuk and Charles K. Warriner, writing an introduction to the Spring 1965 issue of *Sociological Inquiry* devoted to the analysis of voluntary associations, pointed out that the study of voluntary organizations involves at least three concerns: that of the sociologist with the functions of voluntary associations in the social system; that of the social psychologist with voluntary associations as an environment of individual persons; and that of the student of administration with the organizational processes of voluntary associations. Scholars from all of the disciplines cited have evidenced an interest in the phenomenon of participation.

This chapter will be devoted to an overall introduction to the major hypotheses advanced concerning voluntary associations, with the exception of those dealing with the political aspects of voluntary organizations which are treated in the second, third, and fourth chapters.

Although the dividing line between this chapter and the ones that follow is necessarily somewhat arbitrary, in general we have tried to reserve this chapter for "theory" and to leave material which is primarily devoted to reporting data to other chapters.

TYPOLOGIES AND FRAMES OF REFERENCE

In their attempt to understand the nature and role of voluntary associations, scholars have developed a number of classificatory schemes. Although these typologies or frames of reference are not "theory" in any but the loosest sense of the term, they do represent the initial steps and building blocks of theory construction.

Organizations have been classified on the basis of their size, their internal political structure, their independence of or dependence on outside control, their societal functions, the source of their support, their location, the class and other characteristics of their members, and the intimacy of contact among members. All of these classification schemes — none of which seems wholly satisfactory — draw on the concepts of other disciplines.

For example, the influence of Chester Barnard's pioneering theory of organization and management is evident in an article by Peter B. Clark and James Q. Wilson which appeared in the *Administrative Science Quarterly*, 1961. Clark and Wilson classify organizations on the basis of the incentives — material, solidary, or purposive — which are offered to individuals as an inducement to contribute their activity to the group. Although voluntary organizations offer all three kinds of incentives to members, Clark and Wilson believe the distinguishing feature of the voluntary association is its reliance on solidary incentives such as sociability, fun, and prestige.

Peter Blau and Richard Scott, who also work within the field of public administration, have divided formal organizations, including voluntary organizations, into four types according to the beneficiary of the association's activities. In "mutual-benefit associations" the prime beneficiary is the membership; in "service organizations" it is the client; in "common-wealth" organizations it is the public-at-large; and in business concerns, the owners. In addition to their own typology Blau and Scott's book on *Formal Organizations: A Comparative Approach* also provides a useful review of the various other typologies of formal organizations which have appeared in the sociological literature. However, like most students of public administration the authors are primarily concerned with business and government bureaucracies and with the organization as an abstract type rather than with voluntary associations. Because of this, their book is somewhat peripheral to the concerns of the student of voluntary organizations.

Since sociologists have evidenced more interest in voluntary associations than members of other disciplines, most of the typologies we discovered have a sociological orientation. Many sociologists have employed a functional approach to the analysis and classification of voluntary associations. For example, Sherwood Fox, in his dissertation on "Voluntary Associations and Social Structure," defines voluntary associations as private, nonprofit organizations not engaged directly in any activities that are functional prerequisites for the on-going social system, that is, not directly producing goods or supplying a service. He distinguishes three types of voluntary associations: majoral, minoral, and medial. Majoral associations, such as business, professional, scientific, educational, labor, and agricultural organizations, serve the interest of the major institutions of society. Minoral associations, such as ethnic, racial, cultural, women's, and church organizations, serve the interests of significant minorities in the population. Medial organizations, such as veterans' groups and social service organizations, mediate between major segments of the society. In Fox's view, voluntary associations function as "interstitial" social mechanisms, filling in the gaps between the major institutions of society and easing the strains of the system. Fox also maintains that the importance of an association is positively correlated with its degree of integration with the major institutions of society (pp. 357–364). Most of his dissertation is devoted to business and trade associations, which are highly important given his criteria. Since his work is therefore largely concerned with organizations which do not qualify as voluntary associations in terms of our definition, Fox's study is not as valuable to the student of voluntarism as its title indicates. Moreover, Fox's tendency to use jargon unnecessarily; the fuzzy quality of his definitions; and his reliance on the New York *Times* and general sociological literature, as opposed to the literature on voluntary associations, serve to limit the value of his work.

In contrast to the armchair approach of Fox, sociologists Charles K. Warriner and Jane Emery Prather developed their functionally oriented typology on the basis of an extensive study of the organizational life of a community of 30,000. They employed a variety of techniques, ranging from sample surveys to the examination of community newspapers, to identify the community's organizations. A sample of 60 organizations was drawn from the total of 700 which they located, and these were then subjected to further study. On the basis of this work, Warriner and Prather grouped organizations into four types according to the collective value functions (defined as those consequences of activity which are relevant to the collectivity as a whole or common to its members) served by the organizations. In the first type, the activities of the organization provide the members with "pleasure in the performance itself"; in the second or sociability type, the activities are a vehicle for communion among members; in the third, the activities are symbols or signs that evoke and reaffirm a valued belief system; and finally, in the fourth or productive type of organization, the activities involve the production of goods or services or the bringing about of a change in some object or objects. Warriner and Prather give examples of each type and describe the activities, the membership, and organizational or structural features of each in some detail.

Organizations are frequently differentiated on the basis of their "interests" and "purposes," both terms being used interchangeably with the term "function." Thus, sociologists Wendell Bell and Maryanne Force divide formal associations into three categories according to the interests served by the group. The Chamber of Commerce and service clubs such as the Rotary are classified as "general interest associations" since they are devoted, at least manifestly, to the improvement of the general good through civic betterment of some kind. Organizations which directly serve the interests of a particular social group, such as war veterans, are tagged "special stratum interest groups," while organizations which serve member interests that do not directly derive from a shared social status are given the label "special-individual interest groups" (*Social Forces*, 34:347–348). Another sociologist, Walter Goldschmidt, distinguishes organizations which serve socio-economic interests from those which are purely social in character, and from those which are organized around a hobby or game.

Arnold Rose, a leading sociologist who maintained an interest in voluntary associations throughout his life, devoted a chapter of his *Theory and Method in the Social Sciences* to his "theory of the function of voluntary associations in contemporary social structure." Rose believed that there are only two basic types of voluntary associations. Hobby clubs, sports associations, and scientific societies belong in the first category of "expressive groups" since they act to express or satisfy interests which the members have "in relation to themselves." A second group, which he calls "social influen e associations," concentrate their efforts on the society in order to bring about some condition in a limited segment of the social order. It is this second type that interests Rose, and most of his "theory" is in reality an essay bringing together a series of observations and hypotheses about social influence associations (pp. 50–71).

While a number of other sociologists employ the concept of an "expressive" group, they generally contrast "expressive" groups with "instrumental" ones rather than using Rose's "social influence" type. For example, C. Wayne Gordon and Nicholas Babchuk classify organizations as "expressive," "instrumental," and "instrumental-expressive." Within each of their three categories, Gordon and Babchuk further classify groups according to their status and accessibility. Using their categories, the Daughters of the American Revolution would be typed as an expressive association having high status and low accessibility. It is an "expressive" group because its activities are immediately gratifying to the participants. Instrumental associations, in contrast, either provide a service, produce a product, or serve to maintain or create some normative condition. A group is instrumental-expressive if it provides a framework within which both types of activities can take place. A somewhat similar distinction between types of groups is made by George Lundberg and his associates who contrast "leisure" organizations and "instrumental" organizations. The activities of leisure organizations are ends in themselves while those of instrumental organizations are means to a valued goal. Moreover, instrumental organizations are closely allied to work and are viewed as an extension of occupational, income-yielding activities (*Leisure*, pp. 126–127).

The instrumental-expressive typology is of special interest because there have been some attempts to test its utility. On the basis of their research comparing members of expressive and instrumental groups in terms of perception of the group's character, Arthur Jacoby and Nicholas Babchuk concluded that: "the evidence clearly supports the unidimensionality of the instrumental-expressive continuum applied to voluntary groups and suggests the validity of this framework. Members of voluntary groups appear in high agreement with each other regarding the objectives of the organizations of which they are members. Furthermore, such objectives are important in attracting members to join and

participate in voluntary associations. A distinction is made, however, by
the members between organizational objectives and their personal motives for joining and participating" (*Sociology and Social Research*, 47:
470).

When Joan Moore tried to test the applicability of the instrumental-
expressive typology in her study of women serving on hospital boards
in Chicago, she also found it necessary to distinguish between the members' motives and the organizational type as it would be seen by the
outside expert. She found, for example, that middle class women belonged to more expressive organizations than to instrumental ones, but
that the women stressed instrumental factors such as the importance of
the hospital boards' goals when asked why they retained their membership. On the other hand, upper class women emphasized personal gratification, although they belonged to predominantly instrumental
associations. (*American Journal of Sociology*, 66:597.)

In general sociologists have been sensitive to the distinction between
the manifest and latent functions of organizations, and especially to the
differences in the purposes of an organization as they appear to the
scholarly observer in contrast to the purposes as they appear to the
organization members. Lloyd Warner and his students have been particularly anxious to distinguish between the professed purposes of
organizations and the purposes the Warner group regards as "real." In
Democracy in Jonesville, a community study directed by Warner,
Marchia Meeker quite typically comments that some women's groups in
the town "pose as civic clubs, organized to wrestle with a local community problem" while their real "drawing card" is their social events
(pp. 122-123).

Mhyra Minnis, who studied women's organizations in New Haven in
the late forties, came to a similar conclusion. Although the organizations in her sample had a variety of professed purposes, she concluded
that their function was really social in nearly all cases: "The basic purpose of the organization thus appears to be a human need for group
association and the sharing of common experience, even though
ideationally and practically these organizations may accomplish other
goals" ("The Relationship of Women's Organizations to the Social
Structure of a City," p. 103). The women themselves tended to view
their organizations as service groups. To us, this member view seems as
important as the scholar's classification, and we would caution against
the tendency on the part of some sociologists (the Warner group seems

especially prone) to dismiss the member's definition as incorrect. As W. I. Thomas pointed out many years ago, in sociology's infancy, the individual's definition of the situation has real consequences for himself and for the social system.

Some sociologists have been primarily interested in the structural characteristics and organizational processes in voluntary associations and have used these as a basis for classification. David Sills, a leading student of voluntary associations, employed a structural distinction between "corporate-type" and "federation-type" organizations in his pioneering 1957 book *The Volunteers*, which is an analysis of the National Foundation for Infantile Paralysis (see Chapter Seven for a more detailed discussion of this work). In the article on the sociological aspects of voluntary associations which he wrote for the 1968 edition of the *International Encyclopedia of the Social Sciences*, Sills focuses much of his discussion on the four organizational processes he regards as fundamental to the understanding of voluntary associations. These are: institutionalization, minority rule, goal displacement, and goal succession.

Sills uses the concept of institutionalization, or the "unplanned process that turns a loosely organized group of adherents to an idea or a goal into a formal organization," as a tool to study the transformation of individual organizations over time and to classify a variety of organizations at a particular point in time. He has developed a two-dimensional scheme for classifying voluntary associations in terms of the degree to which the association exhibits "formal organization–like" characteristics on the one hand, and the lay or professional status of the association's members on the other. As he sees it: "Some voluntary associations have goals and programs that are oriented toward the gradual improvement of the existing order. Their members therefore bring a relatively low degree of affect to their participation, and the organizational structure is relatively formal and matter-of-fact. Such highly institutionalized organizations may be called formal organization–like associations. Other voluntary associations have goals and programs that are much more radical and ideological, and are more at variance with what the participants believe to be the norms of society; their members bring a relatively high degree of affect to their participation, and the organizational structure is likely to be informal and fluid. These less institutionalized organizations may be called social movement–like associations" (*Encyclopedia*, 16:367–368). It should be noted that Sills is really working

with at least four variables in the above formulation — institutionalization, membership affect, professionalism of the members, and the
radicalism of the organization's goals. Whether or not these variables are
correlated in the ways Sills has assumed in constructing his typology is a
matter for empirical verification.

Minority rule is Sills's label for the phenomenon Robert Michels described with the phrase the "iron law of oligarchy." Both labels refer to
the supposed tendency of organizations to develop nondemocratic internal power structures and we will deal with this in the chapters on
political theory. The term goal displacement is used by Sills to describe
the tendency observed in many organizations for the activities of the
group to "become focused upon the proper functioning or organizational procedures, rather than upon the achievement of the initial
goals." Thus, the means by which the organization originally sought to
achieve its goals become ends in themselves. Goal succession, the last of
the four processes, is closely related to goal displacement. In goal succession, new ends replace the original ones, either because the original
goals have been achieved or because they have become irrelevant or
unobtainable in changing social circumstances.

Using these concepts, Sills has attempted a preliminary classification
of organizations according to their success or failure in functional adaptation. In this classification he also describes and differentiates organizations in terms of the nature of their initial goals; their additional or
secondary goals; the characteristics of the original membership; environmental changes requiring adaptation; new or added goals; and the
consequence of the new goals for the organization (*Encyclopedia*, 16:
370–372).

The processes of change which Sills has analyzed have not gone un-
noticed by other scholars, although the labels by which they characterize them sometimes differ. "Institutionalization," which is called
"bureaucratization" or "formalization" in other theories, has been
studied by scholars interested in general organization theory and to a
lesser extent by scholars specifically interested in voluntary associations.
F. Stuart Chapin, who developed a widely used (but very crude) scale
for measuring the degree of individual participation in voluntary organizations, has hypothesized that "bureaucratic tendencies" are present in
all social institutions and that the "formalization process may be seen in
the history of voluntary organizations of American culture." Following
a discussion of his "formalization hypothesis" in an article on "Social

Institutions and Voluntary Associations," Chapin concludes that: "(a) voluntary associations develop (sometimes spontaneously, sometimes planned) to satisfy some need; and (b) voluntary organizations having once started their life career, grow and gain momentum toward formalization of structure. As growth in size of membership proceeds, structure subdivides into subgroups of smaller size and with different functions. Although relatively large in membership, the voluntary associations may become veritable congeries of small constituent groups with mutually supporting or competitive relationships, within the larger system of the overall group. Attitudes of members then become conditioned to the norms of the groups (often embodied in codes) that stipulate the expected behaviors, to the symbols of the authority and the function of the organization, and to its physical property. An increasing emphasis on conformity and status develops and the voluntary organization begins to have traditions. In short, the process of growth and formalization has run its course and the original "voluntary" organization has become a full-fledged institution" (pp. 263-264). Chapin and his student John Tsouderos studied this formalization process in ninety-one organizations in the Minneapolis–St. Paul area. After interviewing officers of each association and examining the number of meetings, property, turnover in office, membership activity, and other characteristics of the organizations, they concluded that the process of formalization is general and uniform in character and accompanies the growth of an organization's membership (*Social Forces*, 34:344). Tsouderos also studied ten Minneapolis-area organizations in detail. He arrived at a number of theoretical propositions related to the details of the formalization process, such as the relationship between growth in membership and increase in organization staff and property (*American Sociological Review*, 20:206-210).

All of the general, somewhat "theoretical" typologies discussed so far are probably of only limited usefulness at this point in the development of study of voluntary organizations. This is so in part because the very generality of the categories obscures important differences among groups. The majority of surveys and studies therefore employ none of the more "theoretical" typologies; the most frequently used categories are described in everyday, "unscientific" language. The National Opinion Research Center (NORC), to take just one example, has used the following categories in some of its studies: veterans, military, patriotic (and auxiliaries of same); organizations relating to health (except

sick benefit associations); civic or service (other than health); political
or pressure groups; lodges, fraternal, and secret societies, mutual (sick)
benefit associations (and auxiliaries); church, religious; economic, occupational, professional (other than health or labor union); cultural educational, college alumni (other than health); and social, sports, hobby,
recreational (except specifically church-connected). (See Hausknecht,
The Joiners, pp. 131–132.)

ORGANIZATION AND SMALL GROUP THEORY

Although there is a body of theory dealing with the organization, it is
unfortunately of relatively little usefulness to students of the voluntary
association, since organization theorists have largely focused on government bureaucracies and businesses. Their hypotheses appear to be based
on experience with nonvoluntary organizations, and their illustrations
and applications of the hypotheses generally deal with nonvoluntary
organizations. Moreover, as Sanford Lakoff points out in a rather devas-
tating critique of the work on organizations (in Pennock and Chapman,
Voluntary Associations), students in the field have been unable to define "organization" satisfactorily; have been very insensitive to the
political aspects of organizations and to the effect on them of the
political-cultural environment; have been guilty of tautological reasoning and illogical thinking; and, ironically, "in view of their disdainful
attitude toward earlier theorists," often "seem to be involved in nothing
so much as the rediscovery of the most hoary of political truisms, well
known to ancient and modern philosophers," (p. 183). Yet the work of
organization theorists does represent an attempt to understand the
functioning of organizations, and the student of voluntary associations
should have some familiarity with it.

There are a number of books which survey the field of organization
research and theory and can serve as a good introduction and guide.
Two of the best known and most useful are the *Handbook of Organizations* edited by James G. March and *Organizations* by James G. March
and Herbert A. Simon. The *Handbook,* according to its editor, represents
an effort "to summarize and report the present state of knowledge about
human organizations." Its twelve hundred pages contain a collection of
twenty-eight essays by leading scholars from the fields of economics,
political science, psychology, business administration, and sociology,
who attempt to describe the present state of organization research and

theory in the various areas in which they specialize. The contributions deal with methodology, applications, and basic or foundation studies (covering such topics as influence, leadership, and control; decision making and problem solving; small groups and large organizations; social structure and organization); with theoretical-substantive areas such as management theory, economic theories of organization, organizational growth and development, communication in organizations, and organizational decision making and control structure; and with specific types of organizations such as unions, political parties, public bureaucracies, military organizations, hospitals, schools, governmental units, prisons, and business organizations. There is no article devoted to voluntary associations, and there is no entry on voluntary organizations in the index. Apparently no expert has attempted to apply systematically the research findings and theories of organization to voluntary associations, although there is clearly a need for such an attempt. The *Handbook* does not contain a master bibliography, but there are long bibliographies following each article, and there is a discussion of the outstanding and most influential books in the field in the introduction by March.

Although *Organizations*, which appeared in 1958, is considerably older than the *Handbook of Organizations*, published in 1965, in some respects it is more useful. *Organizations* is a thorough, intensive, and compact (just over two hundred pages) survey of organization theory "starting with those theories that viewed the employee as an instrument of physiological automation, proceeding through theories that were centrally concerned with the motivational and affective aspects of human behavior, and concluding with theories that placed particular emphasis on cognitive processes" (p. 21). The authors have extracted propositions about formal organizations from the literature. Frequently they have restated the propositions in more testable form, with particular attention to the operational definition of variables, and they have also at times suggested the kinds of tests that would be relevant and practical in dealing with the propositions.

The authors are both leading advocates of the behavioral approach in political science which emphasizes the importance of methodological rigor and mathematical sophistication. Consequently they pay considerable attention to methodological questions in their discussion, and are careful to separate theory from evidence and to indicate the reliability of the evidence. The entire discussion is pitched at a high level of generalization and does not single out voluntary organizations, nor any other specific type of organization for that matter, for special treatment. However, as March and Simon note in their introductory discussion, voluntary organizations are a type of formal organization and the general theory should apply to them if it is valid.

There are a number of other collections of material on organizations, such as *Reader in Bureaucracy* edited by Robert Merton and others, *Complex Organizations* edited by Amitai Etzioni, and *The Sociology of Organizations* edited by Oscar Grusky and George A. Miller, as well as collections of general interpretations by leading scholars, such as the Blau and Scott book on *Formal Organizations* which was discussed in a preceding section. Of these, there are two which should probably be singled out: *The Government of Associations* edited by William A. Glaser and David L. Sills, and *Human Behavior* by Bernard Berelson and Gary A. Steiner.

Although *The Government of Associations* includes a number of important articles dealing with several aspects of voluntary associations, the bulk of the selections in the book come from the literature of public administration and organization theory and cover such topics as the nature of leadership, organizational structure and processes, communications, decision making, goals and means, internal divisions in organizations, and organizational change. Glaser and Sills note that they have chosen reports of research on voluntary associations whenever possible, but "since not enough research has been carried out exclusively on voluntary associations, some selections concern other private organizations" (p. x). Although the paucity of studies on voluntary organizations is regrettable, the Glaser and Sills book is extremely valuable in that it represents a selection of relevant research in the field of organizations by two responsible scholars interested in voluntary associations.

The Berelson and Steiner inventory of scientific findings, *Human Behavior*, contains a chapter on organizations which reviews a variety of definitions and conceptualizations that can be found in the literature, and summarizes in propositional form a number of findings from studies dealing both with organizations and with the relationships between leaders and members of organizations. Several of the propositions deal specifically with voluntary associations, and, in general, Berelson and Steiner pay more attention to voluntary organizations than is usually the case. However, the inventory has to be used with care since the generalizations presented are based on a limited and apparently unsystematic sampling of the literature rather than on the entire available body of research. Moreover, Berelson and Steiner tend to use the studies they have reviewed somewhat indiscriminately without indicating the degree of reliability of various findings. In this respect, the March and Simon book is superior since the authors are careful to point out the methodological deficiencies.

In addition to Berelson and Steiner's chapter on organizations, there is also material of interest to the student of voluntary associations in their chapter on "Face to Face Relationships in Small Groups." Since a few voluntary associations are small groups, and all voluntary associations include small groups in the form of committees, executive boards, and local chapters within their larger structure, the literature on small groups is relevant to our concerns. There is some overlap between the literature on organization and that on small groups, but for the most part these are two separate areas of investigation involving two different sets of social scientists.

Like organization theory, the literature of small groups (most of which belongs in the field of social psychology) is too vast to be considered in depth here. However, the student of voluntary associations should know something about the work, and for this purpose Berelson and Steiner's inventory of findings and such general reviews of the field as Clovis R. Shepherd's *Small Groups* and Michael S. Olmsted's *The Small Group* are useful. The literature of small group studies between 1900 and 1955 is systematically summarized in A. Paul Hare's *Handbook of Small Group Research*. Joseph McGrath and Irwin Altman have also summarized and classified a sample of that literature. Their synthesis, a comprehensive bibliography of research in the field up to 1962, and an essay on small group research appear in their book *Small Group Research: A Synthesis and Critique of the Field*. A number of theoretical and research articles are collected in *Small Groups: Studies in Social Interaction* edited by Paul Hare, Edgar Borgatta, and Robert Bales. Much of F. Stuart Chapin's article "Social Institutions and Voluntary Associations" written for the *Review of Sociology* is devoted to a review of the writing on small groups. However, although Chapin states that the findings of small group and group dynamics research is of relevance to the understanding of voluntary associations, he makes little attempt to demonstrate that relevance.

In addition, we would recommend Sidney Verba's *Small Groups and Political Behavior*, which provides a review of the literature, particularly that dealing with the phenomenon of leadership, and an excellent discussion of the degree to which findings from laboratory studies of small groups "artificially" created for the purposes of an experiment are applicable to real-life situations in "natural" groups.

THE ORIGINS, GROWTH, AND FUNCTIONS OF
VOLUNTARY ASSOCIATIONS

A number of hypotheses concerning the origins, growth, and functions of voluntary associations have been advanced. We have already touched on many of these in our discussion of typologies and frames of reference, most of which are, necessarily, based on such hypotheses. Probably the best single introduction to sociological thinking on the subject is the essay on "Voluntary Associations" which David Sills wrote for the 1968 *International Encyclopedia of the Social Sciences*. Sills emphasizes the latent functions (those which the participants do not intend or recognize but which can be observed by the outside analyst) as opposed to the manifest functions (those which the participants intend and recognize) of voluntary associations, and distinguishes between the functions of associations for individuals and those for society. In the first instance, associations are thought to be important because they train the individual in organizational skills and help to integrate him into his social milieu. The social interaction experienced by a member of a voluntary association presumably also gives him an opportunity to learn social norms and acquire information, and combats loneliness. In the case of the social system, it is asserted that associations mediate between primary groups and the state; integrate minority groups into the larger society; offer a "legitimate locus for the affirmation and expression of values"; govern "in the sense of making decisions on policy and of providing services to citizens"; initiate social change; and distribute power (16:372–376). As Sills points out, there is some evidence in support of most of these hypotheses, but it is not sufficient to constitute real proof, and in many instances there are contradictory findings from different researchers.

David Horton Smith has also reviewed, in *Sociology and Social Research*, 50:483–494, the contributions of formal voluntary organizations for society, attempting to fit his analysis into a Parsonian framework. He asserts that the organizations perform a role in each of Talcott Parson's four structural-functional categories of analysis thus contributing to societal goal attainment, integration, pattern maintenance, and adaptation. Unfortunately, Smith uses an extremely broad definition of the voluntary organization — including political parties, trade associations, universities, the state-controlled groups of a totalitarian regime, and international organizations such as the United Nations — so that his work is of minimal utility.

The early sociologists tended to see voluntary associations as concomitants of modernization, making their appearance in a society as it is transformed from a folk or traditional social order into an industrial, urban social system. In this view, voluntary associations only become necessary as the ties of kinship, neighborhood, and religion break down and the individual is freed from traditional obligations. The individual needs something to replace the old institutions, and he finds in voluntary associations a partial substitute for former ties. There is a tendency among some of these sociologists to derogate such modern institutions as voluntary associations as cold and inadequate in comparison to the warmth and meaningfulness of the folk community. Drawing on the work of Tonnies, Durkheim, and others who developed the contrasting models of the Gemeinschaft or folk and the Gesellschaft or modern societies, Louis Wirth of the Chicago school of sociology applied these concepts to the analysis of the nature of voluntary associations. His article on "Urbanism as a Way of Life" has now become a classic statement of the thesis. Wirth wrote:

> Urban life is characterized by the substitution of secondary for primary contacts, the weakening of bonds of kinship, and the declining social significance of the family, the disappearance and the undermining of the traditional basis of social solidarity . . .
>
> Being reduced to a stage of virtual impotence as an individual the urbanite is bound to exert himself by joining with others of similar interest into organized groups to obtain his ends. This results in the enormous multiplication of voluntary organizations directed toward as great a variety of objectives as there are human needs and interests. While on the one hand the traditional ties of human association are weakened, urban existence involves a much greater degree of interdependence between man and man and a more complicated, fragile, and volatile form of mutual interrelations over many phases of which the individual as such can exert scarcely any control . . . It is largely through the activities of the voluntary groups, be their objectives economic, political, educational, religious, recreational, or cultural, that the urbanite expresses and develops his personality, acquires status, and is able to carry on the round of activities that constitute

his life career . . . however . . . the organizational framework which these highly differentiated functions call into being does not of itself insure the consistency and integrity of the personalities whose interests it enlists. Personal disorganization, mental breakdown, suicide, delinquency, crime, corruption, and disorder might be expected under these circumstances to be more prevalent. (pp. 46–47)

In somewhat the same spirit, David Riesman wrote more recently that the advocacy of group belongingness in voluntary associations as a remedy for individual loneliness and as a replacement for the primary ties of family and clan and the experience of meaningful work is an admission of the individual's weakness and loss of defenses. Riesman warns that the emphasis on voluntary associations strengthens yet another set of outside powers and adds to the pressure on the individual to submerge himself in a collectivity (*Individualism Reconsidered*, p. 114).

The validity of the assumptions made by Wirth, Riesman, and others as to the modern urban character of voluntary associations now appears quite questionable given the findings of the empirical investigations of the post–World War II generation of social scientists. Although relative latecomers to the field, anthropologists have played a key role in forcing a revision in thinking about voluntary associations. Following the lead of Robert Lowie, who first pointed out the importance of the association or sodalities, anthropologists have built a considerable literature. For the most part, this literature is descriptive in character. Lowie had confined himself to description and discussion, reasoning that: "Since sodalities represent a congeries of diverse associations set off by negative rather than positive criteria, they defy logical classification. Indeed, given their marked fluidity, classification of that sort would wrest asunder phenomena that are genetically related" (*Social Organization*, p. 295).

In a 1971 review of the work of anthropologists, Robert Anderson (himself an outstanding researcher in the field) reports that efforts to generalize about sodalities in the "middle-range" of societal evolution have "not yet yielded very impressive results" so that the best one can do is to characterize associations "broadly and note regularities limited to particular parts of the world or to particularly associational mechanisms such as secrecy or age alignment" (*American Anthropologist*, 73: 213).

Anderson traces voluntary associations back to the very beginnings of human social existence. The earliest sodalities appeared to have had a religious basis and probably emerged sometime in the upper paleolithic period in western Europe or in the nonnomadic mesolithic societies. Sodalities were definitely present in the agricultural villages of the neolithic era. On the basis of the available studies (and he provides a thorough guide to the relevant works), Anderson contends that the first "widespread elaboration and diffusion of common interest associations" began as early as 8000 B.C.

Anderson believes that there was something of a decline in the importance of voluntary associations in preindustrial societies, that the sodalities which did exist were primarily confined to the merchant class, being almost nonexistent among the elite and the peasantry. The state and other institutions such as the family seem to have replaced the village sodalities of the preceding period, while the elite was small enough to constitute a face-to-face society in which sodalities were unnecessary. Michael Banton's essay on the anthropological aspects of voluntary associations in the *International Encyclopedia of the Social Sciences* contains the statement that "voluntary associations become more common and significant as societies advance in technology, complexity, and scale" (16:358); the studies cited by Anderson seem to indicate that Banton's generalization is at best an oversimplification.

It should be noted that some scholars reject the anthropological work on the grounds that the sodalities of the preindustrial, primitive, tribal, and traditional societies are so unlike contemporary voluntary associations that they are a separate kind of institution. For example, Immanuel Wallerstein, an Africanist, asserts that the voluntary association which emerges in modernizing tropical African societies is fundamentally "different in function and structure from the associations found in tribal societies." Those in tribal societies are largely ascriptive, with individuals gaining membership by virtue of ascribed social roles. Moreover the tribal associations functioned primarily as extensions of the government or traditional authority to attain the society's goals, while modern associations have been formed for a limited purpose by groups of individuals recruited on some other basis than traditional social ties. In further contrast, joining the modern association is voluntary and takes place through a formal entry process. (Coleman and Rosberg, *Political Parties and National Integration*, pp. 318–322.) Of course Wallerstein has simply defined the voluntary association in terms of the characteristics of associations found in industrial societies. Given such a definition, his conclusion that the only true voluntary associations are those of the modern society necessarily follows. Most scholars, including Anderson, would agree that there are important differences between modern voluntary associations and those of premodern societies, but unlike Wallerstein they define the voluntary association in broad enough terms to include both types. Anderson, for his part, has stressed the bureaucratization or adoption of rational-legal modes of operation of the association in industrial societies. He defines the rational-legal association as one with: "written statutes clearly defining membership, participant obligations, leadership roles, and conditions of convocation. It normally possesses a legally recognized corporate identity. It is rational in the sense that as a body it is geared to efficiency in making decisions and taking action, particularly as leaders are, in principle at least, impartially chosen by election of the most qualified to take office. It is legal in the sense that compliance in decisions and actions is sanctioned by the impersonal force of law" (*American Anthropologist*, 73:215).

Whether or not one accepts preindustrial sodalities as being "real" voluntary associations, the Wirth thesis still requires revision. While voluntary associations have proliferated in industrial nations, factors other than the degree of urbanization and industrialization have affected their growth, and their role in the lives of individuals has not quite been that envisioned by Wirth. For one thing, rational-legal voluntary associations are found in rural areas and traditional communities of industrial or industrializing nations (see Norbeck 1961). When established in traditional communities, the associations appear to adapt to traditional patterns of action rather than introduce changes in the traditional social organizations (See Levi 1958 and La Palombara 1957).

Their study of a Danish village led Anderson and his wife Barbara Gallatin Anderson to the conclusion that the "impetus to multiplication and elaboration of voluntary associations was as much socially linked with the patterns of the communities past as with the more recent urbanism." In Dragor, voluntary associations had existed and successfully maintained and directed social participation before rapid urbanization. It was therefore "natural" that voluntary associations should be employed as a device for coping with the problems of the twentieth century. (*The Vanishing Village*, p. 121.) When this tradition of voluntary association activity is not present in a society, voluntary associations are less likely to be used to meet modern crises, as Floyd Dotson

found to be the case in Mexico. The Andersons hypothesize: "Voluntary associations appear either to have had pre-urban recognition and a
successful history within the particular population or culture before
their city's 'flowering' or they are hindered in making significant inroads
in the general social structure. In the former case associations multiply
as urban life becomes more complex, in the latter case (as in Guadela-
jara) their development is more erratic, dependent perhaps on selective
acculturative influences . . . The variability in the patterning and pro-
pensities of cultures seem as much a determinant of voluntary associations as the functional link between them and urbanism" (*American
Journal of Sociology*, 65:272).

The urban sociologist Scott Greer has used his own and other studies
to provide evidence that in the United States the conjugal family group
remains strong and that the individual's life tends to be centered around
his family rather than voluntary associations, which play a relatively
limited role in his experience. In Greer's view: "the usual individual's
involvement in formal organizations and work-based friendship is weak;
the mass media are most important in a family context; participation
with kin and friendship circles is powerful, and with neighbors and local
community's groups it varies immensely by area . . . By and large, the
conjugal family group keeps itself to itself; outside is the world — formal
organizations, work, and the communities" (in Young, *Approaches to
the Study of Politics*, pp. 332–333).

In their 1963 book, *The Civic Culture*, which is based on over 5000
interviews conducted in the United States, Great Britain, Germany,
Italy, and Mexico, political scientists Gabriel Almond and Sidney Verba
suggest that differences in the political culture and socialization experiences of the citizenry account for differences in the amount, kind, and
effects of voluntary participation in nations which are equally urban in
character. For example, fewer Germans than Americans belong to
organizations, and of those who belong, a significantly smaller percentage of the Germans are active participating members (46 percent of the
Americans compared with 16 percent of the Germans are active).
Almond and Verba observe that: "Once again we find that in Germany
the structures of a democratic system are well developed, but they do
not yet play significant roles in the perspectives and behavior of citizens" (p. 258). In his studies of German and American high school boys,
the psychologist David McClelland found that the Germans engaged in
significantly fewer extracurricular activities than the Americans, and

attributed this difference in participation to entrenched cultural patterns. McClelland argues that American children are trained to pay attention to the opinions of others and are generally more other-directed than German youngsters who are taught to assert their individuality in solitary pursuits and are trained to focus their attention on traditional institutions. (*The Achieving Society*, pp. 197–199.)

Similarly, Edward Banfield's study of an Italian peasant village led him to conclude that cultural values are a crucial variable in determining the role of voluntary associations in a society. In *The Moral Basis of a Backward Society* he argues that Montegrano's "amoral familism," an ethos stressing loyalty to the nuclear family and distrust of outsiders, is the key to the people's behavior. The villagers eschew all cooperative activities, including participation in organizations. In fact, there are no organizations in the community.

It is significant that Herbert Gans found a similar ethos and absence of participation in activities outside the family circle among the Italian American residents of Boston's West End area. However, in *The Urban Villagers* Gans maintains that the life style of the West Enders is primarily a class phenomenon rather than an ethnic one, since studies of American working class groups of various ethnic origins as well as research in working class areas outside the United States reveal a similar pattern of behavior (see chapter 11).

FURTHER ANTHROPOLOGICAL VIEWS
OF CONTEMPORARY ASSOCIATIONS

Anthropologists have led the way in investigating the functions of voluntary associations in the rapidly changing, urbanizing societies of Africa. Voluntary associations have been found in great number in these societies, particularly in urban areas. According to Michael Banton, the associations function as a means of "organizing people in order to achieve new ends, such as the raising of capital, the regulation of prices, and the provision of extra labor"; they create and institutionalize new roles and relationships, reinforcing new values and behavior patterns; and they serve as substitutes for traditional institutions in the lives of urban newcomers. Very importantly, voluntary associations have also served as the basis of other new major institutions such as political parties, unions, and religious organizations, since, given the circumstances of colonialism, the voluntary association was often the first form taken by these institutions. (*Encyclopedia*, 16:360.)

The bibliography which follows Banton's essay in *The International Encyclopedia of the Social Sciences* provides a short guide to further discussion of the voluntary association in Africa and to other aspects of the anthropological study of voluntary associations. Banton's monograph *West African City: A Study of Tribal Life in Freetown* features a detailed empirical and theoretical discussion of voluntary associations. In addition, Kenneth Little's outstanding *West African Urbanization: A Study of Voluntary Associations in Social Change* should be singled out. Little approaches the analysis of voluntary associations within an "evolutionary" frame of reference emphasizing the displacement of simple systems of integration by more complex systems. He argues that: "The substitution of a market economy for an economy based upon subsistence involves the disturbance of traditional ideas of status. New roles are created whose fulfillment necessitates the interaction of individuals on a basis of common interest in such things as wages, education, religion, and politics rather than genealogical origin and descent. Before, however, the new forms of association can be fully institutionalized there is required a system of relationships which will link the old with the new structures . . . the system of relationships . . . is provided largely by voluntary associations" (pp. 1–2). Little has marshaled detailed evidence from his own studies and the work of others to prove that voluntary associations perform an important role in integrating changing West African societies.

Without denying the validity of the view that voluntary associations often promote the modernization of a society, we should note the evidence that associations may also hinder modernization, or at the very least strengthen traditional social institutions. Robert Anderson suggests that associations may help migrants re-create traditional institutions within their new urban environment; and in the traditional milieu itself, associations may reinforce traditional values and institutions. He also notes that while voluntary associations do provide an education in modern ways, they may do so only for those who are already somewhat modern. In sum, Anderson concludes that voluntary associations do not themselves initiate social change although they may support it. He writes: "They function to adapt the social structure for modern requirements. They function to adapt individuals for modern participation. But they do not create a new social structure in a traditional society, and they do not socialize an individual when circumstances broadly are not favorable" (*American Anthropologist*, 73:218).

HISTORICAL VIEW

The historical literature on voluntary associations is not extensive. Only a few historians appear to have been interested in the history of voluntary associations in modern societies. Among those who have evidenced some concern, Arthur M. Schlesinger, Sr., and Oscar and Mary Handlin have provided informative, but limited, discussions of voluntary associations in the United States. Schlesinger's article "Biography of a Nation of Joiners" (which was later incorporated in his book *Paths to the Present*) contains a general description of the rise of voluntary associations in America. Like Wirth, Schlesinger believed that the growth of associations has been stimulated by the rise of cities and by other modern phenomena such as improved communications, the increase in national identification, and greater leisure time. In contrast to Wirth, Schlesinger stressed the positive rather than the negative functions of voluntary organizations. He believed that voluntary organizations function to train individuals in democratic self-government, to help integrate the nation, to provide a safety valve for the tensions and ambitions generated by modern life, to educate the public, and to promote social reform.

The Handlins also view the voluntary association in generally favorable terms. However, their discussion in *The Dimensions of Liberty* focuses on the political functions of voluntary associations so we shall discuss it more fully in Chapter Two. Here it should be noted that the Handlins provide some historical information in connection with their speculations on the role of associations. Along similar lines, such commentators as Alexis de Tocqueville and James Bryce have provided us with information on voluntary associations in nineteenth and early twentieth century America. But both of these foreign visitors were more interested in political theory, and therefore their observations are more fittingly discussed in Chapter Two.

There is some impressionistic material on the history of voluntary associations in the various entries on the subject in the 1935 *Encyclopedia of the Social Sciences*, edited by Seligman and Johnson; in the

entries by Sieder and Manser in the *Encyclopedia of Social Work*; in a
1911 article by Louis Hartson on education and social voluntary associations in Europe from the twelfth to eighteenth centuries that appeared
in *Pedigogical Seminary*; in the standard historical texts; and in such
general commentaries on the American scene as Max Lerner's *America
as a Civilization*. There is also some historical information in *The Citizen
Volunteer*, a collection of articles edited by Nathan Cohen. This book,
which was sponsored by the National Council of Jewish Women, is
aimed primarily at the volunteer, and most of the articles describe different types of volunteer activities and advise the potential volunteer as
to how and where he can serve. However, some articles by scholars on
the history and functions of voluntarism in America, the motivation of
volunteers, and the future role of volunteers in American society are
also included.

Finally, we should mention the 1927 text *The Rise of American
Civilization* by Charles and Mary Beard since it contains a frequently
quoted account of the impact of voluntary associations on American
life. The evidence available from recent sociological studies indicates
that the description is inaccurate for current America, and that if was
most likely an exaggeration even in the 1920s. The Beards wrote: "It
was a rare American who was not a member of four or five societies.
Every person who evolved a new idea or a variant on an existing
doctrine strove at once to found a fellowship for propaganda and promotion. Any citizen who refused to affiliate with one or more associations became an object of curiosity, if not of suspicion. If he isolated
himself he could hardly hope to succeed in any trade, business, or profession, no matter how great his talents" (p. 731).

BIBLIOGRAPHY

Almond, Gabriel A., and Sidney Verba, *The Civic Culture*. Princeton, Princeton
    University Press, 1963.
Alpert, Burt, and Patricia A. Smith, "How Participation Works," *Journal of Social
    Issues*, 5 (Winter 1949): 3–13. A typology of participation in reference to
    group problem-solving. Functional participation is contrasted with formalistic
    and anarchic participation.
Anderson, Robert, "Voluntary Associations in History," *American Anthropologist*,
    73 (February 1971): 209–222.
—— and Gallatin Anderson, "Voluntary Associations and Urbanization: A Dia-

chronic Analysis," *American Journal of Sociology*, 65 (November 1959): 265–273. Report of a field study of voluntary associations in a Danish village which has been transformed into a suburb of Copenhagen in the last fifty years.

——— and Barbara Gallatin Anderson, *The Vanishing Village*. Seattle, University of Washington Press, 1964. A fuller account of their research in the Danish village Dragor. Most of the material on voluntary associations appeared in the 1959 article.

——— and Barbara Gallatin Anderson, *Bus Stop for Paris*. Garden City, New York, Doubleday, 1965. An "anthropological history" of the French village of Wissous. The Andersons have "joined a genre of historical research, the history of single communities, with a genre of anthropological research, the community study" (p. 3). Considerable attention is paid to the village's voluntary associations.

Babchuk, Nicholas, and John N. Edwards, "Voluntary Associations and the Integration Hypothesis," *Sociological Inquiry*, 35 (Spring 1965): 149–162. The authors have reviewed the literature of sociology and social-psychology which is of relevance to the hypothesis that associations function as integrative entities at both the individual and societal levels. They also present findings from their own survey of associations in Lincoln, Nebraska.

Babchuk, Nicholas, and C. Wayne Gordon, *The Voluntary Association in the Slum*. Lincoln: University of Nebraska, 1962 (University of Nebraska Studies: new series no. 27).

Babchuk, Nicholas, and Charles K. Warriner, "Introduction" to "Signposts in the Study of Voluntary Groups," *Sociological Inquiry*, 35 (Spring 1965): 135–137. A brief discussion of the theoretical concerns involved in the study of voluntary associations.

Banfield, Edward C., with the assistance of Laura Fasano Banfield, *The Moral Basis of a Backward Society*. New York, Free Press, 1958.

Banton, Michael, *West African City: A Study of Tribal Life in Freetown*. London, Oxford University Press, 1957.

——— "Voluntary Associations: Anthropological Aspects," in David Sills, ed., *International Encyclopedia of the Social Sciences*, 16:357–362. New York, Macmillan and Free Press, 1968.

Beard, Charles A., and Mary R. Beard, *The Rise of American Civilization*. Volume II. New York, Macmillan, 1927.

Bell, Wendell, and Maryanne T. Force, "Social Structure and Participation in Different Types of Formal Associations," *Social Forces*, 34 (May 1956): 345–350.

Berelson, Bernard, and Gary A. Steiner, *Human Behavior: An Inventory of Scientific Findings*. New York, Harcourt, Brace, 1964.

Blau, Peter M., "A Formal Theory of Differentiation in Organizations," *American Sociological Review*, 35 (April 1970): 201–218. Blau argues that differentiation enlarges the administrative component in organizations and that increasing organization size generates differentiation at decelerating rates.

Blau, Peter M., and Richard W. Scott, *Formal Organizations: A Comparative Ap-*

proach. San Francisco, Chandler, 1962. A general work in organization theory which includes a brief discussion of voluntary associations as one of a number of organization types.

Boulding, Kenneth E., *The Organizational Revolution: A Study in the Ethics of Economic Organization.* New York, Harper and Brothers, 1953. Although most of Boulding's discussion does not relate to voluntary associations as they are defined here, there are some general comments on organizations that are applicable.

Chapin, F. Stuart, "Social Institutions and Voluntary Associations," in Joseph B. Gittler, ed., *Review of Sociology.* New York, John Wiley, 1957.

—— and John E. Tsouderos, "The Formalization Process in Voluntary Associations," *Social Forces,* 34 (May 1956): 342-344.

Chapple, Eliot Dismore, and Carleton Stevens Coon, *Principles of Anthropology.* New York, Henry Holt, 1942. The authors view voluntary associations as tangential institutions, formed at the point where several institutions or subsystems meet. They also argue that classifying associations on the basis of secrecy is not useful since secrecy occurs to some extent in all institutions and not just in voluntary associations.

Clark, Peter B., and James Q. Wilson, "Incentive Systems: A Theory of Organizations," *Administrative Science Quarterly,* 6 (September 1961): 129-166.

Cohen, Nathan, ed., *The Citizen Volunteer.* New York, Harper, 1950.

Cyert, Richard M., and Kenneth R. MacCrimmon, "Organizations," in Gardner Lindzey and Elliot Aronson, eds., *The Handbook of Social Psychology,* Volume I, second edition, pp. 568-611. Reading, Massachusetts, Addison-Wesley, 1968. An attempt to develop a general framework for the study of organizations integrating the work of a variety of disciplines. There is a bibliography of more than 175 works.

De Grazia, Sebastion, *Of Time, Work and Leisure.* New York, The Twentieth Century Fund, 1962. There a few scattered comments and statistics on organizational memberships in this wide-ranging, somewhat philosophic examination of leisure in our society.

Dotson, Floyd, "A Note on Participation in Voluntary Associations in a Mexican City," *American Sociological Review,* 18 (August 1953): 380-386. Dotson describes participation in Guadalajara on the basis of an exploratory survey.

Dulles, Foster Rhea, *America Learns to Play: A History of Popular Recreation, 1607-1940.* New York, Peter Smith, 1952. There are some references to voluntary association membership as a leisure time activity in this popular history.

Durkheim, Emile, *The Division of Labor in Society.* Translated by George Simpson. New York, Macmillan, 1933.

—— *Professional Ethics and Civic Morals.* Glencoe, Illinois, Free Press, 1960. Contains a discussion of the role of private organizations in mediating between the state and the individual.

Edelstein, J. David, "An Organizational Theory of Union Democracy," *American Sociological Review,* 32 (February 1967): 19-31. Edelstein's formal "structural-procedural" theory of the effectiveness of opposition or competition for organization office might prove useful in suggesting hypotheses for the study of voluntary association democracy.

Etzioni, Amitai, "New Directions in the Study of Organizations and Society," *Social Research*, 27 (Summer 1960): 223–228.

—— ed., *Complex Organizations: A Sociological Reader*. New York, Holt, Rinehart and Winston, 1964. A collection of essays by leading social scientists covering organization theory, the application of theory, organization goals and structures, organization and society, organizational change, and methods for the study of organizations. There are no selections dealing specifically with voluntary associations.

Fox, Sherwood Dean, "Voluntary Associations and Social Structure." Unpublished PhD dissertation, Harvard University, 1952.

Gans, Herbert J., *The Urban Villagers*. Glencoe, Illinois, Free Press 1962. Study of second generation Italian Americans in Boston, based on Gans's eight-month residence in the area as a participant observer.

Gist, Noel P., "Fraternal Societies," in Seba Eldridge and associates, *Development of Collective Enterprise*. Lawrence, University of Kansas Press, 1943. A general review of research and theory related to the subject. Most of the article is a summary of Gist's monograph, *Secret Societies: A Cultural Study of Fraternalism in the United States*, The University of Missouri Studies, 15 (October 1, 1940).

Glaser, William A., and David L. Sills, eds., *The Government of Associations: Selections from the Behavioral Sciences*. Totowa, New Jersey, The Bedminster Press, 1966.

Goldhamer, Herbert, "Voluntary Associations in the United States," in Paul K. Hatt and Albert J. Reiss, Jr., eds., *Reader in Urban Sociology*. Glencoe, Illinois, Free Press, 1951. A short general essay on the functions of voluntary associations in urban society. Goldhamer deals briefly with the potential conflict between voluntary associations and the state.

Goldschmidt, Walter, *As You Sow*. Glencoe, Illinois, Free Press, 1947.

Gordon, C. Wayne, and Nicholas Babchuk, "A Typology of Voluntary Associations," in William A. Glaser and David L. Sills, eds., *The Government of Associations*. Totowa, New Jersey, The Bedminster Press, 1966.

Greer, Scott, "Individual Participation in Mass Society," in Roland Young, ed., *Approaches to the Study of Politics*. Evanston, Northwestern University Press, 1958.

Grusky, Oscar, and George A. Miller, eds., *The Sociology of Organizations: Basic Studies*. New York, Free Press, 1970. Includes sections on classical and current theoretical perspectives, methods of study, substantive problems, and organizations in other industrial societies.

Guetzkow, Harold, "Building Models about Small Groups," in Roland Young, ed., *Approaches to the Study of Politics*. Evanston, Northwestern University Press, 1958. Guetzkow, a political scientist, deals generally with "central trends in the development of miniature theoretical systems in the study of small groups and their relationship to methodological problems involving the dimensions or groups." The essay does not descend to specifics.

Hammond, Phillip E., and Robert E. Mitchell, "Segmentation of Radicalism — The Case of the Protestant Campus Minister," *American Journal of Sociology,* 71 (September 1965): 133–143. The authors discuss the way in which the church segments and isolates radicals thus minimizing the disruption radicals might create without losing the benefit of their potential insights. While dealing specifically with the church, the study seems to have wider implications.

Handlin, Oscar, and Mary Handlin, *The Dimensions of Liberty.* Cambridge, Belknap Press of Harvard University Press, 1961.

Hare, A. Paul, *Handbook of Small Group Research.* New York, Free Press (Macmillan), 1962.

—— Edgar F. Borgatta and Robert F. Bales, eds., *Small Groups: Studies in Social Interaction.* New York, Alfred A. Knopf, 1965.

Harrison, Paul M., "Weber's Categories of Authority and Voluntary Associations," *American Sociological Review,* 25 (April 1960): 232–237. A largely speculative article dealing with the differences among organizations in terms of various types of authority. All of the illustrations are drawn from Harrison's study of the Baptist church.

Hartson, Louis D., "A Study of Voluntary Associations, Educational and Social, in Europe during the Period from 1166–1700," *Pedigogical Seminary,* 18 (March 1911): 10–31. General, impressionistic discussion of guilds, student societies, and other early forms of our present-day voluntary associations in Europe.

Hausknecht, Murray, *The Joiners.* New York, The Bedminster Press, 1962.

Henderson, D. R., "The Place and Function of Voluntary Associations," *American Journal of Sociology,* 1 (1895): 327–334. A commentary on Tocqueville's analysis of voluntary associations in the United States.

Hoebel, E. Adamson, *Man in the Primitive World: An Introduction to Anthropology.* Third edition. New York, McGraw-Hill, 1958. Includes material on voluntary associations in primitive cultures.

Jacobson, Eugene, "The Growth of Groups in a Voluntary Organization," *The Journal of Social Issues,* 12 (Second Quarter, 1956): 18–23. Jacobson outlines an approach to the analysis of the development of groups. He presents no data in the article.

Jacoby, Arthur, and Nicholas Babchuk, "Instrumental and Expressive Voluntary Associations," *Sociology and Social Research,* 47 (July 1963): 461–471.

Jansyn, Leon R., Jr., "Solidarity and Delinquency in a Street Corner Group," *American Sociological Review,* 31 (October 1966): 600–614. Provides a model for dealing with processes of organization and disorganization.

Lakoff, Sanford A., "Private Government in the Managed Society," in J. Roland Pennock and John W. Chapman, eds., *Voluntary Associations.* New York, Atherton Press, 1969.

La Palombara, Joseph, *The Italian Labor Movement.* Ithaca, Cornell University Press, 1957.

Lerner, Max, *America as a Civilization.* Volume II. New York, Simon and Schuster, 1957. An interestingly written, speculative discussion of the "associative impulse" in American life, by a journalist–political scientist. Lerner claims that this impulse is very strong in the United States and that no other civilization has as many groups.

Levi, Carol, *Words Are Stones: Impressions of Sicily.* Translated by Angus Davidson. New York, Farrar, Straus and Cudahy, 1958.

Little, Kenneth, *West African Urbanization: A Study of Voluntary Associations in Social Change.* Cambridge, England, Cambridge University Press, 1965.

Lowie, Robert, *Social Organization.* New York, Rinehart, 1948.

Lundberg, George, Mirra Komarovsky, and Mary Alice McInery, *Leisure: A Suburban Study.* New York, Columbia University Press, 1934.

McClelland, David C., *The Achieving Society.* Princeton, New Jersey, D. Van Nostrand, 1961.

McGrath, Joseph E., and Irwin Altman, *Small Group Research: A Synthesis and Critique of the Field.* New York, Holt, Rinehart and Winston, 1966.

MacIver, R. M., and Charles H. Page, *Society.* Revised edition. New York, Rinehart and Company, 1949. There is a long theoretical discussion on associations and interests.

McKelvey, Blake, *The Urbanization of America (1860-1915).* New Brunswick, Rutgers University Press, 1963. Historian McKelvey provides some information on voluntary associations in American cities of the period, especially those with a charitable goal.

Manser, Gordon, "Voluntary Organization for Social Welfare," *Encyclopedia of Social Work*, fifteenth issue, pp. 823-829. New York, National Association of Social Workers, 1965.

March, James G., ed., *Handbook of Organizations.* Chicago, Rand McNally, 1965.

—— and Herbert A. Simon (with the collaboration of Harold Guetzkow), *Organizations.* New York, John Wiley, 1958.

Marcus, Philip M., "Union Conventions and Executive Boards: A Formal Analysis of Organizational Structure," *American Sociological Review*, 31 (February 1966): 61-70.

Merton, Robert K., Ailsa Gray, Barbara Hockey, and Hanan C. Selvin, eds., *Reader in Bureaucracy.* Glencoe, Illinois, Free Press, 1952. The topics covered by the selections in the reader include: theoretical conceptions of bureaucracy; the basis for the growth of bureaucracy; bureaucracy and power relations; the structure of bureaucracy; recruitment and advance; the bureaucrat; social pathologies of bureaucracy; and field methods for the study of bureaucracy. Lengthy bibliography.

Minnis, Mhyra S., "The Relationship of Women's Organizations to the Social Structure of a City." Unpublished PhD dissertation, Yale University, 1951.

—— "Cleavage in Women's Organizations: A Reflection of the Social Structure of a City," *American Sociological Review*, 18 (February 1952): 47-53. A brief version of the author's PhD dissertation, Yale, 1951.

Moore, Joan W., "Patterns of Women's Participation in Voluntary Associations," *American Journal of Sociology*, 66 (May 1961): 592-598.

Moore, Wilbert, E., *Man, Time and Society*. New York. John Wiley, 1963.

Norbeck, Edward, "Cultural Change and Continuity in Northeastern Japan," *American Anthropologist*, 63. 2 (1961), pt. 1.

Olmsted, Michael S., *The Small Group*. New York, Random House, 1959. A short, clearly written, introductory, interpretive survey of small group studies "focusing on major approaches, assumptions, and problems and organized in terms of a conception of social science deriving ultimately from the work of Talcott Parsons and Robert F. Bales." Olmsted views small group sociology as a "special case of the sociology of all groups."

Palisi, Bartolomeo J., "Some Suggestions about the Transitory-Permanence Dimension of Organizations," *British Journal of Sociology*, 21 (June 1970): 200–206. Palisi outlines his concept of the "transitory organization," an organization intended to be in existence for a short span of time. Such organizations are often voluntary associations and have distinctive structural characteristics.

Pennock, J. Roland, "Epilogue," in J. Roland Pennock and John W. Chapman, eds., *Voluntary Associations*. New York, Atherton Press, 1969. Pennock notes the "paucity of information about and political features of voluntary associations" and lists some of the questions that need to be examined concerning the individual in relation to voluntary associations, the internal composition and workings of organizations, and the effects of associations upon the state.

Redfield, Robert, "The Folk Society," *American Journal of Sociology*, 52 (January 1947): 293–308. In this famous article, Redfield outlines an ideal type of the folk society and contrasts it with the secular, urban society. In the folk society, voluntary associations in their modern form are unknown and unneeded because of the strength of traditional and kinship ties.

Riesman, David, *Individualism Reconsidered and Other Essays*. Glencoe, Illinois, Free Press, 1954. Riesman has some comments on other-directedness, group pressures, and voluntary associations.

Riggs, Fred W., "The Prevalence of 'Clects,'" *American Behavioral Scientist*, 5 (June 1962): 15–18. Riggs briefly discusses various typologies of groups including those of Ferdinand Tonnies, Charles Cooley, and Gabriel Almond, and defines a new type — the clect — in Parsonian terms. The clect is both achievement and ascriptive in character and has diffuse and specific characteristics. The Chinese family name association is an example of a clect.

Rose, Arnold, *Theory and Method in the Social Sciences*. Minneapolis, The University of Minnesota Press, 1954.

——— *Sociology: The Study of Human Behavior*. Revised edition. New York, Alfred A. Knopf, 1965. Chapter 10 deals with voluntary associations, but most of the material is included in *The Power Structure*.

——— *The Power Structure: Political Process in American Society*. New York, Oxford University Press, 1967. In his last major work, Rose analyzes various theories of power in America and deals with the political functions of voluntary associations. A chapter on voluntary associations is largely an updated version of his earlier work.

Schlesinger, Arthur M., Sr., "Biography of a Nation of Joiners," *American Historical Review*, 50 (October 1944): 1–25.

—— *Paths to the Present.* New York, Macmillan, 1949. An essay on voluntary associations, which covers the same ground as Schlesinger's article "A Biography of a Nation of Joiners," is included in this text.

Seligman, Edwin R. A., and Alvin Johnson, eds., *The Encyclopedia of the Social Sciences.* New York, Macmillan, 1935. Although it is dated and has been "replaced" by a new edition, the first encyclopedia of the social sciences contains a number of entries dealing with various types of voluntary associations such as friendly societies, Masonry, clubs, women's organizations, patriotic societies, and so on, as well as discussions of "interests" and "pluralism." Some of the essays are considered classics and have taken on the status of historical documents.

Shepherd, Clovis R., *Small Groups: Some Sociological Perspectives.* San Francisco, Chandler, 1964. A general, introductory, elementary discussion of selected theories, research, and findings in the field of small group study organized "within the perspectives of pure and applied science and within the philosophical positions of symbolic interactions and positivism."

Sieder, Violet M., "Volunteers," *Encyclopedia of Social Work,* fifteenth issue, pp. 830–837. New York, National Association of Social Workers, 1965.

Siegel, Bernard J., "Some Recent Developments in Studies of Social and Cultural Change," *The Annals of the American Academy of Political and Social Science,* 385 (September 1969): 157–174. One section of this review article is devoted to the subject of "Migration, Enclavement and Associations."

Sills, David, *The Volunteers.* Glencoe, Illinois, Free Press, 1957.

—— "Voluntary Associations: Instruments and Objects of Change," *Human Organization,* 18 (Spring 1959): 17–21. Sills argues that associations are limited in their usefulness as instruments for rationally planned change since they are themselves the objects of change.

—— "Voluntary Associations: Sociological Aspects," in David Sills, ed., *International Encyclopedia of the Social Sciences,* volume 16. New York, Macmillan and Free Press, 1968.

Sklair, Leslie, "The Development of the Sociology of Voluntary Association in the United States," *Archives internationales de sociologie de la cooperation et du developpement,* 24 (July-December 1968): 29–53. In this historical account, which is written in French, Sklair describes the shift from early work exploring the place and significance of voluntary associations in society to the more recent empirical studies of participation.

Smith, David Horton, "The Importance of Formal Voluntary Organizations for Society," *Sociology and Social Research,* 50. 4 (1966): 483–494.

Survey Research Center, Research Center for Group Dynamics, University of Michigan, *Institute for Social Research, 1946-56.* Ann Arbor: University of Michigan, 1957. A description of the Institute's extensive research program on organizations, which includes voluntary associations in its scope.

Toffler, Alvin, *Future Shock.* New York, Random House, 1970. In chapter 7, "Organizations: The Coming Ad-hocracy," Toffler argues that bureaucracy is being replaced by a "fast-moving, information-rich, kinetic" organizational structure which is filled with "transient cells and extremely mobile individuals" (p. 144).

Tonnies, Ferdinand, *Community and Society* (Gemeinschaft und Gesellschaft). Translated and edited by Charles P. Loomis. East Lansing, Michigan State University Press, 1957. Tonnies views the voluntary association as a type of special interest group based on contractual obligations. See particularly pp. 213–216.

Tsouderos, John E., "Organizational Change in Terms of a Series of Selected Variables," *American Sociological Review,* 20 (April 1955): 206–210.

—— "Voluntary Association – Past, Present, Future," *Adult Leadership,* 6 (April 1958): 267–270 and 282. A rather impressionistic discussion of the birth, life, and death of a typical association.

Turk, Herman, "Interorganizational Networks in Urban Society," *American Sociological Review,* 35 (February 1970): 1–19. Propositions concerning interorganizational networks were tested in terms of the flow of poverty funds from federal agencies to, and among, organizations in American cities.

Verba, Sidney, *Small Groups and Political Behavior.* Princeton, Princeton University Press.

Vernon, Raymond, *The Myth and Reality of Our Urban Problems.* Cambridge, Harvard University Press, 1952. The director of the New York Metropolitan Region study has some brief comments on intellectuals and the city and on the attraction of the city and its specialized voluntary associations for different classes.

Wallerstein, Immanuel, "Voluntary Associations," in James C. Coleman and Carl G. Rosberg, Jr., eds., *Political Parties and National Integration in Tropical Africa.* Berkeley, University of California Press, 1964.

Warner, W. Lloyd, and associates, *Democracy in Jonesville.* New York, Harper, 1949.

Warriner, Charles K., and Jane Emery Prather, "Four Types of Voluntary Associations," *Sociological Inquiry,* 35 (Spring 1965): 138–148.

Whyte, William Foote, "Social Organization in the Slums," *American Sociological Review,* 8 (February 1943): 34–39. Whyte argues against the thesis that the slum is disorganized, maintaining that the older forms of organization among slum dwellers have been replaced by new forms such as voluntary associations and juvenile gangs.

Williams, Robin M., Jr., *American Society.* Third edition revised. New York, Random House, 1970. This sociology text includes a discussion of voluntary associations which is sometimes referred to by students in the field.

Wirth, Louis, "Urbanism as a Way of Life," in Paul K. Hatt and Albert J. Reiss, Jr., eds., *Reader in Urban Sociology.* Glencoe, Illinois, Free Press, 1951.

—— *Selected Papers.* Edited by Elizabeth Wirth Marvick and Albert J. Reiss, Jr. Chicago, University of Chicago Press, 1956. Speculation by a leading sociologist about the nature of urbanization and the role of voluntary associations in urban life. Wirth's article on "Urbanism as a Way of Life" is the better source for his views.

Wood, J. R., and M. N. Zald, "Aspects of Racial Integration in the Methodist Church: Sources of Resistance to Organizational Policy," *Social Forces*, 75 (December 1966): 255–266. An analysis of the difficulties of introducing policies with low consensus in an organization in which leaders have few sanctions at their disposal. The analysis could be applied to voluntary associations although here it is dealt with in the context of the church viewed as a voluntary organization.

Chapter Two   The Pluralist Thesis

VOLUNTARY ASSOCIATIONS IN THE TRADITION OF POLITICAL THEORY

The political role of voluntary associations has interested political theorists over the centuries, although until recently it has seldom been a central concern or concept in the outstanding theories of the political system. A number of democratic theorists have viewed voluntary associations as a necessary part of a democratic political order, and have discussed their role in maintaining democracy. The voluntary association, as a positive element in the political system, has been, in fact, virtually the exclusive concern of the democrat, since democrats and antidemocrats alike generally assume that voluntary associations can only function successfully in a democratic state. The private association is viewed as a threat by nondemocratic governments and their apologists, and historically the voluntary association has been either outlawed or severely restricted in all nondemocratic states. In their model of the totalitarian regime, political scientists Carl Friedrich and Zbigniew Brzezinski include as one of the six distinguishing traits of totalitarian dictatorship the absence of private, nongovernment organizations. The totalitarian regime, they maintain, is marked by "A central control and direction of the entire economy through the bureaucratic coordination of formerly independent corporate entities, typically including most other associations and group activities" (p. 22).

The philosopher Thomas Hobbes probably has been the most important exponent of the view that groups are a threat to the state. Hobbes rejects the notion that groups have a right to exist by virtue of some

natural right; for him groups exist by virtue of the sovereign's conces-
sion. The Hobbesian position on voluntary associations is discussed in
an informative essay by D. B. Robertson in his *Voluntary Associations.*

The celebration of private associations, including the voluntary associations with which we are concerned, has been the work of the "pluralist" school within political theory. Pluralists maintain that a democratic
system requires a multitude of independent, voluntary, nongovernment
associations as buffers between the individual and the state. These associations prevent the arbitrary exercise of government power and contribute to the maintenance of the polity by educating or socializing the
citizenry. Individuals are said to learn the fundamentals of group and
political action through participation in the governing of their private
organizations. Some theorists go further and argue that participation in
voluntary associations is an essential part of the good life. Participation
is supposed to give the individual a feeling of community with his fellow
man along with the opportunity to make the rules by which he must
abide. This is crucial because, in this view, a man is free only when he
makes and accepts of his own will the rules under which he must live.

THE AMERICAN TRADITION

Ironically, one of the first statements of the positive functions of the
voluntary association in the democratic political system was made by a
French aristocrat, who was not wholly sympathetic to either democracy
or private associations. Having observed the Americans for two years
during his visit in the 1830s, Alexis de Tocqueville concluded that they
were a "nation of joiners" and wrote that "Americans of all ages, all
conditions and all dispositions constantly form associations." He
thought the Americans were even more addicted to associations than
the English. While the English seemed to regard associations as only one
of several "powerful means of actions," the Americans appeared to
regard associations as the only means (II, 107).

Tocqueville perceived a connection between the proliferation of
private groups in the United States and the egalitarian, democratic character of the society. Since individuals in an egalitarian society are weak
(in contrast to the aristocratic individual in the European social order),
the citizens "become powerless if they do not learn voluntarily to help
one another. If men living in democratic countries had no right and no
inclination to associate for political purposes, their independence would

be in great jeopardy, whereas if they never acquired the habit of forming associations in ordinary life, civilization itself would be endangered.
A people among whom individuals lost the power of achieving great
things single-handed, without acquiring the means of producing them
by united exertions would soon lapse into barbarism" (II, 107).

A British observer, James Bryce, helped perpetuate the Tocquevillean
view that the United States was unique in the extent of its organizational life. In *The American Commonwealth* he wrote: "Associations
are created, extended, and worked in the United States more quickly
and effectively than in any other country. In nothing does the executive
talent of the people better shine than in the promptitude wherewith the
idea of an organization for common object is taken up, in the instinc-
tive discipline that makes everyone who joins in starting it fall into his
place, in the practical, business-like turn which the discussions forthwith
take" (pp. 281–282).

Bryce emphasized the role played by associations in American politics,
and was particularly impressed by the power of the temperance societies
in elections and their part in the development of opinion. He observed:
"Such associations . . . rouse attention, excite discussion, formulate
principles, submit plans, embolden and stimulate their members, produce that impression of a spreading movement which goes so far
towards success with a sympathetic and sensitive people . . . the appearance of strength gathers recruits as well as puts heart into the original
combatants. Unexpected support gathers to every rising cause. If it be
true that individuality is too weak in the country, strong and self-reliant
statesmen or publicists too few, so much the greater is the value of their
habit of forming associations, for it creates new centers of force and
motion, and nourishes young causes and unpopular doctrines into self-
confident aggressiveness. But in any case they are useful as indications
of the tendencies at work and the forces behind those tendencies. By
watching the attendance at meetings, the language held, the amount of
zeal displayed, a careful observer can discover what ideas are getting
hold of the popular mind" (p. 238).

As noted in the previous chapter, other observers of the American
scene have tended to view voluntary organizations in much the same
fashion as Tocqueville and Bryce. Native commentators like Schlesinger
have, if anything, placed even greater emphasis on the importance of
associations. For example, historians Oscar and Mary Handlin admit
that voluntarism has entailed "heavy social costs" in waste, inefficiency,

and the duplication of effort, but conclude that these costs are out-weighed by the benefits. They point out that voluntary associations have kept the individual from feeling isolated, protected him from the state, met needs that could not be filled by the government, and pre-served a degree of choice for him. They assert that voluntary associa-tions have made it possible for the economic and social system to recover from mistakes by keeping alternative courses of action open; and have further maintained the flexibility and adaptability of the sys-tem by fostering a high degree of experimentalism. In sum, the Handlins write: "That the voluntary association sometimes served the ends of the state was less important than the fact that it also offered society an alternative to it. By facilitating collective activity of all sorts, freedom of association enabled men to dispense with coercion and also encour-aged an active rather than a passive attitude. It was not necessary to wait for the initiative of a higher authority in the face of the need for action; Americans knew how to set themselves going" (p. 112).

A number of explanations have been offered to account for the im-portance and proliferation of voluntary associations in the United States. The Handlins indicate that the relative weakness of state govern-ments, and their resulting inability to establish strict controls over pri-vate groups, facilitated voluntarism. In contrast to other countries, the right of association is also recognized (by implication) in the Constitu-tion itself, although the Founding Fathers tended to view private groups as a necessary evil rather than a positive good. In the *Federalist* papers, Madison wrote of the danger of factions and the threat they posed to the public interest. However, he claimed that factions must be permitted in a free state, for liberty would suffer more if the government outlawed private groups. He argued that division of power among units of govern-ment and between the government and the people organized in factions or groups is necessary because the imperfections of men make it unwise to trust governments with total power. Given this state of affairs, the "cure" for the danger of factions is to insure the establishment and competition of many groups.

Over the years, American law has come to take a more positive atti-tude toward voluntary associations. Their right to exist and to interact with the government has long been established. A constitutional law of associations has gradually been developed, which is helpfully summa-rized in two monographs: *The Constitutional Right of Association* by David Fellman and *Groups and the Constitution* by Robert A. Horn.

Fellman also provides some comparative data on the rights of associations in Great Britain and the democracies of continental Europe, in addition to his discussions of such topics as unlawful assembly and public meetings; freedom of association; the right of association and exposure by government; and the "bad association" and "bad associates" doctrine in American law. The emphasis in Horn's book is on the modern political theories of association, beginning with Hobbes and Locke, and their relationship to the principles which the Supreme Court has established concerning the rights of groups. While the major part of Horn's work deals with churches, labor unions, and political parties, he has included material relating to voluntary associations.

CLASSICAL PLURALISM

Although there are private associations in other nations, both the theory of pluralism and the extensive development of voluntarism are generally viewed as primarily Anglo-American phenomena. For example, D. B. Robertson, in his essay on Hobbes's theory of association, observes that: "England . . . or more broadly the Anglo-Saxon world, has been the spawning ground for voluntary groups which have characterized modern, Western democratic societies. It is not that non-Anglo-Saxon countries have not had voluntary associations in impressive numbers; it is the function that these groups have performed in the societies which has been the most significant point, and this point has been determinative for the type of society which has developed" (p. 109). Robertson believes that England experienced an "organizational explosion" in the seventeenth century in which for the first time groups took on the function of cushioning the space between the individual and the state, of qualifying and regulating the state's power, as well as recapturing something of the "medieval sense of community."

The great English political theorists of the liberal democratic tradition all assumed that a free society would have private groups within it, although they usually did not write in detail about voluntary associations. The individualist orientation of the early liberal tradition led to a preoccupation with the rights of individuals and to the slighting of the role of groups in the polity. When they did turn to the place of associations, the liberals tended either to write in very general terms or to deal with such institutions as the church and the business corporation. For example, Locke discusses freedom of association in relation to religious bodies in his *Letter on Toleration*. However, as Robert A. Horn points out: "two of his arguments have much broader implications. Most important, Locke assumes that the individual has a natural and unalienable right to associate. He needs no permission from government to exercise this right; indeed civil society has an obligation to protect his right and to limit only on a clear demonstration of necessity. It is this principle which is the foundation of Anglo-American thinking about freedom of association. A corollary of this principle is almost as important: the rights of a group are a derivative from the right of the individual to associate" (*Groups and the Constitution*, p. 8).

Given their individualist orientation, English and American liberals were inclined to defend groups in terms of the benefits they brought to the individual. John Stuart Mill favored voluntary action on the grounds that: "In many cases, though individuals may not do the particular thing so well, on the average, as the officers of government, it is nevertheless desirable that it should be done by them, rather than by government, as a means to their own mental education — a mode of strengthening their active faculties, exercising their judgment, and giving them a familiar knowledge of the subjects with which they are thus left to deal. This is a principal, though not the sole recommendation . . . of the conduct of industrial and philanthropic enterprises by voluntary associations" (*Utilitarianism, Liberty, and Representative Government*, p. 164). In the twentieth century A. D. Lindsay, a leading liberal in the T. H. Green tradition, argued that voluntary associations preserved democracy, and that the experience of interacting with others in an association helped to preserve the individual's personality. Explaining his position, Lindsay wrote: "Within trade unions and perhaps as much in friendly societies, cooperative societies, and working men's clubs and institutes the ordinary member of the rank and file has a chance to make his contribution, to have his work and his particular gift recognized, to earn the personal respect of his fellows . . . The isolated individual is always powerless against great organizations. The ordinary man, if his personality is to have a chance, must have his own small association of which he can be an effective member. He must have his own discussion group if his personality is to hold out against the molder of mass opinion; his own trade union branch if he is to hold his own against the petty tyranny of officials" (*The Modern Democratic State*, pp. 258–259).

Similar views have been expressed by other modern theorists including those who stand in the "humanist" stream of Marxism. Erich Fromm, the psychoanalyst who has drawn on both Marxism and Freudian psychology, is probably one of the most noted of this category. The value of participation in meaningful groups and of exercising individual freedom and spontaneous creativity in associations is a theme running throughout all of Fromm's works. In *The Revolution of Hope*, one of his most recent books, Fromm stresses the need for "participant face-to-face groups" in "all enterprises," whether in business, education, health, political life, or leisure activities, if the human being is to be more than an automaton. Fromm also proposes the formation of a movement of clubs and groups which will serve as the spearhead of the new humanistic society, pointing out that: "Historically, important movements have begun their lives in small groups. It does not matter whether we think of the early Christians, the early Friends, the Masons. I am referring to the fact that groups which represent an idea in its purity and without compromises are the seedbeds of history; they keep the idea alive, regardless of the rate of progress it makes among the majority" (p. 160).

The nineteenth and twentieth century English liberals such as Ernest Barker, G. D. H. Cole, Harold Laski, John Figgis, and Frederic Maitland, who collectively are loosely identified as members of the Pluralist school, strayed from the Lockean individualism of earlier liberalism although they never went so far as the German scholars like Otto Gierke whom they admired. Thus, Ernest Barker in his introduction to Gierke's work expresses sympathy with the German political theorist's concept of "real group personality," but warns that such a concept is only an analogy, and that it can be dangerous if the state itself is regarded as a person. Barker cites events in Germany at the time of his writing, just following the Nazis' accession to power, as an indication of some of the pitfalls of organic theories of the group.

The pluralist position has been well summarized by George Sabine, the distinguished American student of political theory, in the conclusion to his article on "The Two Democratic Traditions" in which he compares French and Anglo-Saxon political theory. "In order to be democratic a society has to be a complex of lesser societies which are corporately or collectively units because they stand for interests that are at once personal to their members and are shared, and such groups have to provide the conditions for giving their members a justified sense of participation. Collectively they have to be self-governing in the sense that they set the standards of their own performance, gauge their own interests, and in general live their own lives in their own way, and at the same time they have to give their members individually a part in forming the collective decision. This is what liberty means, in so far as it is a personal experience in a social organization . . . Society is full of 'rules-making institutions,' but whether rules are oppressive or not depends very much on how they are made and enforced, and particularly on the attitude engendered in a person who is subject to them. If he genuinely feels that they are *his* rules and not merely imposed on him, he is quite likely to think of them as the safeguards of his liberty. Liberty is not simply an attribute of an individual; it is a relationship between a person and the complex of societies to which he belongs. The extent to which freedom of association can be generally and effectively achieved, and the extent to which association can preserve individual spontaneity, are the measures of liberty in any society" (pp. 469–470). Sabine then points out that the "theory candidly accepts the existence of many and diverse interests and of groups with real power to protect them, and also the certainty that diverse interests in many cases will be antagonistic. The theory can lead to a workable policy only if negotiation and mutual adjustment lead to agreements that are at once reasonably acceptable and reasonably stable" (p. 470). Lastly, he notes that the "development of democratic constitutionalism has largely consisted in extending or inventing institutions before which conflicting interests could be made to confront one another under conditions leading to successful negotiation and orderly regulation . . . [this] principle has been steadily and very widely extended. Its fundamental assumptions are that issues are so complex and changeable that parties at interest must be free to make their own case, that deliberation at this level must in the nature of the case take place largely through the spokesman of organized interests" (p. 470).

THE PRIVATE ASSOCIATION IN FRENCH AND GERMAN POLITICAL THOUGHT

In France the growth of voluntary associations differed in extent and character from that in the United States and Britain and the theoretical view was correspondingly different. Rousseau, the political theorist of the French democratic tradition, viewed private associations with some hostility, since he believed that "partial societies" prevented the complete expression of the general will. In the *Social Contract* Rousseau observed: "when factions arise, and partial associations are formed at the expense of the great associations, the will of each of these associations becomes general in relation to its members, while it remains particular in relation to the State . . . It is therefore essential, if the general will is to be able to express itself that there should be no partial society within the State" (p. 27). However, Rousseau reasoned, apparently in the same fashion as James Madison did in Federalist 10, that if it were impossible to eliminate all partial societies, then it was best to have as many as possible and to prevent them from being unequal. Rousseau does not elucidate, but presumably he believed that competing factions would control the effects of faction by preventing any one group, whether a majority or minority, from prevailing over the general will (or "public good" in Madison's terms).

Although Rousseau's theory was certainly not the only cause of the legal restrictions on the rights of associations which have existed in France since the Revolution, it probably helped provide a rationale for the policy. These restrictions and the general status of French voluntary associations, both past and present, are discussed and analyzed in detail by Arnold Rose in a chapter on "Voluntary Associations in France" which appears in his book *Theory and Method in the Social Sciences.* Rose argues that the weak tradition of voluntary associations in France is due to a variety of factors: "(1) the deliberate repression of associations by government, fearful of nonconforming and revolutionary forces; (2) the liberal tradition concerned with the freedom of the individual . . . (3) the general concern over the consequences of mainmort (that is, the hoarding of wealth by associations so that it does not circulate and cannot be taxed); (4) the Catholic tradition of attempting to encompass the individual within the church and of having priests, rather than laymen, active in the welfare and improvement activities of the community; and (5) the strong central government — as opposed to decentralized and even frontier conditions of the United States — which performs many functions left by the United States to local governments, which are closer to the people, or to citizens themselves" (p. 114). Rather ironically, a number of revolutionary underground associations developed in France which repressed associations, but did not appear to the same extent in England and the United States where groups were allowed to function openly in the political arena. Rose believes French revolutionary activity can in part be explained by the government's denial of legitimate channels of operation to private groups. He also points out that the absence of viable voluntary associations cut off one channel for the organization of resistance during the Nazi occupation in World War II. In contrast to a country like Norway where "the organization of the resistance was immeasurably aided by the existence of many voluntary associations," in France the task of organizing the resistance fell largely to the Communist party because it was one of the few strong groups in the nation.

According to Rose's "general theory of voluntary associations," such groups came into existence following the Industrial Revolution in order to fill man's need for fellowship, personal security, and "an explanation of the forces controlling the perceived world." Prior to the Industrial Revolution, these needs had been satisfied by the all-encompassing community, church, and extended family. In contemporary France they are partially met by the modern café, the political party, the conjugal family, the public park, and — to the extent that they have not already disintegrated — by the community and the extended family. Rose believes the church has disintegrated almost completely, and does not serve man's needs at present. All told, he regards modern French institutions as inadequate. They meet the need for fellowship, but not the need for security or for explanation. Although he does not actually claim that the alleged failure of French society to satisfy human needs and to maintain its own stability is due to the weakness of its voluntary associations, Rose implies that this is the case and quotes with approval Durkheim's pronouncement that: "A nation can be maintained only if, between the state and the individual, there is intercalated a whole series of secondary groups near enough to the individuals to attract them strongly in their sphere of action and drag them, in this way, into the general torrent of social life" (Rose, p. 115).

The German theory of voluntary association tended to develop in a different direction from that of Anglo-Saxon liberalism, as we have already indicated in our comments concerning Barker's essay on Gierke. According to Georg Iggers, a historian writing on early nineteenth century German liberal thought, Germany lacked both a conception of a society consisting of voluntary associations and a "tradition of voluntary association in her political, religious, and to an extent her economic life." While German liberal theorists of the nineteenth century did deal with voluntary associations, their position was corporatist as opposed to individualist. They viewed groups "not as associations formed or maintained by individuals for common purposes, but as ends in themselves."

In the course of time, doctrines of natural sovereignty became the focal point of German liberal theory, and the rights of the individual were increasingly subordinated to those of the community and of the state. In his paper published in Robertson's *Voluntary Associations,* Iggers traces the various stages in this progressive development from Wilhelm von Humboldt through Johann Droysen and Gierke, concluding that by 1871 the democratic view of voluntary associations had completely given way to an organismic, corporate concept, which stressed inequality, hierarchical organization, and restricted participation. The crucial ideas of natural law and of the state as an association of limited purposes were absent from German political theory. Iggers writes: "it is difficult to escape the thought that the radical repudiation of natural law and of the theory of voluntary association left Germany more prone than the Western democracies to political nihilism and totalitarianism" (p. 157). However, Iggers notes that it is important to distinguish between theory and practice since there were voluntary associations in "German political, cultural, philanthropic, educational, economic and athletic life" in nineteenth century Germany. Unfortunately, he does not try to explain this seeming contradiction between theory and practice.

CONTEMPORARY AMERICAN PLURALISM

It is probably fair to say (although we cannot provide full documentation here) that pluralism has been the unspoken ideology of American political practice for much of the nation's history. Certainly the New Deal acted on pluralist assumptions, as did John F. Kennedy and Lyndon Johnson, and Richard Nixon has made it a point to emphasize his faith in voluntary action (as opposed to government initiatives) in all spheres of the society. Perhaps the Johnson administration's insistence on working with organized groups, even if it meant the government had to organize the groups, provides the strongest evidence of the American belief in the nongovernment association.

However, despite the widespread acceptance of pluralist thinking, it is impossible to identify a single contemporary theorist, or group of theorists, as the spokesmen for liberal democratic pluralism today. In addition to George Sabine, there are a number of semiphilosophic commentators on the contemporary social and political scene who have expressed pluralistic views, but none has developed a systematic or complete statement of the position. For example, Robert Nisbet, a sociologist with the temperament of a political theorist, has written on the political theory of the community and the association and advanced his own views on the importance of participation, in *Community and Power* (originally called *The Quest for Community*). Nisbet is critical of those liberal democrats who regard the individual as the basic unit of society. He believes that the group, especially the small and relatively informal group, is the fundamental unit of society, and reasons that: "The liberal values of autonomy and freedom of personal choice are indispensable to a genuinely free society, but we shall achieve and maintain these only by vesting them in the conditions in which liberal democracy will thrive — diversity of culture, plurality of association, and division of authority" (p. 279).

There is also a section on the pluralist society in the Rockefeller panel report on *The Power of the Democratic Idea,* which summarizes much of the thinking about the positive contributions of voluntary associations in a democratic polity. The pluralist society is described as a society of greater freedom since it has private associations which protect and support the individual and educate him in democratic habits, especially the art of compromise. Together with the media of communication and the political parties, voluntary associations are seen as serving democratic purposes by defining political issues for the public. Thus they bear the "crucial responsibility of determining whether the political dialogue will be serious or merely superficial, informed or studiously ignorant." In sum, the pluralist society: "provides conditions in which the habit of compromise has a chance to develop and opportunities for reasonable and rewarding compromises are likely to flourish. In such a society the citizen has many different interests and associations; no center of power and interest embraces all the others; no single issue becomes so dominant that all other issues pile up around it. When an individual has many interests and belongs to many groups, he is unlikely to risk everything on a single issue, and he is likely to bring an external perspective to the struggles in which he engages. Some of his interests may overlap those of men and women who are among the innocent bystanders. Some even may be identical with those of members of the group directly opposed to his own. Wittingly or unwittingly, in consequence, he is likely to see things a little from the outside and to rehearse the larger social issue in an inner debate in his own mind" (p. 36).

Many social scientists operate on pluralist assumptions, but fail to spell out their premises. Arnold Rose, whose ideas we have already mentioned at several points, and William Kornhauser are among the few who have tried to develop a systematic pluralist theory. In *Theory and Method in the Social Sciences* Rose postulates that social influence groups (those organized to change some aspect of the system) play a major role in supporting American democracy by: (1) distributing power over social life among a large proportion of the people; (2) encouraging a sense of satisfaction with democratic processes through helping the individual see how these "processes function in limited circumstances, of direct interest to himself, rather than as they grind away in a distant, impersonal and incomprehensible fashion"; and (3) providing a social mechanism for "continually instituting social changes" (p. 51). In a later work, *The Power Structure*, Rose adds to this list, postulating that voluntary associations also serve (4) "to tie society together and to minimize the disintegrating effects of conflict" — the social cohesion function; (5) to give the individual a feeling of identification with a smaller group than he can fully understand and can influence, thus helping to give meaning and purpose to the individual's life — the function of personal identification; and (6) to enhance an individual's social status — the function of social and economic advancement (pp. 250-251).

Rose argues that voluntary associations are generally to be found only in urban and democratic societies, and that (as we have seen in our discussion of France) associations serve in these societies as something of a replacement for the weakened family, church, and community. The individual turns to the voluntary association for security, for "self-expression," and for "satisfaction of his interests." He concludes that: "If this is the case, the voluntary association would tend to contribute to the democratic character of American society, since strong family systems, churches, and communities tend to be totalitarian in their influence over the individual, whereas voluntary associations distribute and diversity power and influence" (*Theory and Method*, p. 59).

While Rose notes that none of his hypotheses have been fully established, he cites evidence in their support, and it is clear that on the whole he feels his theory actually describes the American system. Thus, he ends his chapters on voluntary associations in both *The Power Structure* and *Theory and Method in the Social Sciences* by writing: "Fortunately for the United States, participation in associations is voluntary and the associations are able to compete for their share of real power in the society."

Like Rose, William Kornhauser sees voluntary associations as vital in supporting the democratic polity and preventing the development of a "mass society." The concept of mass society has been variously defined, but here it can best be thought of as an extension of the view that urbanization promotes anomie and results in an atomistic society without a sense of community or a meaningful role for the individual. Kornhauser's book on *The Politics of Mass Society* is designed in part to answer the "aristocratic" critics of pluralist democracy who regard participation by the average man as a threat to true civilization and one of the causes of the totalitarian mass society.

In Kornhauser's schema, society is divided into three levels. The voluntary association and the local community fall in the intermediate level, sandwiched between the family (in the first level of primary or personal relations) and the state (on the third level of societal relations). In the pluralist society containing a wide variety of independent, limited function or noninclusive groups, this intermediate level maintains democracy and freedom in several ways. By meeting many of the people's demands, intermediate institutions protect elites from excessive pressure by the masses and preserve their effective leadership. Moreover, as long as the aims of the group are not actually subversive, group leaders help "shore up the larger system of authority to which their own authority is inextricably bound." Conversely, by providing the social basis for free and open competition for leadership posts, widespread participation in the selection of leaders, restraint in the application of pressures on leaders, and self-government in many areas of social life, intermediate groups curb the power of the elites and prevent them from exploiting the masses. Kornhauser expands on this theme, arguing that:

> intermediate groups help to protect elites by functioning as channels through which popular participation in the larger society (especially in the national elites) may be directed and restrained. In the absence of intermediate groups to act as representatives and guides for popular participation, people must act *directly* in the critical centers of society, and therefore in a manner unrestrained by the values and interests of a variety of social groups. [Moreover] . . . the opposition among such groups restrains one another's power, thereby limiting the aggregate intervention in elites; that is, a system of social checks and

balances among a plurality of diverse groups operates to protect elites as well as non-elites in ways we have indicated. Furthermore, the separation of the various spheres of society — for example, separation of religion and politics — means that access to elites in one sphere does not directly affect elites in other spheres. The various authorities are more or less autonomous in their own spheres, in that they are not directly determined in their membership or policy by authorities in other spheres. These same factors protect non-elites from elites, since independent groups guard their members from one another, and since overlapping memberships among groups, *each of which concerns only limited aspects of its member's lives,* restrains each group from seeking total domination over its membership. (p. 78)

While groups prevent the state from tyrannizing the individual, it should be noted, the state for its part prevents the private group from dominating the individual member.

Turning from sociologists to political scientists, one probably finds an even greater tendency to accept pluralism, both as an accurate description of the United States at present and as a model for the good society. Although we have no statistics to cite as proof, an examination of the major works in political science until the mid-1960s reveals a pronounced inclination to justify American institutions in general and their pluralist character in particular. As Grant McConnell notes in his critique of political scientists and the political system they defended, this boosterism was "particularly strong in discussions of the place of interest groups in the large political order. It has been marked among social scientists by the disinterment of the work of Arthur Bentley, revived use of the word 'pluralism', revulsion against ideology — even against any large goals in politics — and cynicism about the meaning of "the public interest." It has also involved discovery of a beneficient order in the workings of the pluralism of interest groups. The virtues of this order have been variously perceived as the guarantee of freedom, the preservation of diversity, the limitation of power, protection against mass movements and irrationality in politics, and the provision of meaning in common life" (*Private Power and American Democracy*, p. 353).

It is impossible here to discuss at length the work of contemporary political science, or even of the study of pressure groups. However, a few comments are in order. One must first distinguish between those scholars who identified themselves as advocates of a Bentleyan-type of group theory and the large body of political scientists who simply proceeded on pluralist assumptions in their work. There are relatively few individuals in the first camp. In fact, until recently there were almost no "group theorists" in the strict sense. *The Process of Government,* in which Arthur Bentley argued that the raw material of politics is group activity, and that the focus of political science must therefore be on the activity of political interest groups, was largely ignored when it was first published in 1908. It was not until the 1950s that Bentley's theories were revived by a number of scholars, who also updated his ideas, and *The Process of Government* was reissued, receiving high praise in a review by Bertram Gross in the *American Political Science Review.* David Truman's *The Governmental Process* was the most influential of the later Bentleyan works; Earl Latham's *The Group Basis of Politics* also deserves mention.

Truman and Latham both accept Bentley's methodology as well as his view of the significance of groups. Both also defend the legitimacy of a pluralist system in which policy is the product of group struggle and the government plays the role of a broker among competing groups. While Truman is not unaware of the possible abuses of the pluralist political system, he maintains that the system is self-corrective. Its evils are counteracted in large part through overlapping memberships which prevent any one group from developing an excessive hold on individual members, and through the emergence of "potential groups." Such groups, "based upon interests held widely throughout society," supposedly appear whenever those fundamental interests are threatened. Although Truman's book contains considerable descriptive material, he really cannot be said to have proven any of his major contentions.

While the literature of political pressure groups is generally excluded from consideration in the study of voluntary associations, it cannot be completely ignored since voluntary organizations do sometimes act as pressure groups and there is consequently some overlap of concern. In addition to the books cited above, several other works provide a good introduction to the field of interest group study. The recognized text in the area is V. O. Key's *Politics, Parties, and Pressure Groups.* Along with the theoretical discussion, Key describes the activities of various interest groups, including voluntary associations, when they act as pressure groups. Two shorter, more recent works devoted exclusively to interest groups, Abraham Holtzman's *Interest Groups and Lobbying* and Harmon Zeigler's *Interest Groups in American Society*, both provide introductory summaries as well as bibliographies. The Zeigler book has a chapter on "Interest Groups in the Literature of Political Science." *Pressure Groups in American Politics*, edited by H. R. Mahood, brings together essays by leading groups theorists such as Latham and articles on various pressure groups.

Descriptive data on lobbyists and information on the laws regulating the lobbying activities of interest groups can be found in the Congressional Quarterly Service publication *Legislators and the Lobbyists*. A more comprehensive view of the role of the Washington representative is given by Lewis Anthony Dexter in *How Organizations Are Represented in Washington*. Dexter's book is one of those rare works which can be of use to scholars seeking to understand the interaction of government and private groups and to the groups and their representatives seeking to improve their position vis à vis the government structure.

Since the pluralist model of the American political system has functioned as both a normative and empirical frame of reference for many political scientists, it is not surprising that "politics" itself is defined as a pluralistic process in one of the major books in the field, Vernon Van Dyke's *Political Science: A Philosophical Analysis*. Van Dyke wrote that: "politics can be defined as: (1) activity occurring within and among groups (2) which operate on the basis of desires that are to some extent shared, (3) an essential feature of the activity being a struggle of actors (4) to achieve their desires (5) on questions of group policy, group organization, group leadership, or the regulation of intergroup relationships (6) against the opposition of others with conflicting desires" (p. 134).

Like many other political scientists (particularly those identified with the behavioral movement), Van Dyke also takes the position that the scientist, qua scientist, is not qualified to determine the ultimate ends of society or the nature of the public interest since these are ethical rather than empirical matters. While there is no compelling logical reason that this view of the role of the scientist should lead to an acceptance of the American political system in which goals are determined by various private interests, in many cases this has been the result. A good illustration is provided in the work of Edward Banfield. In *Political Influence* Banfield compares central decision systems (in which decisions are made by responsible officials acting to realize system goals) with the "social choice process" of decision making (in which decisions are the "accidental by-product" of a struggle among interest groups seeking to attain their own ends). Banfield concludes that the social choice or pluralistic system is preferable because it provides a "single ultimate criterion: the distribution of influence" among competing groups, whereas the central decision process allows the decision maker to choose on the basis of his own biased, subjective concept of the good society, given the impossibility of objectively determining the public interest. Banfield recognizes that all ends may not be given consideration and that the outcome representing the greatest "total benefit" to all parties may not be the result of the pluralist process, but he believes these handicaps can be (and are, in fact) overcome by combining the social choice process with a central decision maker who lays down some guidelines. In the Chicago political system that Banfield is analyzing, Mayor Daley acts as the central decision maker; presumably the President would serve a similar purpose in the national system.

Charles E. Lindblom's work on the nature of public policy making provides a good illustration of pluralist thinking vis à vis the national decision making structure. Like Banfield, Lindblom compares two alternative decision making processes. In the "rational-comprehensive" process, the administrator proceeds by considering all alternative ends, choosing one end, and then, through empirical and theoretical analysis, choosing the policy that can be shown to be the best means to the chosen objective. In the "incremental" process of "successive limited comparisons," ends and means analysis are intertwined and the choice is made among policies each of which brings about some slight, incremental change in existing policy. The test of a "good policy" in incrementalism is typically that the participants in the process can agree on it. There is no overall goal or concept of the public interest to serve as a criterion. Lindblom rejects the rational comprehensive method, saying it is impossible to carry out, since the value problem is always one of adjustments at a margin and "there is no practicable way to state marginal objectives or values except in terms of particular policies." Moreover, the attempt to agree on the public interest only results in unnecessary conflict; it is enough that agreement can be found on specific policies. Lindblom sees the American system, and indeed any other democracy, as a system in which policy changes through incremental adjustments and policies are the result of "negotiation between groups" in a "highly fragmented" pluralist decision making process. All that is necessary to assure justice in such a system is that each interest has its watch dog, and that there is an agency within the government structure to represent its point of view.

Lindblom and Banfield are atypical only in their attempt to spell out their assumptions, not in the assumptions themselves. However, even they do not develop a true philosophical defense of the position. Americans, unlike Europeans, have tended to take pluralism for granted as a fact of life and therefore have found no need to develop a normative doctrine of pluralism similar to the Europeans. Among social scientists, pluralism was, as Henry Kariel charges in *The Decline of American Pluralism*, unconsciously adopted in the guise of a purportedly non-normative functionalism. Moreover, since stability and equilibrium are posited as system goals in the functionalist frame of reference, consciously or unconsciously political scientists (and other social scientists) adopted these goals as characteristics of the good society. In thus accepting and defending the status quo, American social scientists were inevitably inviting criticism from all those who saw the present order as something far less than a good society. In retrospect, it is only surprising that it took the reaction until the late 1960s to develop strength and become a viable threat to the Social Science establishment.

BIBLIOGRAPHY

Abernathy, Glenn, *The Right of Assembly and Association.* Columbia, University of South Carolina Press, 1961. A discussion of the law of associations in the United States and the value of associations to the social system.

Adams, James Luther, "Civil Disobedience: Its Occasions and Limits," in J. Roland Pennock and John W. Chapman eds., *Political and Legal Obligation: Nomos XII*, pp. 293–331. New York, Atherton Press, 1970. Comments on the relationship between civil disobedience and the voluntary association which, for Adams, includes churches.

—— "The Protestant Ethic with Fewer Tears," in Bernard Landis and Edward S. Tauber, eds., *In the Name of Life: Essays in Honor of Erich Fromm.* New York, Holt, Rinehart and Winston, 1971. In this provocative critique of Max Weber's conceptualization of the Protestant ethic Adams argues that Weber overlooked the Puritan concern for the whole social order and the importance they placed on forming voluntary associations to reform different aspects of the social system.

Banfield, Edward C., *Political Influence.* Glencoe, Illinois, Free Press, 1961. Banfield presents seven case studies of controversies in Chicago politics in 1957–58, and an analytical and theoretical framework from which to view the urban political scene. The case studies contain references to voluntary associations involved in the controversies, and the theory views voluntary associations as playing an important role in the initiation of the controversies.

Bentley, Arthur, *The Process of Government: A Study of Social Pressures.* Bloomington, Indiana, The Principia Press, 1949 (originally published by the University of Chicago Press in 1908).

Boonin, Leonard G., "Man and Society: An Examination of Three Models," in J. Roland Pennock and John W. Chapman, eds., *Voluntary Associations.* New York, Atherton Press, 1969. Boonin analyzes the organic and atomistic models and develops his own "persons-in-relation" theory of society as a "community of subjects." He points out that each model leads to a different conceptualization of the nature of voluntary associations.

Bryce, James, *The American Commonwealth.* Volume II, fourth edition. New York, Macmillan, 1910.

Chapman, John W., "Voluntary Association and the Political Theory of Pluralism," in J. Roland Pennock and John W. Chapman, eds., *Voluntary Associations.* New York, Atherton Press, 1969. A very general, rambling essay in which voluntary associations are defined in the broadest possible terms.

Congressional Quarterly Service, *Legislators and the Lobbyists.* Second edition. Washington, D.C., May 1968. A compendium of information on lobbying laws and activity plus several case studies on lobbying in Congress.

Dexter, Lewis Anthony, *How Organizations Are Represented in Washington.* Indianapolis, Bobbs-Merrill, 1969.

Edel, Abraham, "Commentary: Shared Commitment and the Legal Principle," in J. Roland Pennock and John W. Chapman, eds., *Voluntary Associations.* New York, Atherton Press, 1969. A criticism of Lon Fuller's essay on the principles of association (see Fuller entry in this bibliography). Edel also deals with the problem of classifying associations, especially in reference to their legal status.

Fellman, David, *The Constitutional Right of Association.* Chicago, University of Chicago Press, 1963.

Fox, Daniel M., *Voluntarism, Localism and Competition for Power.* Occasional Paper Number 3, Center for a Voluntary Society, Washington, D.C., October 1970. Fox argues that the debate over public versus private or voluntary activity simply masks the real struggle over the distribution of power and influence. "The pertinent questions are how different clusters of institutions affect individuals and groups at particular times" (p. 6).

Friedrich, Carl J., and Zbigniew K. Brzezinski, *Totalitarian Dictatorship and Autocracy.* Second edition, revised by Carl J. Friedrich. Cambridge, Harvard University Press, 1965.

Fromm, Erich, *The Revolution of Hope: Toward a Humanized Technology.* New York, Harper and Row, 1968.

Fuller, Lon L. "Two Principles of Human Association," in J. Roland Pennock and John W. Chapman, eds., *Voluntary Associations.* New York, Atherton Press, 1969. Fuller, a law professor, distinguishes between two principles of human association — shared commitment and the legal principle — and indicates how

these are related to each other. His comments are general and apply to all
types of organizations. He is especially concerned with the problem of apply-
ing law to cases involving private associations.

Gierke, Otto, *Natural Law and the Theory of Society, 1500-1800.* Volume I. Translated and with an introduction by Ernest Barker. Cambridge, England, Cambridge University Press, 1934.

Goldschmidt, Maure L., "Rousseau on Intermediate Associations," in J. Roland
Pennock and John W. Chapman, eds., *Voluntary Associations.* New York,
Atherton Press, 1969. Goldschmidt argues that Rousseau was not totally hostile to intermediate groups and cites instances in which Rousseau praised
certain groups.

Gross, Bertram, "The Process of Government" (a book review), *American Political
Science Review,* 44 (September 1950): 742-748. An extensive review, sum-
marizing and praising Arthur Bentley's *The Process of Government* which
Gross calls "one of the most important books on government ever written in
America."

Hagan, Charles B., "The Groups in a Political Science," in Roland Young, ed., *Approaches to the Study of Politics,* Evanston, Northwestern University Press,
1958. An advocate of the group as a focal point in political analysis explains
and defends the usefulness of the "group concept" that "values are authori-
tatively allocated in society through the process of the conflict of groups."

Hamilton, Alexander, John Jay, and James Madison, *The Federalist.* New York,
Random House (Modern Library), 1937. The rationale for dividing power
among groups and other "factions" is set forth in various essays in this fundamental work justifying the American constitutional system.

Handlin, Oscar, and Mary Handlin, *The Dimensions of Liberty.* Cambridge, Belknap
Press of Harvard University Press, 1961.

Harris, H. S., "Voluntary Association as a Rational Ideal," in J. Roland Pennock
and John W. Chapman, eds., *Voluntary Associations.* New York, Atherton
Press, 1969. Harris, a philosopher, engages in a rather confusing dialectic,
emerging with the conclusion that the good society is a voluntary one.

Hobbes, Thomas, *Leviathan.* Edited with an introduction by Michael Oakeshott.
Oxford, Basil Blackwell, 1957.

Holtzman, Abraham, *Interest Groups and Lobbying.* New York, Macmillan, 1966.
A short general introduction to the subject. There are chapters on interest
groups in society; the strengths and weaknesses of organization; interest
groups in Great Britain, Italy, and the United States; groups and the legislators; the executive and the judiciary; and group techniques of direct legislation.

Horn, Robert A., *Groups and the Constitution.* Stanford, Stanford University Press,
1956. Horn reviews modern political theories on voluntary associations and
"relates them to principles which are emerging from Supreme Court decisions
concerning the rights of groups." He also deals with the application of these
principles to various groups and provides some information on the right of
association in other nations.

Hurst, Willard, "Commentary: Constitutional Ideals and Private Associations," in

J. Roland Pennock and John W. Chapman, eds., *Voluntary Associations.* New York, Atherton Press, 1969. A commentary on the paper by H. S. Harris (see Harris entry in this bibliography) stressing the importance of controlling private, as well as public, associations. Hurst agrees with Harris that the American constitutional ideal places a high value on voluntarism, and that this is as it should be.

Iggers, Georg G., "The Political Theory of Voluntary Association in Early Nineteenth-Century German Liberal Thought," in B. Robertson, ed., *Voluntary Associations: A Study of Groups in Free Societies.* Richmond, Virginia, John Knox Press, 1966.

Kariel, Henry S., *The Decline of American Pluralism.* Stanford, Stanford University Press, 1961.

Kateb, George, "Some Remarks on Tocqueville's View of Voluntary Associations," in J. Roland Pennock and John W. Chapman, eds., *Voluntary Associations.* New York, Atherton Press, 1969. Kateb argues that Tocqueville's views on voluntary associations are largely obsolete since Tocqueville failed to distinguish between parties and other associations and devoted most of his attention to small business firms when dealing with civil associations. Moreover, Kateb feels that Tocqueville lacked a basic understanding of the democratic ideal of the sovereign individual, which led him in turn to misunderstand the role of voluntary associations.

Key, V. O., *Politics, Parties, and Pressure Groups.* Fourth edition. New York, Thomas Y. Crowell Company, 1958.

Kornhauser, William, *The Politics of Mass Society.* Glencoe, Illinois, Free Press, 1959.

Laski, Harold J., "Freedom of Association," *Encyclopedia of the Social Sciences,* 6:447–450. New York, Macmillan, 1935.

Latham, Earl, *The Group Basis of Politics.* Ithaca, Cornell University Press, 1952. In addition to theoretical chapters, there is a long case study of the struggle in the 80th and 81st Congress to enact "basing-point" legislation. Latham sees Congress as a group functioning in an environment of groups, both official and unofficial. He argues that policy emerges as a by-product of group action.

Lindblom, Charles E., "The Science of 'Muddling Through'," *Public Administration Review,* 19 (Spring 1959): 79–88.

Lindeman, Eduard C., *The Democratic Man,* edited by Robert Gessner. Boston, Beacon Press, 1956. This collection of essays by a well-known sociologist and educator include several statements on the role of voluntary associations in a democracy.

Lindsay, A. D., *The Modern Democratic State.* London, Oxford University Press, 1943.

Locke, John, *The Second Treatise of Civil Government and A Letter Concerning Toleration.* Edited and with an Introduction by J. W. Gough. Oxford, Basil Blackwell, 1948. The classic statement of the liberal philosophy. The *Letter,* in particular, deals with the freedom of association.

McBride, William Leon, "Voluntary Association: The Basis of an Ideal Model, and the 'Democratic' Failure," in J. Roland Pennock and John W. Chapman, eds.,

Voluntary Associations. New York, Atherton Press, 1969. McBride, a philosopher, sees voluntary associations as "ideal social forms because they ideally promote responsibility in their members" and argues that the principle of voluntariness should be extended to society as a whole.

McConnell, Grant, *Private Power and American Democracy.* New York, Alfred A. Knopf, 1967.

Mahood, H. R., *Pressure Groups in American Politics.* New York, Charles Scribner's Sons, 1967.

Mill, John Stuart, *Utilitarianism, Liberty, and Representative Government.* London, J. M. Dent, 1910.

Miller, Arthur Selwyn, "The Constitution and the Voluntary Association: Some Notes toward a Theory," in J. Roland Pennock and John W. Chapman, eds., *Voluntary Associations.* New York, Atherton Press, 1969. Miller makes some comments on the constitutional law of voluntary associations.

Nisbet, Robert A., *Community and Power.* New York, Oxford University Press, 1962. First published by Oxford in 1953 under the title *The Quest for Community.*

Pickering, George W., *Voluntarism and the American Way.* Occasional Paper Number 7, Center for a Voluntary Society, Washington, D.C., October 1970. Pickering objects to the cooptation of voluntary associations by government and the tendency to view the associations as mere interest groups. To Pickering voluntary associations are essential in a democratic society which depends upon them for protecting significant differences. "Voluntary associations are the citizen's means for citizen participation in the shaping of our common life" (p. 11).

Rice, Charles E., *Freedom of Association.* New York, New York University Press, 1962. A study of the constitutional law of associations which deals with religious, labor, and other voluntary associations in their role as pressure groups.

Robertson, D. B., "Hobbes's Theory of Associations in the Seventeenth-Century Milieu," in D. B. Robertson, ed., *Voluntary Associations: A Study of Groups in Free Societies.* Richmond, Virginia, John Knox Press, 1966.

Rockefeller Panel, *The Power of the Democratic Idea.* Sixth Report of the Rockefeller Brothers Fund Special Studies Project. Garden City, New York, Doubleday, 1960.

Rose, Arnold, *Theory and Method in the Social Sciences.* Minneapolis, The University of Minnesota Press, 1954.

—— *The Power Structure: Political Process In American Society.* New York, Oxford University Press, 1967.

Rousseau, Jean Jacques, *The Social Contract and Discourses.* Translated by G. D. H. Cole. New York, E. P. Dutton, 1950.

Sabine, George, "The Two Democratic Traditions," *The Philosophical Review,* 61 (October 1952): 451–474.

Schlesinger, Arthur M., Sr., "Biography of a Nation of Joiners," *American Historical Review,* 50 (October 1944): 1–25.

Tocqueville, Alexis de, *Democracy in America.* Two Volumes. The Henry Reeve

Text as revised by Francis Bowen and further corrected and edited by Phillips Bradley. New York, Alfred A. Knopf, 1947.

Truman, David B., *The Governmental Process.* New York, Alfred A. Knopf, 1951.

Van Dyke, Vernon, *Political Science: A Philosophical Analysis.* Stanford, Stanford University Press, 1960.

Zeigler, Harmon, *Interest Groups in American Society.* Englewood Cliffs New Jersey, Prentice-Hall, 1964.

Chapter Three   Pluralism: Attack and Defense

The volume of criticism has decidedly increased in the last decade, but the assumptions of pluralism have never been completely accepted in all quarters. The American tradition has from its beginning included those who viewed the state as "unified and positive" in character. Both in theory and practice some Americans have taken the Burkean position that a strong government is not "the sole source of injustice [and] that a feeble government which gives free rein to factious nongovernmental groups may be just as oppressive." Alexander Hamilton was a leading early exponent of this outlook. According to Henry Kariel, Americans in general have not hesitated to rely on a reservoir of positive power in the state. Large scale associations have been regulated and made to comply with constitutional standards of procedure when they assumed a public role, although in Kariel's view this regulation has been neither sufficiently extensive nor effective. (*The Decline of American Pluralism,* pp. 192–212.)

As Grant McConnell documents in *Private Power and American Democracy,* progressivism represents a post–Civil War version of the recurring opinion that private groups are dangerous to the public interest. However, as McConnell further notes, neither the critics of private groups nor their more numerous defenders have produced an "authoritative text" defining their point of view. The critics have been hampered by the character of the orthodoxy, which is unstated, strongly established, and believed with an almost religious reverence. McConnell explains: "The orthodoxy supporting the resulting political arrangements is an unstable amalgram of different ideas. One is simply satisfaction with the performance of the economy and the general prosperity. Another is the vaguely expressed feeling that present arrangements are the result of much evolution and should not be rashly disturbed. Another is the belief that without the existing array of private organizations the nation might be subject to a host of evils culminating in anomie and totalitarian mass movements. Yet another is the conviction that these associations balance and counterbalance each other, with automatic benefit to society. The most important, however, has been a deep-seated faith in the virtue of small units of social and political organization" (pp. 4–5).

Robert Michels laid down his "iron law of oligarchy" more than fifty years ago (in *Political Parties,* first published in 1913). Yet the acceptance of this law and the demonstration of its operation within nongovernment organizations is more widespread today than it was in the early part of the century. Similarly, the thesis that society is always dominated by an elite is as old as political theory and received expression within sociology from such theorists as Comte, Pareto, and Michels long before the present expansion of the social sciences. But it is only since World War II that the thesis has been applied to the United States to any great degree. Led by C. Wright Mills in sociology, significant numbers of social scientists have come to see American pluralism as a facade which hides a ruling power elite. In political science, scholars like McConnell, Kariel, and Theodore Lowi have also questioned the view that nongovernment groups restrict government power and prevent its abuse. And, of course, the New Left and militant black spokesmen from Herbert Marcuse to Rap Brown have all agreed that there is an "Establishment" which effectively robs the people and their genuine organizations of any real influence over policy. For example, in *One Dimensional Man* Marcuse, who is sometimes regarded as the unofficial philosopher of the student revolt, maintains that the United States is really a totalitarian society so dominated by its technology that meaningful choice does not exist. Addressing himself to the Galbraith contention that countervailing powers prevent the tyranny of any single power, Marcuse writes that: "Advanced industrial society is indeed a system of countervailing powers. But these forces cancel each other out in a higher unification — in the common interest to defend and extend the established position, to combat historical alternatives, to contain qualitative change. The countervailing powers do not include those which counter the whole. They tend to make the whole immune against negation from within as well as without; the foreign policy of containment appears as an extension of the domestic policy of containment" (p. 57).

OLIGARCHICAL AND MASS ORGANIZATIONS

The tendency of organizations to develop internally nondemocratic and bureaucratic structures as they grow older is generally accepted today as fact by social scientists. Michels' "iron law," which grew out of his study of the German social parties and labor movements, is included in the Berelson and Steiner inventory of findings from the sciences of human behavior as a well-established proposition, applicable to all types of organizations (p. 366). Paradoxically, Michels himself undertook his study because he found the internal failure of democracy in organizations fighting for a democratic society both disturbing and significant. His work led him to an unhappy conclusion: "It is organization which gives birth to the dominion of the elected over the electors, of the mandatories over the mandators, of the delegates over the delegators. Who says organization says oligarchy" (p. 401).

A good summary of the contemporary view of the process of bureaucratization in voluntary organizations can be found in Bernard Barber's article "Participation and Mass Apathy in Associations." (The work on organization theory cited in the first chapter is also helpful.) Barber points out that most voluntary associations are run by a few officials and staff members, even though the organizations have parliamentary, democratic forms such as decision by vote, elections, and other procedures for removing officials who are not responsible to the membership. Since the modern voluntary association is specific and segmental in character, it engages only part of the individual member's involvement. The average member therefore tends to have only limited interest in the organization and is quite apathetic and inactive. He is willing to let the group be run by the elected officials and hired staff, who do have a greater concern with the organization and are willing to work hard. The result is an oligarchy which retains power for many years without any significant challenge to its reign. Structural factors such as specialization and a hierarchical structure of authority, which develop to enable the organization to deal more effectively with its environment, contribute to the development of oligarchy too. Those who fill positions in the hierarchy acquire knowledge and skills — and, not least, a personal interest in maintaining their positions — which differentiate them from the average member and make it possible for them to hold on to these positions.

The social scientist will undoubtedly recognize the influence of Max Weber, as well as Michels, in Barber's analysis. In fact all students of organization structure are to some extent indebted to Weber and his pioneering analysis of bureaucracy and the "routinization of charisma" in organizations. Weber's most important work on bureaucracy can be found in the collection edited by H. H. Gerth and C. Wright Mills; there is a good selection of his writings on routinization in the collection edited by S. N. Eisenstadt.

Some analysts have seen a tendency for organizations to develop beyond mere oligarchy into "mass organizations" in which power is centralized in the hands of a national elite and autonomous (and even semi-autonomous) subgroups have disappeared. Philip Selznick, a sociologist known for his organization studies, defines the mass organization as "one in which participation is segmental, mobilization is high, and the membership is relatively unstructured save by the formal devices of managerial control and by unmediated emotional attachments to a centralized elite" (*The Organizational Weapon,* p. 286). Such mass organizations are said to contribute to the development of atomization, mass society, and totalitarianism. In *The Politics of Mass Society,* William Kornhauser claims that when members feel their organizations are remote, they become prime targets for mobilization by totalitarian elites. He explains that "In the absence of a structure of smaller groups, formal organizations themselves become remote from their members, and as a result cannot deeply influence them nor command their loyalties. Consequently, members of excessively bureaucratized organizations may become mobilized by totalitarian elites" (p. 95).

It is easy to see why Kornhauser proceeds to recommend more membership participation in organizations as an antidote to the mass society, although it is not so easy to see how this can be achieved. All of the evidence (as will be seen in the next chapter) points to the almost universal existence of apathy and oligarchy. The International Typographical Union, which was studied by Seymour Lipset (with Martin Trow and James Coleman), is the one widely known exception to the rule of oligarchy. According to Lipset, writing in *Union Democracy,* the ITU is the only labor organization (and probably the only large private organization of any kind) which has maintained both a democratic two-party political system and an internal network of voluntary associations. This network, which was created to satisfy the members' social and recreational needs, in turn is paralleled and supported by a large informal group structure. Lipset and his colleagues found that the informal and formal activities of the union members functioned to increase the individuals' knowledge of and involvement in union politics, and to provide an arena within which potential leaders could acquire political skills and build a following. In addition the clubs enforce the democratic rules of union politics since officials know that the clubs can take independent action and could challenge them effectively if they violate the rules. In combination with the institutionalized party system that they help to support, the clubs thus play a key role in maintaining internal democracy in the ITU (pp. 77–79, 114–116).

VOLUNTARY ASSOCIATION AND THE MASS SOCIETY

The theory that a plurality of private groups prevents the rise of totalitarian movements and the development of a mass society has been questioned by a number of writers. There is an excellent summary and critical analysis of the theory as advanced by William Kornhauser, one of its major advocates, in an essay by W. Alvin Pitcher of the University of Chicago Divinity School. Pitcher rejects Kornhauser's assertion that *The Politics of Mass Society* is a scientific, descriptive work free of concern with values, and argues that, in fact, Kornhauser does deal with value questions, but does so inadequately since he neither defines nor defends his values. Pitcher is especially critical of what he sees as Kornhauser's failure to deal with questions relating to the quality of the elite and the validity of the ends which the elite pursues. He also questions Kornhauser's central assumption that persons who belong to groups are not available for mobilization in a mass movement. Pitcher believes that participation, by increasing an individual's interest and understanding of politics, may actually contribute to the individual's disillusionment with politics and lead to privatization insofar as the individual realizes the extent to which he and his groups lack real power and independence of action. From his Christian viewpoint, Pitcher further questions Kornhauser's belief that increased participation in private groups is an adequate guarantee of a good society. Contending that an increase in the numbers of decision makers insures neither their good will nor their ability, Pitcher rejects the pluralist's faith in process and the competition of groups. In Pitcher's view, "participation in intermediate organizations . . . represents a sickness of the soul rather than its health." Finally, he comments: "For better or for worse, and inevitably, we believe, the state permeates the life of our times. The personnel and programs of an increasing number of institutions are influenced by political institutions. Increasingly the state influences the substance of our lives. Is it not, therefore, to beg the question, to suggest that the state is neutral, merely an institution to provide a framework in which other institutions determine the substance of life?" (in Robertson, *Voluntary Associations*, pp. 258-259).

In another critique of Kornhauser, Maurice Pinard argues that the voluntary associations of a pluralist society may facilitate the advance of totalitarianism by mobilizing support for a totalitarian movement, or may alternatively remain neutral, doing nothing to hinder such a movement. Voluntary associations can aid in the diffusion of a mass movement, serving to communicate its message. Whether or not the groups do support a mass movement depends in great part on the strains that exist within a society. Pinard suggests that where there are strains, the movement may progress more rapidly in the pluralist society since it is easier to mobilize individuals already integrated into organizations by taking over these organizations than it is to reach and mobilize the atomized individual in the mass society. He argues: "If the strains are severe and widespread, alienated groups will tend to be particularly active; moreover, either conformist groups will tend to move from a restraining position to a more neutral or even to a mobilizing position or their members will tend to elude restraining effects. Their communicating role, on the other hand, will be working fully. To the extent that this prevails, I would predict that integrated individuals and pluralist societies will be more prone to social and political movements than atomized people and mass societies" (*American Journal of Sociology,* 73:689). However, he adds that once attracted to a new movement, the more integrated individuals will probably exhibit greater control of their behavior and be less likely to engage in extreme or violent acts.

Pinard's argument parallels that advanced by Joseph R. Gusfield, a sociologist who has done extensive research on voluntary associations. Gusfield maintains that extremism can, and does, occur within pluralist political structures. Groups that feel excluded from society and unfairly treated are likely to employ violent, extremist tactics (as black militants and student protestors have amply demonstrated). Moreover, a pluralist competitive structure requires some cohesive element to counterbalance the conflict of groups, if it is to retain its tranquility. The peace of a pluralist society is always fragile, and the society is ever vulnerable, particularly to those within it who reject the fundamental "rules of the game" which enable the system to survive.

THE ABUSE OF PRIVATE POWER

A number of social scientists have criticized the American pluralist system. For example, Grant McConnell has documented the dangers of power held without adequate checks by private interest groups. In *Private Power and American Democracy* he points out that private groups run by oligarchies wield power over their own members and over matters affecting the larger community, and warns that: "Far from providing guarantees of liberty, equality, and concern for the public interest, organization of political life by small constituencies tends to enforce conformity, to discriminate in favor of elites, and to eliminate public values from effective political consideration. The service of a multitude of narrowly constituted political associations is often genuine. However, this service lies in the guarantee of stability and the enforcement of order rather than in support for the central values of a liberal society" (p. 6).

Using a series of case studies McConnell demonstrates how private groups have gained power and established their control over public authority, largely by isolating particular government agencies. McConnell sees this process as a threat to the public interest. He does not accept the argument, made by proponents of the system such as David Truman, that potential interest groups will organize themselves and protect the segments of the public which had been threatened by the power of the private groups first entering the pluralist political arena. McConnell expresses doubt that potential groups will always be able to organize and observes that even if they can, "the existing inequalities will tend to be perpetuated with only minor redistribution." As he sees it, reform will have to come from forces outside the pluralist political pattern in which "groups already having power are coopted by the conferring of benefits not available to those without power" (p. 159).

Although McConnell draws his illustrations from the history of "functional groups" such as unions, professional organizations, and trade associations, he treats voluntary associations in the general, theoretical sections of his work and would seem to assume that they act much as other private groups do. While McConnell takes issue with the defenders of American pluralism, it should not be assumed that he therefore accepts the C. Wright Mills position that America is run by a power elite. Actually, McConnell believes that there are elites in the United States, but that there is no single cohesive elite, power being distributed among a number of effectively organized, relatively homogenous groups, each of which has considerable influence over "particular areas of public policy through close collaboration with segments of government." To McConnell the narrow-constituency private association — rather than any potential mass movement — presents the greatest threat to individual liberty and equality in the United States today. In his view institutions such as the major political parties and the presidency, which have large national constituencies, are much more likely to serve as the bulwarks of national cohesion and freedom than are the private associations so dear to the heart of the pluralist.

Interestingly, E. E. Schattschneider has challenged both the pluralist theorists and their critics such as McConnell, stating that the pressure system is subordinated to party politics. We cannot do justice to the theory Schattschneider weaves in *The Semi-sovereign People,* but his basic argument is that political conflict among special interests spreads or expands in scope beyond the groups most immediately interested. The pressure system, composed of special-interest, exclusive groups and dominated by business and the upper class, is very small and has to go to the parties because only the parties can mobilize a majority to win an election. Once the issue does enter party politics its outcome "is inevitably different from that of pressure politics" (p. 56).

Drawing on the work of McConnell, Theodore Lowi, also a political scientist, has traced the "degeneration" of the American pluralist ideology (and the traditional liberal and conservative positions) into a vulgarized "interest-group liberalism" which makes the following assumptions: "(1) Organized interests are homogeneous and easy to define, sometimes monolithic. Any "duly elected" spokesman for any interest is taken as speaking in close approximation for each and every member. (2) Organized interest groups pretty much fill up and adequately represent most of the sectors of our lives, so that one organized group can be found effectively answering and checking some other organized group as it seeks to prosecute its claims against society. And (3) the role of government is one of ensuring access particularly to the most effectively organized and of ratifying the agreements and adjustments worked out among the competing leaders and their claims" (*American Political Science Review,* 61:12). When no countervailing group appears on its own, the government (according to the tenets of "perverse pluralism") is actually under an obligation to foster and create an opposition organization.

Lowi contends that the most important differences between the two parties and between so-called "liberals" and "conservatives" today lie in the interest groups with which they are aligned. Political decision makers, he charges, are "guided" by the organized interests they "have taken for themselves as the most legitimate; and that is the measure of the legitimacy of demands" (p. 13).

While Lowi is not hostile to "genuine" pluralism, he expresses concern over the consequences of the "pathological" version of the philosophy which he believes to be the operative principle of government at present. As he sees it, interest-group liberalism sidesteps the problem of defining the legitimate ends of power by parceling out the determination of these ends to private interests on the false grounds that the participation of private groups is equivalent to genuine popular government. Lowi feels that the costs of interest-group liberalism are high. The ideology results in the "atrophy of institutions of popular control" by handing over control of programs to organized groups, thereby shutting out the public and its representatives in Congress and in the presidency; it also helps to maintain and create new structures of privilege; and it results in conservatism insofar as resistance to change is strengthened. This tendency to keep confrontation at a minimum, combined with the unlikelihood that potential groups will be able to organize themselves to combat particular, short-run injustices, indicate to Lowi that the pluralistic political system is not self-corrective, but must be fought by: (1) exposure of its workings, (2) encouraging group confrontation, (3) insulating administrative agencies from full group participation, (4) setting a limit on the existence of programs, and (5) requiring that an "applicable and understandable set of general rules must accompany every program." Lowi would, in short, restore "pluralism as an effective principle of democratic politics" by "destroying it as a principle of government." He would take government programs out of the hands of the "interested parties" and return them to the "appropriate level of government" (p. 94).

Many of the points made by Lowi and McConnell are, as both acknowledge, elaborations of arguments first enunciated by Henry S. Kariel in *The Decline of American Pluralism,* which was published in 1961. Kariel's work is somewhat more theoretical in character, but he does marshal evidence to support his contention that private organizations have been allowed to exercise public power irresponsibly. He also gives extensive coverage to constitutional questions.

Kariel feels that the fragmentation of power brought about by our constitutional system has allowed "perverse pluralism" to flourish anachronistically at the very time that the technological system works inevitably toward the consolidation and concentration of power. However, the procedural rights guaranteed by this same constitution have been applied to regulate the public activities of private organizations in the past, and Kariel believes and hopes that they will be used even more stringently in the future.

While Kariel, like Lowi and McConnell, focuses on economic organizations, his ideas are framed so as to apply to all private groups. The sections in which he reviews the theory of pluralism in the United States and Europe deal with nongovernment groups as a whole, and are highly recommended as an introduction to the subject. Many of his arguments are similar to those of Herbert Marcuse in *One Dimensional Man* (which appeared after Kariel's work), but are expressed with far greater clarity and cogency in Kariel's writing than in Marcuse's heavy, Germanic, Hegelian obfuscations.

THE ELITIST POSITION

Probably the best known and most influential attack on pluralism has been that of the elitist school of sociologists. Although many of the community studies (see Chapter Six), beginning with the Lynds's famous works on Middletown (Muncie, Indiana), pictured power structures in elitist terms, the names most frequently identified with the school are those of C. Wright Mills and Floyd Hunter.

Hunter utilized the "reputational method" to locate key influentials in his studies of local (Atlanta, Georgia) and national power structures. In his national study he began by asking the executive secretaries of some associations for the names of individuals whom they believed to be top leaders. In this manner he compiled a master list of leaders — most of them businessmen, although it contains some names of teachers, heads of voluntary organizations, social workers, state governors, and lawyers. (The list is printed in Hunter's *Top Leadership, USA*.) Hunter then sent questionnaires to all of those on the list and personally interviewed a select sample. On the basis of his research he concluded that "There is a general network of individuals who stand behind and sometimes aloof from the formal associations but who use the associations as foils in policy making . . . The total informal, top level

network has been estimated by various informants as being between 100
and 300 men. I believe about 200 men would easily constitute the
nucleus of the network of which I speak . . . National leaders have a
wide acquaintanceship among other leaders. Some men are recognized
as top policy makers, others as second- and third-rate figures amenable
to reason through informal discussions with the higher-ups, still others
as front men for specific interests . . . Friendships, committee work,
club and recreation associations, customer relations, and financial problems all tend to intertwine into definable action patterns" (in Young,
Approaches to the Study of Politics, pp. 360–362).

Hunter's methodology, and therefore his conclusions, have been the
subject of extensive criticism, but C. Wright Mills accepted Hunter's
data largely at face value. Mills used the data, plus his own limited research and decided opinions, to formulate and support his thesis that
America is run — ineptly and most likely disastrously — by a power
elite.

According to Mills, the members of the elite are distinguished from
the rest of the population because they hold positions which make it
possible for them to transcend the environment of ordinary people and
to mold American life by their decisions. "In so far as national events
are decided, the power elite are those who decide them." In the United
States at present the elite is purportedly formed by the leading men in
each of three main power domains: the economic, political, and military
orders. "At the top of the economy, among the corporate rich, there
are the chief executives; at the top of the political order, the members
of the political directorate; at the top of the military establishment, the
elite of soldier-statesmen clustered in and around the Joint Chiefs of
Staff and the upper echelons" (*The Power Elite*, pp. 8–9). The men in
these posts do not form three separate and competing elites, but rather
a kind of coordinated interlocking directorate. The circles of power tend
to converge; and power, wealth, and prestige cumulate for the individual
member of the elite. Moreover, power in one domain can be "translated" into power in another domain. The successful general becomes
president of a major university and then president of the United States.
The heads of institutional hierarchies become part of a ruling stratum —
a "set of groups whose members know one another, see one another
socially and at business." Those who belong to the elite "feel themselves
to be, and are felt by others to be, the inner circle of the 'upper social
classes'" (p. 11).

In Mills's world view the power elite makes history. Mills relegates Congress and voluntary associations to the "middle" rungs of power, and the majority of citizens to the bottom level where he sees the emergence of a mass society. Theories of balance or "romantic pluralism," as he calls them, are rejected by Mills, who singles out David Riesman's concept of veto groups for special attack. Riesman had argued in *The Lonely Crowd* that no one really runs things in America, that power is dispersed among a number of "veto groups" each of which is strong enough to prevent the others from leading, but not strong enough to lead itself. In one passage, Riesman had written that the future in the United States "seems to be in the hands of the small business and professional men who control Congress . . . of the military men who control defense and, in part, foreign policy; of the big business managers and their lawyers, finance-committee men, and other counselors who decide on plant investment and influence the rate of technological change; of the labor leaders who control worker productivity and worker votes; of the black belt whites who have the greatest stake in southern politics; of the Poles, Italians, Jews, and Irishmen who have stakes in foreign policy, city jobs, and ethnic religious and cultural organizations, etc." (pp. 254–255).

In *The Power Elite,* Mills retorted that Riesman failed to see the entire structure of power and therefore overlooked the elite which makes the big decisions. The "pressure groups" which play such an important role in the pluralist schema have, according to Mills, "either been incorporated in the personnel and in the agencies of the government itself, both legislative and executive or become the instruments of small and powerful cliques, which sometimes include their nominal leaders but often do not. These facts go beyond the centralization of voluntary groups and the usurpation of power of apathetic members by the professional executives. They involve, for example, the use of the NAM by dominant cliques to reveal to small-business members that their interests are identical with those of big business, and then to focus the power of business-as-a-whole into a political pressure" (p. 247). Mills then dismisses voluntary associations: "From the standpoint of such higher circles, the voluntary association, the pressure group, becomes an important feature of a public-relations program. The several corporations which are commanded by the individual members of such cliques are themselves instruments of command, public relations, and pressure, but it is often more expedient to use corporations less openly, as bases of power, and to make of various national associations their joint operating branches. The associations are more operational organizations, whose limits of power are set by those who use them, than final arbiters of action and inaction" (p. 247).

The top men may belong to associations but, according to Mills, they are seldom active members. At most, the associations are used by the top men as vehicles for putting into effect the policy line worked out at higher levels — "training groups in which young hustlers at the top prove themselves." Sometimes at the local level, voluntary associations serve as recruiting groups for the elite. Mills also sees Congress as relatively insignificant when compared to the executive. In his judgment many of the most fundamental issues never reach Congress and the pressure system. The fate of mankind, the issues of war and peace, are not decided on the middle levels where checks and balances may still to some extent operate. At most, those in the middle may "'get in the way' of the unified top, but no one of them has a chance to come into the top circles" (p. 268).

As will shortly be made clear, many "established" social scientists have been highly critical of the Mills-Hunter elite thesis. However, "radical" groups in the social sciences have sympathized with the view. *The New Sociology,* edited by Irving Louis Horowitz, and dedicated to the memory of C. Wright Mills, contains a number of essays in this vein; while in the field of history, such figures as Staughton Lynd and Christopher Lasch have seen America in a similar light. Outside of academic circles, the existence of a "power elite" of a "military-industrial Establishment" is no longer questioned among the New Left and Black Power groups, and the New York *Times Magazine* features articles such as Richard Kaufman's description (and condemnation) of the relationship between private organizations and the Defense Department.

THE PLURALIST DEFENSE: ELITIST DEMOCRATIC THEORY

Even if one rejects, as many have, the elitist picture of power in America on the grounds that the evidence is inadequate and the research methods questionable, there is still an extensive body of data which throws doubt on the validity of the pluralist position. With the development of modern research techniques, social scientists have accumulated data pointing to the existence of irresponsible elites, both public and private; to the growth of large, hierarchical, oligarchical organizations; to

widespread apathy toward public and private governments on the part
of their constituents. Membership in voluntary associations has been
shown to be class-based, with upper and middle class individuals much
more likely to hold memberships than lower class individuals. Moreover,
the membership of given groups has been found to be largely homogeneous in terms of class, ethnicity, and religion; the voluntary character
of many groups now appears to be questionable given the pressures
to join that have been uncovered; and the activities of many groups
were found to be somewhat frivolous in character, serving to distract
members from social and political affairs rather than drawing them into
and preparing them for community activity. The rise of the mass movement, with its "true believers," whose individuality is smothered rather
than nurtured by the group, also led to questions about the value of
participation to the democratic system and the individual. Defenders of
pluralism and the American pluralist system have had to deal with all of
these facts (as well as with the elitist power structures purportedly
found by some investigators) and with the criticisms based upon them.

Their fundamental line of defense has taken the form of redefining
democracy in such a way that the pluralist system can continue to be
labeled democratic. The classical model of democracy in which an informed and concerned citizenry governs has been abandoned as unreal-
istic and unsound psychologically, politically, and philosophically. In its
place, an "elitist" model, characterized by the competition of responsible elites for the vote of the people, has been developed. Although
some leading advocates of the theory such as Robert Dahl have objected
to being called "elitist democrats," we are using the term here because
it seems to us to summarize the essence of the thesis.

According to Joseph Schumpeter, who initially formulated the theory
in his 1942 book *Capitalism, Socialism and Democracy,* elitist democracy is more realistic because it acknowledges the inevitable existence of
elites, the role of leadership, the minimal concern of the average man
with politics, and the impossibility of agreement on a single definition
of the public interest. In elitist democratic theory, democracy is defined
in terms of the procedures by which officials are chosen. The people are
no longer given the impossible task of actually governing; they are asked
only to choose those who will govern for them. Elites acquire the power
to make political decisions through a competitive struggle for the
people's vote. As E. E. Schattschneider puts it in his book *The Semi-
sovereign People*: "The problem is not how 180 million Aristotles can

run a democracy but how we can organize a political community of 180 million ordinary people so that it remains sensitive to their needs. This is a problem of *leadership, organization, alternatives and systems of responsibility and confidence*" (p. 138, Schattschneider's emphasis).

Given the elitist model, it is possible to call both the American pluralist system and its large private associations democratic institutions. The elitists argue that the political system is democratic because there are in fact competing elites which must submit to the electoral process. While the proponents concede that the masses do not participate in the manner envisioned by a Paine or Jefferson (or practiced in a New England town meeting), they do not view this absence of participation as negating the democratic character of the system. Many elitist democrats regard mass participation as dangerous rather than desirable. They advocate a system in which a small layer of activists and intermediate associations intervene between the masses of the people and the state, thus protecting the leadership from mass whims and moods. As the critics would certainly point out, here as elsewhere the pluralist social scientist has merged empirical and normative theory. Analysts of the American political scene commonly divide the populace into several strata on the basis of their political activity, generally employing three major divisions. For example, V. O. Key distinguishes among: (1) the political activists at the top, the "professional politicians, the semiprofessionals, and the highly placed individuals in corporate, associational, and community life who have political sidelines and connections"; (2) a middle group of individuals who engage in such political acts as attending rallies and meetings and may enter into the active ranks on occasion; (3) the inactive mass at the bottom composed of individuals whose major political act is voting and of those who take no interest at all in politics (*Public Opinion,* p. 184).

Within the elitist democratic system, politicians act as nonideological "brokers" for the competing elites who ultimately determine the ends that the government pursues. These elites represent the various interests in the society, and are largely the heads of big, private organizations. Elitist democrats tend to assume that the interests of the masses are sufficiently represented as long as the heads of the large associations to which many citizens belong participate in the decision-making process, although some proponents have not failed to recognize the problem of the representativeness of the leaders of these private associations. Charles Frankel, a philosopher who identifies with the Pragmatist school, even notes in *The Democratic Prospect* — a book largely devoted to restating and defending the elitist democratic version of pluralism — that the problem of insuring representativeness is further complicated by the existence of "implicit associations." These are associations which speak for a class of individuals although the individuals in question have never actually joined an organization or chosen leaders. The "scientific community" and its self-appointed spokesmen are an example of an "implicit association." Sometimes formally organized associations such as the American Medical Association will also claim to speak for all the members of a profession or class even though all the individuals neither belong to the association nor regard the view of the leaders as representing their own opinions. Frankel comments that "The implicit voluntary association . . . carries even further the tendency which the large, explicitly organized voluntary association also exemplifies. On one side, decisions affecting great numbers are made by a relatively small group of individuals occupying key positions, official or otherwise; on the other side, the influence of these individuals derives from the fact that they 'represent' a large and inactive following that can only infrequently do anything but take what it gets" (p. 60).

However, many elitist democrats view voluntary associations as playing an important role in maintaining the democratic political system even though the associations are sometimes nonrepresentative and oligarchical. Voluntary associations are seen as especially important because they function as socializing agents for the elite and activists who are believed to be the most crucial elements of the system. While it may be regrettable that voluntary associations do not reach the masses, it is not crucial to the maintenance of democracy that they do so.

Apathy on the part of the mass of citizens and the mass of members in various organizations is not regarded by the elitist democrat as evidence of the decay of democracy. Instead apathy is actually seen as beneficial and functional in the democratic political order. Together with the multiple group memberships and allegiances which dilute the strength of any single loyalty, apathy gives the system a flexibility it would not otherwise have. Apathetic individuals without strong allegiances are willing to live with the compromises made by the elites and do not make impossible (nonnegotiable) demands on their governors. All in all, apathy and multiple allegiances lead to a political system in "equilibrium." Stability, it will be recalled, is a highly valued condition from the functionalist point of view. The individual is also seen as benefiting from the system; by letting others take care of his political concerns and his organizational affairs, he is freed for things that are more important to him and avoids the pitfalls of being smothered by the group and the polity.

Although elitist democrats express admiration for the professional politician and the activist in some of their writings, they are ambivalent and tend to be somewhat apprehensive about the individual who seeks personal fulfillment in groups and in politics. Sometimes they see him as a potential convert to a fascistic mass movement; at other times they picture him as somewhat neurotic and abnormal. A leading pluralist spokesman, Robert Dahl, has written that the average man is "not by nature a political animal and will turn to politics only when his primary goals are threatened." A political activist therefore is seen as being in some sense abnormal. While Dahl does not paint the sort of pathological portrait of the political actor drawn by Harold Lasswell in such early writings as *Psychopathology and Politics* (1930), he does speculate that the political professional is distinguished by "an inordinate capacity for multiplying human relationships without ever becoming deeply involved emotionally" (*Who Governs?* pp. 225–229). Robert Lane, another pluralist political scientist of note, has characterized the individual who seeks intimacy in a group as a person who yearns for a totalitarian order. Lane believes that the American pluralist system demands that the individual "shed the qualities of the community man and assume the role of the independent, isolated individual," adding that "in the nation-state some identity diffusion and a touch of anomie is necessary for democracy to survive" — an observation which seems to raise a few questions about the value of a form of government making such demands.

To avoid being accused of flailing a straw man, it may be well to end this summary of the elitist democratic thesis by quoting an advocate, Lester Milbrath, who has put the theory in neat outline form in the final pages of his inventory of knowledge concerning *Political Participation.*

(1) Most citizens in any political society do not live up to the classical democratic prescription to be interested in, informed about and active in politics. (2) Yet, democratic governments and societies continue to function adequately. (3) It is a fact that high participation is

not required for successful democracy. (4) However, to insure responsiveness of officials, it is essential that a sizable percentage of citizens participate in choosing their public officials. (5) Maintaining open channels of communication in the society also helps to insure responsiveness of officials to public demands. (6) Moderate levels of participation by the mass of citizens help to balance citizen roles as participants and as obedient subjects. (7) Moderate levels of participation also help balance political systems which must be both responsive and powerful enough to act. (8) Furthermore, moderate participation levels are helpful in maintaining a balance between concensus and cleavage in society. (9) High participation levels would actually be detrimental to society if they tended to politicize a large percentage of social relationships. (10) Constitutional democracy is most likely to flourish if only a moderate proportion of social relationships (areas of life) are governed by political considerations. (11) Moderate or low participation levels by the general public place a special burden of responsibility on political elites for the successful functioning of constitutional democracy. (12) Elites must adhere to democratic norms and the rules of the game and have a live-and-let-live attitude toward their opponents. (13) A society with widespread apathy could easily be dominated by an unscrupulous elite; only continuous vigilance by at least a few concerned citizens can prevent tyranny. (14) Elite recruitment and training is an especially important function. (15) To help insure final control of the political system by the public it is essential to maintain an open communications system, to keep gladiator ranks open, to make it easy for citizens to become active should they so choose, to continue moral admonishment of citizens to become active, and to keep alive the democratic myth of citizen competence. (pp. 153–154)

A SAMPLE OF ELITIST DEMOCRATIC THEORY: LIPSET

Elitist democratic theory, in one version or another, has been adopted, refined, and defended by many well-known social scientists including Robert Dahl, Edward Banfield, William Kornhauser, and Seymour Lipset; Lipset has been particularly closely identified with the thesis. Even in *Union Democracy* Lipset points out that institutionalized democracy in private governments such as that he and his associates found in the International Typographers Union may weaken the democratic process in the larger society. In *Political Man* he draws on his union research to argue that oligarchic organizations may be more responsible both to their members and to society than the organizations directly controlled by their memberships since "The members may want their 'selfish' objectives pursued even if achieving them will hurt others or endanger the organization. Employers know well that the more democratic a union — that is, the more opposition to the incumbent leadership, the more factions, the more turnover in office — the more irresponsible the union will be" (p. 396).

The study of the International Typographers Union indicated that certain conditions associated with membership participation (and therefore with internal democracy) also appeared to weaken democracy in the larger society. Lipset explains:

> to the extent that members of an association have a diffuse set of relationships with the organization, to the extent that a large part of their lives is lived within its influence, to the extent that its members interact with each other, to that degree are the chances for a high level of concern and participation increased. But these same factors isolate the members of the group from cross-pressures and exposure to diverse values and influences, and, as we have seen in the case of those in "isolated" industries like miners or longshoremen, heighten the intensity of their political beliefs. This again poses a dilemma for us. Integration of members within a trade-union, a political party, a farm organization, a professional society, may increase the chances that members of such organizations will be active in the group and have more control over its policies. But extending the functions of such organizations so as to integrate their members may threaten the larger political system because it reduces the forces making for compromise and understanding among conflicting groups. Trade-unions like those of the miners or the printers, which are characterized by high membership involvement and loyalty deriving largely from the existence of an "occupational" community, exhibit less concern for the values of other parts of the community than do unions whose members are less isolated and hence less committed. (pp. 395–390)

Lipset sees other positive features in oligarchic associations. Oligarchy and bureaucracy in voluntary associations can strengthen the pluralistic democracy insofar as the professionally led and bureaucratically managed organization is better able to protect the interests of its members in struggles with business and government organizations led by professionals and managed by bureaucrats. A small, completely voluntary and democratic group led by untrained members working in their spare time could not compete with General Motors. Moreover, Lipset contends, many of the decisions made by voluntary associations in their role as political pressure groups are similar to the foreign policy decisions of national governments. Therefore unity and secrecy in decision-making are as desirable in associations as in the government (although the voluntary groups also face the same danger of losing feedback when policy-making is not open and democratic). Lipset argues further that oligarchic voluntary associations have "facilitated political education and opposition by training new leaders, organizing and communicating opinions, and representing their members to other groups and the state. Many such groups acquire trained leaders who are better informed, even when not full-time officials, concerning the problems of the organization and ways to serve its members than are the less educated and less aware rank and file members" (pp. 395–396). In sum, while oligarchy may not be appealing from an ethical standpoint, it can serve the cause of democracy well. And Lipset reasons (or rationalizes?) that even the most dictatorial association is a better protector of its members' interests than no association would be, provided the association is free of government or other outside control; even the most dictatorial leaders must be somewhat responsible to the members' needs, or the association will begin to lose its members.

The apathy which accompanies oligarchy in the fragmented modern society also has its functions. Lipset observes: "Multiple and politically inconsistent affiliations, loyalties, and stimuli reduce the emotion and aggressiveness involved in political choice . . . The available evidence suggests that the chances for stable democracy are enhanced to the extent that groups and individuals have a number of crosscutting, politically relevant affiliations. To the degree that a significant proportion of the population is pulled among conflicting forces, its members have an interest in reducing the intensity of political conflict . . . such groups and individuals also have an interest in protecting the rights of political minorities" (pp. 88–89). It should be noted that Lipset's comments here are to some extent based upon the data collected by students of voting behavior. In fact, two of the most important of the voting studies — *Voting* by Berelson and his colleagues and *The American Voter* by Campbell and other members of the Survey Research Center — present versions of elitist democratic theory that are similar to Lipset's.

THE DEBATE OVER COMMUNITY POWER STRUCTURES

Pluralists have not accepted as valid the elitist picture of the power structure of local communities. They have made their own studies of power structures, and these in turn have been questioned by social scientists employing new methods and models which incorporate features of the elitist-stratification and the elitist-democratic models. As a result, an extensive literature has been amassed and a new field carved out. Here we can do more than indicate the character of the controversy among those studying community power structures and the nature of the pluralist research. The interested reader can find a number of reviews of the literature including Nelson Polsby's *Community Power and Political Theory,* which is written in defense of pluralism, and Thomas R. Dye's essay on "Community Power Studies," which is more recent and somewhat more balanced.

In general the pluralist research has been designed to demonstrate that the elitist-stratificationists are wrong in their belief that power is largely held by a single, small, permanent, unified elite based largely on control of economic resources, sharply differentiated from the masses and not responsible to them (see Dye, p. 36). Robert Dahl's study of New Haven in *Who Governs?* is a good example of the pluralist work. The book was awarded the American Political Science Association's Woodrow Wilson Foundation Award in 1962, and it has been widely read and highly influential.

Dahl utilizes a series of case studies of key political decisions in New Haven plus information from surveys, interviews, and historical and statistical sources to support his thesis that New Haven no longer is controlled by a real elite, although one did exist in the very early days of the city when the Congregational patrician families ruled. Dahl believes that New Haven is typical of a number of old American cities in having experienced an "extended and peaceful revolution" which changed the system from one of "cumulative inequalities" to one of "dispersed inequalities" in the political resources. In this system of dispersed inequalities, many kinds of resources are available to different citizens for use in influencing officials. These resources are, with few exceptions, unequally distributed so that individuals who have the greatest access to one type of resource have little or no access to other resources. No single influence resource dominates the others in all, or even most, of the key decision areas. Rather, an influence resource is effective in some areas or in some specific decisions, but not in others. Moreover no citizen, and certainly no group of more than a few citizens, is entirely lacking in some influence resources. Individuals at the lower end of the scale lack money, social prestige, and occupational skills as individuals, but together — as voters — they make up for their individual deficiencies through numbers. With their votes, the masses can influence policy through elections, which Dahl argues do influence the direction of policy. Despite the inequality in New Haven, and the cumulative deprivation of those at the bottom of the social scale who fail to use even their one resource of numerical strength, Dahl labels New Haven a pluralistic and democratic system. Although only a few individuals have much direct influence, many more are potentially influential, and a great many exert indirect influence on decisions through their electoral participation.

The differences in Dahl's findings and those of an elitist such as Hunter may reflect actual differences in the power structures of the cities they studied or, as many commentators have suggested, may be due to differences in the initial assumptions and the methodology employed by pluralists and elitists. Pluralists tend to assume that power has many bases and often use case studies of important political decisions as a research tool. Not surprisingly, they generally discover pluralistic power structures. Elitist-stratificationists are more likely to assume that an economic elite exists and dominates political action from behind the scenes, and they often use some variation of Hunter's reputational method. Not surprisingly, they generally discover elitist power structures. This relationship between method and results has been documented by John Walton on the basis of his examination of thirty-three community studies (*American Journal of Sociology*, 62:430–438).

As a result, there has been a trend toward comparative studies and toward employing a variety of methods in studying a single town. The former is exemplified by Agger, Goldrich, and Swanson's massive study of four communities over a period of fifteen years; the latter by Robert Prethus' examination of a small New York town, which led him to the conclusion that the elitist and pluralist methods are "mutually supportive," neither being capable of uncovering the entire power structure of a community by itself.

ELITIST DEMOCRATIC THEORY: FURTHER CRITICISMS

Those theorists associated with the elitist democratic school of thought do acknowledge certain difficulties with their position. Obviously, the elitist system can be only as good as its elite. As V. O. Key wrote in *Public Opinion and American Democracy,* "the critical element for the health of a democratic order consists in the beliefs, standards, and competence of those who constitute the influentials, the opinion leaders, the political activists" (p. 558). Further, the system retains its democratic character only so long as the elite is ultimately responsive to the electorate and loyal to those democratic values such as free speech and the toleration of dissent which elitists identify as "fundamental rules of the game." The elitists contend that the American elite is, in fact, responsive to the basic wishes of the mass, and that members of the elite have a better understanding of and a greater willingness to live by democratic norms than do the mass of ordinary citizens.

Having thus disposed of the first difficulty, the elitist theorists are faced with the problem of dealing with the discrepancy that exists between their view of the citizen's role and the place of the citizen in the classical model of democracy. The average man whose compliance is required if the system is to function may be hard put to understand how the elitist democratic system qualifies as the "government of the people, by the people and for the people" which the schools taught him to revere. The elitist democrat candidly recognizes that given this discrepancy, a certain amount of illusion or (the critics would say) "sham" is needed to preserve the system. The elitists find (to their own satisfaction) that the necessary illusion is present in the American system and that the average man does have the requisite feelings of efficacy largely as a result of his ignorance of the realities — that is, the elitist character — of the political order.

It is perhaps not amiss to remark here that the reaction of many young people upon discovering what to them are the realities — that is, the "perverted," elitist pluralism of Lowi's America — seems to indicate that the system which depends on a noble lie may not be so stable after all. Research on student protest suggests a clear relationship between attraction to the movement and a perceived disparity between the American political system and democratic ideals. Richard Flacks, a sociologist who has studied and participated in the New Left, reports that student activists tend to come from homes where liberal, democratic values predominate, and that the students have used these values in judging society (pp. 13–14).

While an elitist democrat such as Milbrath sees American democracy as a "realistic adjustment to the nature of modern society" (*Political Participation,* p. 154), the critics view both the elitist democratic theory and the American practice as perversions of true democracy. The critics also view the work of the elitist democrats as a perversion of the scientific method in that the elitists have accepted reality as an ethical norm, allowing the "is" to determine the "ought" — thereby joining the ranks of all those guilty of the "naturalistic fallacy." Jack Walker, writing "A Critique of the Elitist Theory of Democracy" in the *American Political Science Review* accused contemporary political scientists of "having stripped democracy of much of its radical elan and having diluted its utopian vision, thus rendering it inadequate as a guide to the future." In addition, Walker charged that emphasis on the stability of the American system has led political scientists to "ignore manisfestations of discontent not directly related to the political system" (p. 295). It might be added that the complete failure of American social scientists to predict the current student revolt and unrest and (to a lesser extent) the militancy in the black community can be seen as evidence of the dangers of reading apathy as a sign of content rather than alienation. Walker's article, and a number of others taking elitist democrats (and political scientists in general) to task for their hidden ideology, have been collected by Charles A. McCoy and John Playford in a useful volume, *Apolitical Politics: A Critique of Behavioralism.*

CONCLUSION

There can be no satisfactory ending to this account of the political theory of voluntary associations. It would probably be fair to say that the elitist democrats have failed to make a totally convincing case for the system as it now stands, while the critics have failed to present any viable alternative to the present system. Several of the critics simply opt for a kind of palace revolution, urging that the present Establishment be replaced by one more to their liking. A careful reader of C. Wright Mills will find that he wished to substitute enlightened intellectuals for the military and corporate chieftains of the power elite. Herbert Marcuse proposes that the vanguard of revolutionaries, largely composed of students and such oppressed minorities as black people, replace the traditional Marxian dictatorship of the proletariat with their own interim dictatorship until a truly free society is established. Some New Leftists want to skip even this stage of the dictatorship of the knowing. The revolution would be followed immediately by a system which somehow combines anarchy, participatory democracy, and individual self-realization. Ironically, the New Leftists have thus come almost full circle, back to the ideal of the early pluralists who also wanted a society of small meaningful groups and of maximum fulfillment for the individual in a communitarian setting.

The academic critics of pluralism like Kariel, Lowi, and McConnell also turn out to be frustrated pluralists of a sort. In the final analysis all of them advocate reforms which will bring a pure pluralism to America. Groups should be truly voluntary and more democratic and should cease to function largely as political entities. The control of government and of private associations in their public acts should be restored to the people. Thus, we find Kariel arguing that the "morally neutral multi-interest state composed of multi-interest groups which in turn are composed of multi-interest individuals" who are committed "to the institution of politics not for the realization of a shared purpose but for bringing conflicting purposes first into public view and then into the harmony," is the ideal one, given modern conditions (*Decline of American Pluralism*, p. 255).

BIBLIOGRAPHY

Agger, Robert E., Daniel Goldrich, and Bert Swanson, *The Rulers and the Ruled.* New York, John Wiley, 1965.

Allock, J. B., "Voluntary Associations and the Structure of Power," *The Sociological Review,* 16 (March 1968): 59–81. On the basis of a study of the relation between the church and broadcasting bureaucracies in the United Kingdom, Allock questions the mediation hypothesis, arguing that voluntary association elites may enter into alliance with government elites rather than intervening between government elites and the public. He warns that the social integration of groups and the integration of the political system must not be equated.

Banfield, Edward C., *Political Influence.* Glencoe, Illinois, The Free Press, 1961.

Barber, Bernard, "Participation and Mass Apathy in Associations," in A. W. Gouldner, ed., *Studies in Leadership.* New York, Harper, 1950.

Bell, Daniel, *The End of Ideology.* New York, Free Press, 1961. Bell defends pluralism and criticizes the concept of the mass society and the power elite thesis of C. Wright Mills.

Berelson, Bernard R., Paul F. Lazarsfeld, and William N. McPhee, *Voting.* Chicago, The University of Chicago Press, 1954.

Berelson, Bernard R., and Gary A. Steiner, *Human Behavior: An Inventory of Scientific Findings.* New York, Harcourt, Brace, 1964.

Campbell, Angus, Philip E. Converse, Warren E. Miller, and Donald E. Stokes, *The American Voter.* New York, John Wiley, 1960.

Craig, John G., and Edward Gross, "The Forum Theory of Organizational Democracy," *American Sociological Review,* 35 (February 1970): 19–33. The authors suggest that the forum theory of internal democracy may be applicable to voluntary associations, although their own empirical research dealt with the Saskatchewan Wheat Pool.

Dahl, Robert A., *Preface to Democratic Theory*. Chicago, University of Chicago Press, 1956. An attempt to construct a realistic, empirical theory of democracy which will fit the "facts" and be applicable to the American system.

—— *Who Governs?* New Haven, Yale University Press, 1961.

—— "Further Reflections on the 'Elitist Theory of Democracy'," *American Political Science Review*, 60 (June 1966): 296-305.

—— *Pluralist Democracy in the United States*. Chicago, Rand McNally, 1967. A basic text by a leading political scientist of the pluralist persuasion which describes and analyzes the American system. Good for a view of the system as seen by the pluralist.

Dye, Thomas R., "Community Power Studies," in James A. Robinson, ed., *Political Science Annual*. Volume II. Indianapolis, Bobbs-Merrill, 1970.

Eisenstadt, S. N., ed., *Max Weber on Charisma and Institution Building*. Chicago, University of Chicago Press, 1968.

Flacks, Richard, "The Liberated Generation: An Exploration cf the Roots of Student Protest," Working Paper Number 1, Youth and Social Change Project, University of Chicago, August 1966.

Frankel, Charles, *The Democratic Prospect*. New York, Harper and Row, 1962.

Gerth, H. H., and C. Wright Mills, *From Max Weber*. New York, Oxford University Press, 1946.

Gusfield, Joseph R., "Mass Society and Extremist Politics," *American Sociological Review*, 27 (February 1962): 19-30.

Horowitz, Irving Louis, ed., *The New Sociology*. New York, Oxford University Press, 1964. A volume of essays in honor of C. Wright Mills.

Hunter, Floyd, "Studying Associations and Organization Structures," in Roland Young ed., *Approaches to the Study of Politics*. Evanston, Northwestern University Press, 1958. Hunter describes the same research on which *Top Leadership* is based.

—— *Top Leadership, USA*. Chapel Hill, University of North Carolina Press, 1959.

Kariel, Henry S., *The Decline of American Pluralism*. Stanford, Stanford University Press, 1961.

—— "Commentary: Transcending Privacy," in J. Roland Pennock and John W. Chapman, eds., *Voluntary Associations*. New York, Atherton Press, 1969. A criticism of Lon Fuller's essay on principles of associations in the same volume. Kariel argues that the open, heterogeneous organization is preferable to the closed homogeneous association.

Kaufman, Richard F., "As Eisenhower was saying . . . 'We Must Guard Against Unwarranted Influence By the Military-Industrial Complex'," *New York Times Magazine*, June 22, 1969. A description of the power exercised by the "complex" operating outside both the pressure system and normal political processes in the executive and congressional branches.

Key, V. O., Jr., *Public Opinion and American Democracy*. New York, Alfred A. Knopf, 1964.

—— with the assistance of Milton C. Cummings, Jr., *The Responsible Electorate:*

Rationality in Presidential Voting, 1936-60. Cambridge, Harvard University Press, 1966.

Kornhauser, William, _The Politics of Mass Society._ Glencoe, Illinois, Free Press, 1959.

—— "'Power Elite' or 'Veto Groups'?" in Seymour Martin Lipset and Leo Lowenthal, eds., _Culture and Social Character: The Work of David Reisman reviewed._ Glencoe, Illinois, Free Press, 1961. A comparison and critique of Mills and Reisman. Kornhauser has some telling points to make in reference to the ideas of both theorists concerning the power of private associations in America.

Lane, Robert, _Political Ideology._ New York, Free Press, 1962.

Lasswell, Harold D., _Psychopathology and Politics._ Chicago, University of Chicago Press, 1930. An application of Freudian theory and techniques to the analysis of political actors. Lasswell views the activist as a damaged individual whose activities compensate for his failure to manage basic life conflicts.

Lipset, Seymour Martin, _Political Man._ New York, Doubleday, 1960.

—— _The First New Nation._ New York, Basic Books, 1963. Although most of this study of the United States at its founding is not relevant to our topic, Lipset does make some scattered comments in reference to voluntary associations.

—— Martin Trow, and James Coleman, _Union Democracy._ Glencoe, Illinois, Free Press, 1956.

Lowi, Theodore, "The Public Philosophy: Interest-Group Liberalism," _American Political Science Review,_ 61 (March 1967): 5-24.

—— _The End of Liberalism._ New York, Norton, 1969. An expansion of his earlier paper.

Lynd, Staughton, "The New Left," _Annals of the American Academy of Political and Social Science,_ 382 (March 1969): 64-72. An analysis of the influence of C. Wright Mills on the New Left and the New Left's commitment to participatory democracy (as opposed to corporate liberalism).

Marcuse, Herbert, _One Dimensional Man._ Boston, Beacon Press, 1964.

McConnell, Grant, _Private Power and American Democracy._ New York, Alfred A. Knopf, 1967.

—— "The Public Values of Private Associations," in J. Roland Pennock and John W. Chapman, eds., _Voluntary Associations._ New York, Atherton Press, 1969. A summary of the views McConnell advances in his book _Private Power and American Democracy._

McCoy, Charles A., and John Playford, _Apolitical Politics: A Critique of Behavioralism._ New York, Thomas Y. Crowell, 1967. Section II contains several articles critical of "bourgeois pluralism" and "local pluralism" as put forth in the work of Dahl, Banfield, Truman, Kornhauser, and other "elitist democrats."

Michels, Robert, _Political Parties._ Reprinted, Glencoe, Illinois, Free Press, 1949.

Milbrath, Lester W., _Political Participation._ Chicago, Rand McNally, 1965.

Mills, C. Wright, _The Power Elite._ New York, Oxford University Press, 1956.

—— _Power, Politics and People: The Collected Essays of C. Wright Mills._ Edited by Irving Louis Horowitz. New York, Oxford University Press, 1963. There are scattered, typically Millsian comments on voluntary associations in this volume.

Parenti, Michael, "Power and Pluralism: A View from the Bottom," in Marvin

Surkin and Alan Wolfe, eds., *An End to Political Science*. New York, Basic Books, 1970. A radical political scientist's view of pluralism as it functions in the urban ghetto.

Perrow, Charles, "The Sociological Perspective and Political Pluralism," *Social Research*, 31 (Winter 1964): 411–422. A general critique of Kornhauser and other advocates of political pluralism and of such critics of Kornhauser as Joseph Gusfield. Perrow argues that political pluralism fails in that it overlooks the role of economic interest, minimizes the role of power, fails to come to grips with data indicating low group membership, and is inadequate as an explanation of the political behavior both of group members and of those outside the group nexus.

Perrucci, Robert, and Marc Pilisuk, "Leaders and Ruling Elites: The Interorganizational Bases of Community Power," *American Sociological Review*, 35 (December 1970): 1040–1057. Power is viewed as a property of interorganizational ties which are described in terms of resource networks.

Pinard, Maurice, "Mass Society and Political Movements," *American Journal of Sociology*, 73 (May 1968): 682–690.

Pitcher, W. Alvin, "'The Politics of Mass Society': Significance for the Churches," in D. B. Robertson, ed., *Voluntary Associations: A Study of Groups in Free Societies*. Richmond, Virginia, John Knox Press, 1966.

Polsby, Nelson W., *Community Power and Political Theory*. New Haven, Yale University Press, 1963.

Presthus, Robert, *Men at the Top*. New York, Oxford University Press, 1964.

Riesman, David, with Nathan Glazer and Reuel Denney, *The Lonely Crowd: A Study of the Changing American Character*. New Haven, Yale University Press, 1950.

Rogin, Michael, "Nonpartisanship and the Group Interest," in Philip Green and Sanford Levinson, eds., *Power and Community: Dissenting Essays in Political Science*. New York, Random House, 1970. The first part of the essay is a trenchant critique of David Truman's work in *The Governmental Process*.

Schattschneider, E. E., *The Semi-sovereign People: A Realist's View of Democracy in America*. New York, Holt, Rinehart and Winston, 1960.

Schumpeter, Joseph, *Capitalism, Socialism, and Democracy*. New York, Harper, 1942.

Selznick, Philip, *The Organizational Weapon: A Study of Bolshevik Strategy and Tactics*. Glencoe, Illinois, Free Press, 1960. (Originally published by the Rand Corporation in 1952.) A largely theoretical study of the archetypal mass organization focusing on its organizational characteristics as they affect strategy and tactics in political combat.

Sidorsky, David, "Commentary: Pluralism, Empiricism, and the Secondary Association," in J. Roland Pennock and John W. Chapman, eds., *Voluntary Associations*. New York: Atherton Press, 1969. Sidorsky, a philosopher, criticizes Grant McConnell's essay on pluralism, arguing that the flaws in American democracy are not the result of pluralism per se but result from the particular distribution of power among groups.

Somit, Albert, and Joseph Tanenhaus, *The Development of American Political Science*. Boston, Allyn and Bacon, 1967. Sections of the book deal briefly with the influence of Arthur Bentley in American political science and with the subject of group theory.

Walker, Jack L., "A Critique of the Elitist Theory of Democracy," *American Political Science Review*, 60 (June 1966): 285–295.

—— "A Reply to 'Further Reflections on "The Elitist Theory of Democracy"'," *American Political Science Review*, 60 (June 1966): 391–392. Walker further defends his criticism of the elitist theory in light of Dahl's criticism of the original Walker critique.

Walton, John, "Substance and Artifact: The Current Status of Research on Community Power Structure," *American Journal of Sociology*, 62 (January 1966): 430–438.

Chapter Four   Voluntary Associations and the Political System: Data

While there has been some theoretical speculation concerning the relationship between voluntary associations and political behavior, relatively little is actually known about the political role of associations. Much of the information which is presently available is conveniently summarized in Robert Lane's survey of *Political Life* and the more recent survey of *Political Participation* by Lester Milbrath. The latter contains an extensive (but not annotated) bibliography and a propositional inventory of the major findings on the relationship between political participation and membership in organizations. Almost all of this research indicates that "persons who are active in community affairs are much more likely than those not active to participate in politics." As Milbrath points out, the "evidence suggests that political participation can be thought of as a special case of general participation in social and community activities. Not everyone who is active socially is likely to become active in politics, but it is probably easier for a person who enjoys social activity to enter politics than it is for a person who shuns social and community participation" (p. 17). The evidence also indicates that the relationship between group activity and participation in politics is partly a function of the role that many organizations play in mobilizing their members for political action. However, membership in organizations can lead to decreased political participation if the individual belongs to an organization that discourages political activity or if he belongs to organizations which pull him in opposite directions politically. A number of studies demonstrate that such cross pressures frequently result in withdrawal from the political arena (Milbrath, pp. 131–132).

There is some evidence from a study by Robert Salisbury which was published after Milbrath put together his inventory that political party activists may not be "joiners." Salisbury found that 118 members of Democratic ward and township organizations in the St. Louis area whom he interviewed had relatively low rates of participation. His subjects tended to specialize in politics. More than half were "inactive in nonpolitical organizations, belonging at most to one other organization, usually a church, and taking no active part even in that." Eleven percent had no other memberships; only 15 percent were very active, belonging to social organizations and taking an active role in some of them (in *Political Parties*, pp. 54–55). However, other investigations of party members yielded dissimilar results and it is not clear if the St. Louis group is simply a deviant one, or if it represents a new trend.

Robert Lane's book, although relatively old (it was first published in 1959) for a book of its type, is still highly useful. Lane deals with a much wider range of subject matter than Milbrath. He discusses both theory and research in treating the following topics: the mechanisms by which groups influence their members' political activity; the characteristics of groups and of their members which determine the degree of influence that a group has on its members' political activity; the effect of such factors as the degree of an individual's activity in groups, the number of group memberships held by an individual, and the extent to which an individual holds leadership positions in voluntary associations on his political activity; the effect of a community's power structure on civic and organizational participation; and the political effects of membership in ethnic associations. Lane makes a number of generalizations that coincide with statements by Milbrath. In addition, he reports research which indicates that the smaller a group is the more democratic its character, and the more political its raison d'être, the more likely it is to affect the political behavior of its members. The effect of an organization also depends upon its degree of importance to the individual and the extent of individual identification with it, and is further related to the social homogeneity of the organization since politics is more likely to be discussed in homogeneous associations than in heterogeneous groups in which political topics could serve as a divisive factor (pp. 191–193).

Perhaps the single most important work on the political effects of voluntary association membership is Almond and Verba's survey of citizen attitudes in the United States, Germany, Mexico, Italy, and Great Britain. In each of the five nations, a representative sample of

1000 individuals was interviewed. The results, as reported in *The Civic Culture,* provide strong support for the theory that voluntary associations "play a major role in a democratic political culture." On the basis of their extensive research, Almond and Verba concluded that "The organizational member, compared with the nonmember, is likely to consider himself more competent as a citizen, to be a more active participant in politics, and to know and care more about politics. He is, therefore, more likely to be close to the model of the democratic citizen. We have also shown that it makes a difference which type of organization an individual belongs to; political organizations yield a larger political 'dividend' than do nonpolitical organizations. And it makes a difference how active an individual is within his own organization: the active member displays a greater sense of political competence than does the passive member. But perhaps the most striking finding is that any membership — passive membership or membership in a nonpolitical organization — has an impact on political competence. Membership in some association, even if the individual does not consider the membership politically relevant and even if it does not involve his active participation, does lead to a more competent citizenry. *Pluralism, even if not explicitly political pluralism, may indeed be one of the most important foundations of political democracy"* (pp. 320–322; emphasis added).

There were a number of differences among the various countries. For example, Germany had a rate of organizational membership which was almost as high as the United States' and Britain's (Italy and Mexico were both considerably lower), but the proportion of active, participating members (as measured by the holding of office) was significantly lower. Almond and Verba interpret this difference to mean that "in Germany the structures of a democratic system are well developed, but they do not yet play significant roles in the perspectives and behavior of the citizens" (p. 315). It is of interest, too, given the comments of many observers about the United States, that it did have the highest rate of organizational participation of the five countries. The total number of members and the number of individuals who are members of several organizations (and of women members) were highest in the United States (p. 320).

In a separate investigation, published in *Journal of Politics,* 27:467–497, Sidney Verba employed the five-nation survey findings to test the familiar hypothesis that multiple group memberships reduce the intensity of political conflict by exposing individuals to a more heterogeneous political environment, thereby increasing the likelihood of cross-pressures which should reduce the intensity of political feelings. Verba found that the data did not support the hypothesis. Instead, it appeared that politics was simply avoided in heterogeneous groups. Moreover, in the United States (where there is considerable multiple, overlapping membership in organizations) hostility toward members of the opposition party was not decreased as a result of group membership. In Italy, where groups are largely homogeneous, hostility to the opposition party was reinforced by group membership.

The data from the Almond and Verba study, plus some new data from a survey conducted in India, were used by Norman Nie, G. Bingham Powell, Jr., and Kenneth Prewitt to further analyze the relationships among organization membership, political participation, and economic development. Using a number of sophisticated analytical techniques such as causal modeling, they determined that economic development leads to greater rates of political participation because "associated with economic development is an expanding organizational infrastructure. Social class and organizational life are the components of economic development which most strongly affect mass political participation" (*American Political Science Review*, 63:370). Contrary to the expectations of many theorists, urbanization did not explain either organizational growth or political participation.

Organizational involvement appeared to have a stronger impact on political participation than social status. In addition, social status and organizational involvement seemed to "operate through different causal paths in affecting political participation." While "virtually all the relationship between social status and political participation is explained by the intervening linking attitude variables" such as efficacy and attentiveness, a very large part of the relationship between organizational involvement and participation is unexplained by any attitude variable (*American Political Science Review*, 63:811). This direct link between organizational involvement and political participation, bypassing as it does social status, could be highly significant. As Nie, Powell, and Prewitt note, "organizational involvement may represent an alternative channel for political participation for socially disadvantaged groups" (63:819).

A number of other studies of lesser scope have contributed evidence in support of the generalization that participation in voluntary associations and political activity are positively correlated. These include: Herbert Maccoby's investigation of a small county recreational association in Virginia; Philip Hastings' examination of voters and nonvoters in Pittsfield, Massachusetts; William Buchanan's study of a small southern municipality; Wayne Dennis' comparison of members of the Daughters of the American Revolution in Lansing, Michigan, with non-members of similar economic status and with a general sample of women in the area; and Basil Zimmer and Amos Hawley's survey in Flint, Michigan. In addition to providing support for the generalization, Maccoby also found that active participation in organizations was linked with positive, nonfatalistic sentiments toward the social environment; general interest and activity in public affairs, without at the same time "getting too worked up" about politics; having parents who regarded voting as important; and defining the role of citizen in a democracy in political terms. Maccoby discovered too that participants were recruited for new organizations because they were known to be "actives," (*American Sociological Review*, 23:530–531).

Some unpublished data from the surveys conducted by the University of Michigan's Survey Research Center show that joiners are more affluent, better educated, and more active in politics than nonjoiners (quoted by V. O. Key, *Public Opinion*, p. 504). Berelson, Lazarsfeld, and McPhee report in *Voting* that they found that organizations in Elmira, New York, helped bring out the vote of their members. In view of Verba's findings, it is also of interest that the research team found that individuals in Elmira tended to belong to organizations which offered a congenial political environment by way of the class and religious homogeneity of the members (p. 52). Similar results were reproted in the earlier voting study *The People's Choice*, by Lazarsfeld, Berelson, and Gaudet.

The results of Robert McWilliams' research on five voluntary associations in a small Detroit suburb indicated that the more politically oriented a group, the greater the member's sense of political obligation, his feeling of political efficacy, his interest in politics, and his political activity. It also appeared that the more active the member in the group, the greater was his political participation. In his report, which is based primarily on questionnaires filled out by organization members, McWilliams deals with other aspects of the relationship between political behavior and social group membership as well. A study by William Erbe of three small Iowa towns (*American Sociological Review*, 24:198–

215) yielded positive correlations between political participation and organizational involvement in both expressive and instrumental organizations. Erbe, who employed highly sophisticated methods, also found that social-economic status and organizational involvement were important antecedents of political participation.

While all of the studies discussed thus far (with the exception of *The Civic Culture*) are American, similar research projects have been undertaken abroad. Scandinavian scholars have been particularly active in the area of election research. In Norway, native scholars and Americans from the University of Michigan Survey Research Center have jointly carried out an extensive research program. Stein Rokkan, who headed the study team, has reported that an initial analysis of the data indicated that party members hold more nonpolitical memberships than nonparty members, and that party members at all educational levels are more likely than nonparty members of similar socio-economic status to have been decision makers in nonpolitical organizations. The difference between party and nonparty members in organization activity was most pronounced for men and did not even appear in women educated beyond primary school. (*Acta Sociologica*, 4:32–33.) In the same article Rokkan cites a UNESCO-sponsored survey of West Germany which indicated that belonging to nonpolitical organizations increased the likelihood of an individual's holding membership in a political party (p. 33). Some results from the joint survey and from later research in southwestern Norway are utilized in a book on *Political Parties in Norway* co-authored by Henry Valen of the Oslo Institute for Social Research and Daniel Katz of the Michigan Survey Research Center. Although Katz and Valen report differences among the parties in the number of organization memberships held by party voters and leaders, they also note that "No matter what the party allegiance, leaders have more ties to other organizations than do voters." The Labor party voters and leaders were found to have fewer memberships than the adherents of other parties who generally were of higher socio-economic status. Politics appeared to be only one of the many community activities of the Liberal party leaders who were discovered to be much more involved in "religious, charitable, humanitarian and community centered organizations than the leaders of other parties." Interestingly, Liberal party officers did not seem to be able to utilize their position as community leaders to mobilize support for their party (pp. 318–319).

The Valen and Katz book also contains a discussion of the political role of Norwegian interest groups. Although the groups are ostensibly neutral politically, in actuality they are linked to the parties through overlapping leadership structures and through the operation of informal groups within the parties. The relationship of interest groups to the government is analyzed too as is the way in which organization members perceive the political role of the association. In general, members were reluctant to admit that their organization took positions on political issues or had an influence on their political behavior.

There has been some research outside the Scandinavian countries, but it is more limited in character. Yasumasa Kuroda surveyed a small suburb of Tokyo, systematically interviewing 287 voters. He found the familiar relationship between political activity and participation in voluntary associations. The Japanese "joiners" were more likely to take on active political roles than the nonjoiners, and individuals active in politics tended to remember their parents' being active in community affairs during their youth. A Yugoslavian investigator, Stanislaw Skrzypek, reports that university students in his country listed the leaders of student organizations as an influence on their political behavior (*Public Opinion Quarterly*, 29:91). And in England, R. D. Jessop found that individuals exhibiting low involvement in voluntary associations tended to deviate from the class norm of "traditionalism" for upper and middle class individuals or "radicalism" for working class individuals (*British Journal of Political Science*, 1:21).

To our knowledge, only one study indicated a negative correlation between participation in a nonpolitical organization and political participation. Suzanne Berger found that some members of a French rural cooperative were kept out of politics by the organization, which functioned to reinforce the political isolation of the French rural populations. As Miss Berger observes, her findings suggest that great care must be taken in extending generalizations from the American political system to other, different political systems. It is her belief that the character of the state — in the French case the state being one which has failed to integrate the political community — and of the culture critically affect the role played by voluntary associations (in Pennock and Chapman, *Voluntary Associations*, p. 282).

THE VOLUNTARY ASSOCIATION AS A SOCIALIZING AGENT

It is often asserted that the voluntary association is a major agent of political socialization in a democracy. Associations are supposed to give their members training and practice in political skills and to inculcate in them the beliefs and values required to keep the political system functioning properly. The association structures the primary group relations which communicate and develop political orientations, and functions as a political reference group for the individual member. (See Dawson and Prewitt, *Political Socialization,* pp. 198–199.)

Some qualification has to be added to these claims from the start since it has been found that one third to one half of the United States population does not belong to voluntary associations so whatever the benefits of membership, they clearly do not go to the entire populace. However, with this limitation in mind, there is evidence to support the assertion. It has also been found that the socializing effect increases with an increase in activity in associations. A widely cited study by Samuel Stouffer showed that the leaders of a community's major voluntary associations were more tolerant of political nonconformity (which Stouffer classifies as a democratic value stance) than were a cross section of the community's members. On the basis of comparisons between the results of a nationwide survey based on probability sampling in which 6000 people were interviewed and of a special sample of selected community leaders (including those of voluntary associations), Stouffer concluded that the leaders were more strongly committed to the civil-libertarian ideals he believed to be vital to democracy. "The community leaders, being especially responsible and thoughtful citizens, are more likely than the rank and file to give a sober second thought to the dangers involved in denying civil liberties to those whose views they dislike" (*Communism, Conformity, and Civil Liberties,* p. 27). Stouffer also found that community leaders were more likely to be worried about and to discuss world problems and were less likely to be "rigid categorizers" or to endorse "authoritarian or conformist attitudes toward child-rearing" (p. 105). However, it is important to note that veterans who belonged to the American Legion and the Veterans of Foreign Wars were somewhat less likely to be tolerant than were veterans who did not belong. Although Stouffer does not dwell on this finding, it appears to suggest that where organizations do not support civil-libertarian values, the socialization process works to inculcate similar nonsupport in the members. One cannot automatically assume that organizations socialize individuals in a single direction — the direction is a function of the "culture" of the organization.

An exploratory study by Arnold Rose in Minnesota yielded results similar to Stouffer's. Rose compared leaders of statewide instrumental associations (questionnaires were mailed to the presidents of all such organizations) and a cross section of the married population of St. Paul–Minneapolis (mailed questionnaires were utilized and those who failed to respond were interviewed in their homes). In *The Power Structure* Rose reports that the leaders, as compared to the "mass" were better educated and were more likely to hold managerial or professional positions; to identify themselves as members of the upper classes; to participate in churches, occupational organizations, and voluntary associations other than the one they led; to have social knowledge and not to feel confused or bewildered about the functioning of society; and to have a sense of power in the community and to feel free to take independent action, although in this last instance the differences were slight. The leaders were less likely to express a need to avoid social contact or exposure; less likely to be alienated or anomic or to express intergroup prejudice; less satisfied with their achievements in leadership roles, although more satisfied with their occupational choice. In sum: "Group leaders manifest more satisfaction with democratic processes both in that their behavior is more in accord with what might be expected of a citizen in a democracy and in that their attitudes are more likely to include a belief that the government is responsive to the wishes of the people" (p. 178). Despite these differences between the leaders and the led, Rose thinks the distinction between the two groups is not great enough to justify labeling the leaders an "elite." Furthermore, he believes that the differences result from the leaders' participation and group activity rather than from any basic personality traits, although he admits that he does not have enough evidence to prove the point.

In *The Power Structure* Rose also analyzes the voluntary association memberships held by congressmen, utilizing information reported in the Congressional Directory and data gathered by Donald R. Matthews for his book *U. S. Senators and Their World.* The evidence of the extensive memberships held by congressmen and Rose's own experience in political office led him to speculate that: "Politicians must be great joiners, for many reasons. Affiliations provide them with channels of personal contact with portions of the electorate, and provide the latter with a sense of personal identity with their public officials. Thus, membership in voluntary associations helps a politician get elected. Politicians tend to be gregarious. If a person does not like to associate with others, he is unlikely to go into politics. An affiliation with some social influence associations sometimes provides the extra bit of motivation and self-confidence that leads a man to try for public office" (p. 87).

Turning from leaders to the ordinary members of organizations, Robert Lane interviewed "in depth" fifteen "common men" living in a middle income housing development in an eastern city. All of the men were white, married, voters. Ten were blue collar workers; five were white collar workers. In *Political Ideology* Lane attributes the support for democratic norms which he found to the subjects' being better off than their fathers in an economic and social sense and to a "second kind of experience which is more specifically related to an enduring affection for the ways of democracy: it is experience in democratic procedures in small groups. Their church, it seems, leads them into this understanding only a little way; their schools a little way further. The voluntary groups that men belong to, the labor unions, the veterans' organizations, the community councils and Parent-Teacher Organizations catch the men at different ages. They mean different things and serve as vehicles for a variety of needs, but almost all of them have elected officers, parliamentary procedures, majority rule tempered by minority rights, and other aspects of what might be said to be popular government. People are often facetious about these aspects of their organizations; sometimes they are cynical. The men of Eastport were neither" (pp. 92-93). Lane quotes several comments which the men made, expressing approval of the democratic procedures of their organizations, and notes that the men's endorsement of their organization extends from the union to social clubs, writing that, "it is so usual that the men sometimes wonder whether there is another way" (than elections and so forth). In summing up, Lane generalized far beyond his limited data: "On balance, the Legion posts, the lodges and the unions, the PTA's and the community councils are schools for learning, in an enclosed space, what the wider democracy of the nation requires. Not the least of all, they teach the imperfections, the hesitations, the halting progress of democracy, and so prepare their members for a more realistic and informed view. At least in part, popular government survives less because men are aware of its crowning virtues than because they are adequately prepared for its galling vices" (p. 94).

Lane also found that the existence of nongovernment associations played a crucial role in the men's acceptance of the American political system. His subjects believed that any American could be powerful if he had the skills and the desire. However, they also felt that obtaining power depended upon organization as well as effort. "Power is dependent on organization and effort; those whom the gods would make powerful they first must organize. But the decision is your own; you have the right to organize, protected by freedom of association. This view offers a political principle of some importance to these men. *Freedom of association provides in the political field the basis for a rationale of relative power positions, just as free enterprise provides this basis for relative wealth in the economic field.* If one has little power at any given time, it is his own fault for failing to organize his interests" (p. 143; the emphasis is Lane's). With the exception of four of their number, the "common men" did not perceive a power elite in America.

There are several other studies, less intensive than Lane's and less extensive than Stouffer's, on the effects of voluntary association membership on political behavior and politically relevant attitudes. Sorace and Seeman found that civil rights activists, both black and white, have more interracial contacts than nonactivists (*Social Forces*, 46:197-207). In their careful study of New Haven whites, Curtis, Timbers, and Jackson report that "independently of education, age, and other social position, participation in secondary structures is associated with reduced prejudice" and that "the secondary participation most markedly associated with reduced prejudice" takes the form of "primary interactions between persons who are brought together by common membership in an external organization: club, neighborhood or workform," while primary relationships with family and friends may actually reinforce prejudice (*American Journal of Sociology*, 72:243-244). However, a survey in four diverse cities utilizing large random samples of whites and blacks, which was conducted as part of the Cornell Studies in Intergroup Relations, indicated that the positive correlation between membership and reduced prejudice disappeared when education was controlled. No positive correlation between reduced prejudice and membership was found at all for blacks. In Watts, blacks who experienced more social contacts with whites, including contacts through voluntary association membership, appeared to be less likely to engage in racial violence than were isolated blacks, according to an attitude survey conducted by H. Edward Ransford (*American Journal of Sociology*, 73: 581-591). Some evidence that Swedish and American workers who belong either to a union or to another organization are less likely to have feelings of powerlessness or to be low in political knowledge than are unorganized workers was uncovered by Melvin Seeman, who also found that the officers of organizations were even lower on the powerlessness scale and higher on the political knowledge scale than were the members (*Public Opinion Quarterly*, 30:353-367).

Several researchers, including the team headed by Angus Campbell which was responsible for *The American Voter,* have argued that social isolation, as in the case of the farmer, for example, is associated with political apathy (see Campbell, in Dreyer and Rosenbaum, *Political Opinion*). Such isolation is also supposed to be associated with political extremism. However, a study of individuals attending the "radical right" San Francisco Bay Region School of Anti-Communism held in January-February 1962 indicated that social isolation and sympathy for "anti-democratic" movements were not necessarily correlated. Eighty-nine percent of the 294 persons interviewed at the school by Raymond Wolfinger and his students belonged to at least one voluntary association (in Dreyer and Rosenbaum, *Political Opinion*). This rate of participation was somewhat higher than that of comparable professional, business, and clerical respondents in the 1952 nationwide survey of the Survey Research Center. These figures indicate once more that caution is in order in generalizing about the socialization role of voluntary associations in a democracy.

AFRICAN STUDIES

The growing literature on modernization and urbanization in Africa includes a surprising number of studies of the political and social functions of voluntary associations. Most observers assign an important, if not crucial role to voluntary associations in the political development of the new African nations.

Thomas Hodgkin was one of the first Africanists to call attention to the contribution of voluntary associations to the growth of nationalism in the continent, pointing out that the associations allowed Africans to "recover within the urban context, the sense of common purpose which in traditional African society was normally enjoyed through tribal organizations." Hodgkin saw a parallel between the African associations and those of the English new towns in the early nineteenth century. In both cases, the associations represent a growth of democracy in that they are institutions created by the people to help them live in an unfamiliar urban world (*Nationalism in Colonial Africa*, pp. 84–85, p. 91).

Like Hodgkin, Immanual Wallerstein, another authority in the field, sees voluntary associations serving as the basis of nationalist, revolutionary movements (even though the organizations were frequently established by the colonial powers to serve as administrative adjuncts). The associations brought together the educated, urbanized elements of the population and gave them experience in office-holding and other organizational skills. The associations also functioned as communication networks through which new ideas could circulate, partly by providing an excuse for travel and contact.

As political consciousness grew, many of the voluntary associations evolved into distinctly political organizations such as parties and nationalist groups. The nationalist movements generally tried to use the network of voluntary associations for political purposes and to absorb them into the movement. They were largely successful in thus penetrating the society and becoming mass parties despite the efforts of the colonial governments to prevent this from happening.

The nationalist movements further tried to undermine the legitimacy of the colonial regime by having their own affiliate voluntary groups recognized by the various international associations of voluntary organizations. These pressures from African nationalists, combined with the cold war competition between communist and noncommunist groups, in turn led to an increasing politicization of the international voluntary associations themselves. A number of outside organizations supported the nationalist cause with material aid as well as resolutions.

The politicization of African voluntary associations begun during the colonial era was intensified after independence. The new governments pressured the organizations to support the regime and sometimes incorporated private groups into the party and government structure. Wallerstein explains: "In the years immediately following independence, there has been an almost total politicization of voluntary associations. Yet their old frameworks are being maintained. National voluntary groups are in fact being strengthened in terms of finance and organization. Today they are closely linked to the single-party structure, but they remain separate organizations and may in fact serve as useful channels for the expression as well as the restraint of dissent. The trend toward specialization of voluntary associations, with its almost inevitable long-run consequence of depoliticization, has been checked or reversed by the growth of single-party structures to meet the problems of the post independence era. With, however, the increased social differentiation that accompanies economic development, it is likely that voluntary associations will again turn in the direction of multiplicity, specificity, and autonomy" (in Coleman and Rosberg, *Political Parties and National Integration*, p. 339).

Wallerstein's view of the political functions of African voluntary associations is supported by the various monographs on specific cities and

regions such as Claude Meillassoux's study of voluntary associations in
Bamako, the largest city in the Republic of Mali; Kenneth Little's work
on west Africa; Michael Banton's study of Freetown, the capital of
Sierra Leone; and A. L. Epstein's research on the Copperbelt towns of
Northern Rhodesia.

The most important of these is Kenneth Little's book on *West African
Urbanization.* Little makes many points which are similar to those of
Wallerstein. He also argues that voluntary associations have enabled
younger men to play a more significant role in politics than they tra-
ditionally would have been able to. By giving young men, as a class and
as individuals, the opportunity to exercise national influence, voluntary
associations have helped restructure the society's age relationships. In
the associations, individuals get a chance to display leadership qualities
in office. In turn, office-holding gives the potential political leader an
opportunity to recruit a personal following and to widen his contacts in
the society. In the voluntary association, the young man can also develop his skills as an intermediary between the modern and traditional
worlds, a role he must play vis à vis the illiterate mass. Associations have
also helped to bring women into community affairs and to give them a
political voice. A number of women have become important in the
political parties, particularly as spokesmen for and organizers of other
women. Finally, the voluntary association itself may participate directly
in politics as a pressure group (pp. 103–118).

Claude Meillassoux's study of Bamako, *Urbanization of an African
Community,* illustrates the manner in which the functions of voluntary
associations may change following political independence. Before independence the voluntary associations in Mali flourished, meeting many
needs of the people and participating in the political struggle. Since independence, the government has taken over many of the functions of
the associations and has attempted to restrict those activities of associations which were not made an official part of the government. Unofficial associations still exist, but they operate somewhat covertly and
tend to avoid political activities. Most of them are either mutual aid
groups or entertainment associations, although there are also regional
and youth groups which Meillassoux feels meet a need for social differentiation.

SOCIOLOGICAL STUDIES

There are a number of studies by sociologists working largely in the
C. Wright Mills–Floyd Hunter tradition which deal with voluntary as-

sociations or the voluntary activities of various classes in relation to the power structure of a community. In "Cibola," a small midwestern community with a population of 20,000, Robert Schulze examined the role of "economic dominants" in voluntary associations and public life; the nature of the "public leaders" and their involvement in voluntary associations; and the attitudes and activities of the "absentee firm dominants" toward voluntary associations. The heads of local voluntary associations were asked to identify "public leaders" (those persons who exercise major influence and leadership in community affairs as distinguished from the "economic dominants" or those who occupy the top positions in the major economic units in the community). Schulze found, upon investigation, that there was a gradual withdrawal of the economic dominants from participation in community affairs and positions as public leaders as the economic life of the town came to be dominated by outside corporations. Individuals who did serve as public leaders were generally long-time residents of the town who were also very active in its voluntary associations, frequently having been president of at least one association.

While the executives of absentee-owned firms in Cibola were not active in local government or voluntary associations, the fifty southern metropolitan area executives interviewed by Roland Pellegrin and Charles Coates were. Their firms encouraged, and in some cases required, that the executives participate in the most important local voluntary associations in order to protect and further the company's interests. Membership in voluntary associations was seen by the executives themselves as part of their job, and apparently they did not resent the close control the company exercised over their volunteer activities (*American Journal of Sociology*, 61:413–419).

Similarly, in Syracuse, New York, and the surrounding metropolitan area research teams led by Linton Freeman and Charles Willie found that business executives from both local and nonlocal firms were involved in community organizations as much, or more, than in the past. Charles Willie and his associates believe that the difference in size between Syracuse, a city of 250,000, and the smaller Cibola may partially account for the differences in the participation pattern of executives (*Sociology and Social Research*, 48:289–300). However, a national survey conducted by the Center for a Voluntary Society indicated a general trend toward increased business executive participation (see Fenn, *Harvard Business Review*, March-April 1971).

Delbert Miller, who employed the reputational method (as did Pellegrin and Coates) compared the "influentials" of an American city in the Pacific northwest with the "influentials" in a southwest English city. Miller discovered that the American influentials were more active in voluntary associations than their British counterparts. He attributes this to the greater reliance Americans place on voluntary associations as a means of exercising power in community decision-making (*American Sociological Review*, 23:9-15).

Two studies comparing formal, organizational leaders with informal and reputational leaders yielded conflicting and inconclusive results. Laskin and Phillett (*Sociological Inquiry*, 35:176-185) identified formal group leaders and leaders chosen by informants (reputational influentials) in four small Canadian towns. Although the two lists of leaders overlapped from 38 to 77 percent, and all of the leaders belonged to formal organizations, no consistent relationship between formal leadership and reputational influence appeared. James E. White compared formal and informal leadership in a rural New York community and found that the two kinds of leadership were not closely related (*American Sociological Review*, 16:50-60). A study by Barth and Abu-Laban (*American Sociological Review*, 24:69-72) also used the reputational method to locate influential individuals and organizations in the black subcommunity of a large northwest city. All of the influential individuals were active in organizations, and particularly in the influential organizations. However Barth and Abu-Laban felt that the black leaders they located did not, in fact, make the key decisions that affected the subcommunity (thereby casting doubt on the value of the reputational method in uncovering a community's power structure).

Lastly, in a brief article (in Wilson and Kolb, *Sociological Analysis*) C. Wright Mills himself described the political dominance of the Chamber of Commerce in middle-sized cities (population between 25,000 and 100,000) and the control of white collar workers and small businessmen by big businessmen. Mills's description is based on some interviewing and on statistical data.

OTHER STUDIES

There is some information on the political role of voluntary organizations in Edward Banfield's *Political Influence* and in Robert Dahl's *Who Governs?* Banfield's seven case studies of Chicago politics led him to believe that many civic controversies arise out of the maintenance and enhancement needs of organizations — both voluntary and other types — and that voluntary associations are frequently employed as intermediaries in political disputes. Political actors also use voluntary associations to build support for their policies. However, in general, Banfield maintains, the associations are reluctant to become involved in controversy although they have to give the appearance of being active in order to retain their members (pp. 250–270). Dahl discusses the role of such organizations as the PTA in providing subleaders and followings for leaders in public affairs, and as a channel through which potential leaders may gain experience and move into political affairs.

A study of the various characteristics associated with the prestige accorded the forty-three organizations of a small New York community by the town's leaders led Ruth Young and Olaf Larson to conclude, somewhat speculatively, that high prestige organizations function to integrate the community and to tie it to the wider state and national social and political structure by channeling information into and out of the community (*American Journal of Sociology*, 71:178–186). Other characteristics of high, medium, and low prestige organizations are also discussed.

While Peter Rossi, who studied a midwest industrial city of 45,000 people, also sees voluntary associations as playing an integrative role, he emphasizes the political functions of organizations. On the basis of data collected through personal interviews with approximately fifty businessmen and community leaders and with fifteen members of the general public, Rossi argued that: "The voluntary associations ranging from the more permanent varieties — the Community Chest, Chamber of Commerce, and service clubs — to the ad hoc Citizens' Committees, have taken over many of the functions of initiating social change and marshaling community support for changes that are formally allocated to local government and to political parties. Although it is often true that voluntary associations eventually must move local authorities, the initial spark and a great part of the task of mobilizing public opinion have been performed for these authorities in advance" (Etzioni, *Complex Organizations*, p. 302). In addition voluntary associations provide a "framework for social life, opportunities for interaction and for gregarious pleasure"; a "context in which businessmen may build up the right access to one another and to community leaders"; and in turn give community leaders easy access to those who control the economic institutions. Lastly, the system of community participation "provides a means of ordering firms and individuals who have no intrinsic ordering relationships among themselves" (pp. 302-305).

Howard Freeman and Morris Showel attempted to measure the political influence of voluntary associations by determining which organizations individuals would turn to for political advice (*Public Opinion Quarterly*, 15:703-714). A sample of 441 adults in the state of Washington chosen on the basis of an area-probability design was interviewed, but the study is of limited usefulness both because the measure of influence is a restricted one and because most of the organizations in the final list ordering associations according to their influence are not voluntary associations at all. The list included such groups as the Democratic and Republican parties, the Catholic Church, and the American Federation of Labor, as well as veterans' groups, the Grange, and the PTA. As we reported in Chapter Three, Floyd Hunter constructed a similar but more elaborate list of 106 organizations ranked according to their potential influence in national policy development as rated by some executive secretaries of national associations. In this case, Hunter himself questions the validity of the list (which is printed in his *Top Leadership USA*) since other investigations led him to conclude that voluntary associations are not as influential as their secretaries believe. In Hunter's opinion, voluntary associations function primarily as coordinators and "clearing houses" and as "community links" in the process of policy development. They are also used by the top leadership to mobilize support for policy and as "foils" in policy making. (See Hunter's essay in *Approaches to the Study of Politics*, p. 360.)

There is some evidence that government officials see voluntary associations as links between the government and the citizen. A 1963 case study by James Rosenau of a conference of national, nongovernment leaders organized by the government to create support for the foreign aid program revealed that 41 percent of those invited were association leaders. Rosenau believes the main function of voluntary association leaders in national policy making is that of supporting or vetoing policy alternatives developed within the federal government structure, although leaders do sometimes advise the government in early stages of policy making and may play a role in the initial creation of an issue calling for government action (*National Leadership and Foreign Policy*, pp. 17-19). The Rosenau case study is a companion to an earlier, theoretical volume, *Public Opinion and Foreign Policy* (1961). There he hypothesized that the heads of voluntary associations frequently are opinion makers by virtue of their access to the mass media and to associational channels of opinion such as the organization newspaper, and that associational opinion makers quickly become experts in the development of consensus (or at least the appearance of consensus) due to the necessity of juggling the variety of demands made by members (pp. 41-65). The book also contains a discussion of the probable effects of various organizational channels of communication on the members' opinions (see pp. 83-96).

The extensive voluntary activities of precinct workers in a midwestern industrial city are detailed by Rossi and Cutright (in Janowitz, *Community Political Systems*). Bromley, Kornberg, and Smith in an unpublished paper compared women in the party hierarchies with members of the League of Women Voters. They found that the political party officials had been reared in a more politicized environment and tended to be of lower socio-economic status and educational attainment than the League women.

Personality variables are dealt with in the famous Berkeley study by Adorno, Frenkel-Brunswick, Levinson, and Sanford and in a more recent study of high school students in an Oregon industrial blue-collar community of 22,000 by David Ziblatt (*Annals of the American Academy of Political and Social Science*, 361:20-31). The Berkeley group found that individuals with authoritarian personalities are not very active in politics and tend not to join community organizations nor to become leaders in those they do join, but their results are subject to question since socio-economic status was not controlled (see Christie, in Christie and Jahoda, *Studies in Scope and Method*). Ziblatt's rather involved results indicated that participation in high school extra curricular activities is correlated with the individual's having a feeling of being integrated into the high school status system, which in turn is correlated with social trust. Social trust is correlated with a positive attitude toward politics, so in an indirect way participation and positive feelings about politics are related.

Finally, we might mention that there is an interesting discussion based on extensive urban research of various types of community actors and the role they play in politics and voluntary associations in Scott Greer's *The Emerging City*, in an article on "The Mass Society and the Parapolitical Structure" which he wrote with Peter Orleans, and in his later book *Metropolitics*. Greer divides individuals into three types: community actors who are members of locally based voluntary organizations and are informed about the community's affairs; neighbors, who participate in the neighborhood but not in the local community; and isolates, who are not involved at either level. The results of a sample survey in the metropolitan St. Louis area indicated that community actors were most involved and also most competent politically and isolates least involved and least competent. More importantly, the study indicated that a parapolitical or intermediary structure of voluntary associations did exist between the citizen and the state, and that the citizens who were not involved in this structure but interacted with the political system largely through the mass media were "far from a majority" (Greer and Orleans, p. 645).

BIBLIOGRAPHY

Abu-Laban, Baha, "Leader Visibility in a Local Community," *Pacific Sociological Review*, 4 (Fall 1961): 73–78. Includes a section on the relationships between the residents' group memberships and their awareness of leaders.

Adorno, T. W., Else Frenkel-Brunswick, Daniel J. Levinson, and R. Nevitt Sanford, *The Authoritarian Personality*. New York, Harper and Row, 1950.

Agger, Robert C., "Power Attributes in the Local Community: Theoretical and Research Considerations," *Social Forces*, 34 (May 1956): 322–331. Data from his study in Oregon indicate formal organizations are important influence channels in the community.

Alford, Robert R., and Harry M. Scoble, "Sources of Local Political Involvement," *American Political Science Review*, 62 (December 1968): 1192–1206. In a sample survey of the electorate of four middle-sized cities in Wisconsin it was found that social status and organization activity were the most important personal characteristics associated with local political involvement.

Almond, Gabriel A., and Sidney Verba, *The Civic Culture*. Princeton, Princeton University Press, 1963.

Austen, Ralph A., *Northwest Tanzania under German and British Rule*. New Haven, Yale University Press, 1968. Contains a discussion of voluntary associations in the area.

Banfield, Edward C., *Political Influence*. Glencoe, Illinois, Free Press, 1961.

―――― and James Q. Wilson, *City Politics*. Cambridge, Harvard University Press and The M.I.T. Press, 1963. This text includes a discussion of the role of voluntary associations in urban politics. Banfield and Wilson compare voluntary associations to other permanent organizations on the city political scene in terms of the incentives offered by the associations, their membership, the role of the staff, and their effectiveness.

Banks, Arthur S., and Robert B. Textor, *A Cross Polity Survey*. Cambridge, The M.I.T. Press, 1963. Banks and Textor rated (in collaboration with other experts) each of the 115 independent polities in terms of fifty-seven characteristics. Two of these "raw characteristics" deal with voluntary associations in the polity ("interest articulation by associational groups" and "freedom of group opposition"). All of the characteristics were then compared with each other, and the book itself consists of a computer printout of all the important information produced by cross tabulation. The value of the book depends on the validity of the authors' judgments in rating, and we are given no information which would enable us to check the ratings' validity.

Banton, Michael, *West African City*. London, Oxford University Press, 1957.

Barth, Ernest A. T., and Baha Abu-Laban, "Power Structure and the Negro Sub-Community," *American Sociological Review*, 24 (February 1959): 69–72.

Berelson, Bernard R., Paul F. Lazarsfeld, and William N. McPhee, *Voting*. Chicago, University of Chicago Press, 1954.

Berger, Suzanne, "Corporative Organization: The Case of a French Rural Association," in J. Roland Pennock and John W. Chapman, eds., *Voluntary Associations*. New York, Atherton Press, 1969.

Beveridge, W. H., and A. F. Wells, eds., *The Evidence for Voluntary Action*. London, Allen and Unwin, 1949. An assessment of the role of voluntary association in British society, particularly in carrying out welfare programs in the postwar era.

Bonjean, Charles M., and David M. Olson, "Community Leadership: Directions of Research," *Administrative Science Quarterly*, 9 (December 1964): 278–300. A general review of the literature on community power published between 1953 and 1963.

Boynton, George Robert, "Southern Conservatism: Constituency Opinion and Congressional Voting," *Public Opinion Quarterly*, 29 (Summer 1965): 259–269. Includes a table relating membership in various types of associations to a measure of social welfare liberalism. There are also some other data on the relationships between voting and social class and voluntary association membership.

Bromley, David, Allan Kornberg, and Joel Smith, "Variable Partisan Commitment among Politically Active Women." Paper delivered at Midwestern Political Science Association meeting, May 1968.

Buchanan, William, "An Inquiry into Purposive Voting," *Journal of Politics*, 18 (1956): 281–296. Study of voters in a small municipality in the South. Voters were more likely to belong to organizations than nonvoters, and purposive voters, that is, those who felt their vote was an effective technique of influencing community affairs, were more likely to be participants than nonpurposive voters.

Campbell, Angus, "The Passive Citizen," in Edward C. Dreyer and Walter A. Rosenbaum, eds., *Political Opinion and Electoral Behavior*. Belmont, California, Wadsworth, 1966.

——— Philip E. Converse, Warren E. Miller, and Donald E. Stokes, *The American Voter*. New York, John Wiley, 1960. This study of the American electorate in 1952 and 1956 does not focus on voluntary association participation, but it does shed light on the manner in which any group affiliation can affect voting behavior.

Christie, Richard, "Authoritarianism Re-Examined," in Richard Christie and Marie Jahoda, eds., *Studies in the Scope and Method of the Authoritarian Personality*. Glencoe, Illinois, Free Press, 1954. Christie refers to studies which indicate that authoritarian personalities are not active in politics or voluntary associations.

Clark, Peter B., *The Businessman as a Civic Leader*. Glencoe, Illinois, Free Press, 1964.

Clark, T. N., "Power and Community Structure: Who Governs, Where and When?" *The Sociological Quarterly*, 8 (Summer 1967): 291–316. Clark argues that a variety of voluntary organizations (along with other factors) in a community provide structural support for a plurality of competing elites and make the power structure more pluralistic. Moreover, in a small community there need not be a great deal of structural support for citizens to challenge policies of the community leadership.

Curtis, Richard F., Dianne M. Timbers, Elton F. Jackson, "Prejudice and Urban Social Participation," *American Journal of Sociology*, 72 (September 1967): 235–244.

Cutler, Stephen Joel, "Membership in Voluntary Associations and the Theory of Mass Society." Unpublished PhD dissertation, University of Michigan, 1969. Cutler's survey of 1013 urban males indicated that voluntary association membership had no effect on the individual's feelings of powerlessness, his dogmatism or conformity to societal norms.

Dahl, Robert A., *Who Governs?* New Haven, Yale University Press, 1961.

D'Antonio, William V., and William H. Form, *Influentials in Two Border Cities*. South Bend, Indiana, University of Notre Dame Press, 1965. A study of the decision making elites in El Paso, Texas, and C. Juarez, Mexico, which deals briefly with the role of voluntary associations in several civic controversies and with the memberships held by influentials in the two cities.

Dawson, Richard E., and Kenneth Prewitt, *Political Socialization*. Boston, Little, Brown, 1969. There is a brief discussion of the role of secondary groups such as voluntary associations in political socialization.

Dennis, Wayne, "Registration and Voting in a Patriotic Organization," *Journal of Social Psychology*, May 1930, pp. 317–318. Comparing members of the DAR with a sample of women over twenty-one and another group of women who were neighbors of DAR members, Dennis found that the DAR women were registered and voted in elections to a greater extent than did either of the other two groups. All of the women were residents of Lansing, Michigan.

DiPalma, Giuseppe, *Apathy and Participation*. New York, Free Press (Macmillan), 1970. An analysis of mass politics in Germany, Italy, Britain, and the United States, employing data collected by Almond and Verba for *The Civic Culture*. In various sections of the book DiPalma discusses organization affiliation and political participation.

Edinger, Lewis J., *Politics in Germany*. Boston, Little, Brown, 1968. A "system-functional" analysis of German politics including the role of organized interest groups. However, Edinger deals almost entirely with religious groups, agricultural associations, and organized labor. There are also a few comments on voluntary associations in contemporary Germany.

Ehrmann, Henry W., ed., *Interest Groups on Four Continents*. Pittsburgh, University of Pittsburgh Press, 1958. This volume, an outgrowth of a conference sponsored by the International Political Science Association, includes reports on interest groups, a few of which are voluntary associations, in Australia, Finland, France, Germany, Great Britain, Japan, Sweden, Yugoslavia, and the United States.

Epstein, A. L., *Politics in an Urban African Community*. Manchester, England, University of Manchester Press, 1958. A detailed study, based upon extensive field work and historical research, of a Copperbelt mining town in Northern Rhodesia. There is some limited information on voluntary associations, especially the Welfare Societies.

Erbe, William, "Social Involvement and Political Activity," *American Sociological Review*, 24 (April 1964): 198–215.

Fanelli, A. Alexander, "Typology of Community Leadership Based on Influence and Interaction within the Leader Subsystem," *Social Forces*, 34 (May 1956): 332–338. Fanelli found some evidence that community leaders were linked through their ties in formal community organizations in the small Mississippi town he studied.

Fenn, Dan H., Jr., "Executives as Community Volunteers," *Harvard Business Review*, March-April 1971, pp. 4–16, 156–157.

Flacks, Richard, "The Liberated Generation: An Exploration of the Roots of Student Protest," Working Paper No. 1, Youth and Social Change Project, University of Chicago, August 1966. Flacks reports on research he conducted with Bernice Neugarten. Data were gathered on a sample of student activists and their parents, a control sample of nonactivists and their parents, and from samples of University of Chicago students who had taken various positions in a sit-in (protestors, nonprotestors, and antiprotestors).

Freeman, Howard E., and Morris Showel, "Differential Political Influence of Voluntary Associations," *Public Opinion Quarterly*, 15 (Winter 1951): 703–714.

Freeman, Linton C., Thomas Fararo, Warren Bloomberg, Jr., and Morris H. Sunshine, "Locating Leaders in Local Communities: A Comparison of Some Alternative Approaches," *American Sociological Review*, 28 (October 1963): 791–798. The researchers employed different techniques for locating leaders, and found that each technique revealed a different set of individuals. One group of leaders are individuals active in voluntary associations who take part in community decision making largely on the basis of their role in voluntary groups. The research was carried out in Syracuse, New York.

Gans, Herbert J. *The Urban Villagers*. Glencoe, Illinois, Free Press, 1962. Gans analyzes the political effects of nonparticipation among Boston's working class Italian Americans.

Gilbert, Claire, "Community Power Structure: Propositional Inventory and Tests," in Terry N. Clark, ed., *Community Structure and Decision Making*. San Francisco, Chandler, 1969. A secondary analysis of power structure data from 166 communities in the United States. The role of community organizations is one of the variables considered.

Gosnell, Harold F., *Machine Politics*. Chicago, University of Chicago Press, 1937.

Gosnell reports that nearly one half of the party workers he studied had fraternal affiliations.

Greer, Scott, *The Emerging City*. Glencoe, Illinois, Free Press, 1962.

—— with the advice and assistance of Norton E. Long, *Metropolitics*. New York, John Wiley, 1963. An analysis of campaigns for metropolitan government in the St. Louis, Cleveland, and Miami metropolitan areas.

—— and Peter Orleans, "The Mass Society and the Parapolitical Structure," *American Sociological Review*, 27 (October 1962): 634-646.

Hastings, Philip, "The Non-Voter in 1952: A Study of Pittsfield, Massachusetts," *Journal of Psychology*, 38 (October 1954): 301-312.

—— "The Voter and the Non-Voter," *American Journal of Sociology*, 62 (November 1956): 302-307. In comparing voters, nonvoters and sometime voters in Pittsfield, Massachusetts, in 1952 and 1954, Hastings found voters to be significantly more likely to belong to associations than were nonvoters, with sometime voters falling in between the other two groups.

Haug, Marie, "Social and Cultural Pluralism as a Concept in Social Systems Analysis," *American Journal of Sociology*, 73 (November 1967): 294-304. Cultural pluralism (as opposed to political pluralism) is explored as an analytic concept through reanalysis of *A Cross Polity Survey* data on 114 world polities. Pluralism appears to be related to other variables such as population type, Gross National Product, political instability, geographic size, and literacy.

Hero, Alfred, *Voluntary Organizations in World Affairs Communication*. Volume V. Boston, World Peace Foundation, 1960. In addition to information on the subject indicated by the title, this monograph contains an introductory chapter which provides an excellent short review of the literature on voluntary associations.

Hillman, Arthur, "Urbanization and the Organization of Welfare Activities in the Metropolitan Community in Chicago," in Ernest W. Burgess and Donald J. Bogue, *Contributions to Urban Sociology*. Chicago, University of Chicago Press, 1964. A summary review of the author's PhD dissertation which documents the trends toward professionalization and the assumption by the government of responsibility for welfare services which were originally provided by voluntary agencies.

Hirschfield, Robert S., Bert E. Swanson and Blanche D. Blank, "A Profile of Political Activists in Manhattan," *Western Political Quarterly*, 15 (1962): pp. 489-507. The researchers found that the New York amateur Democrats were "joiners"; only 3 percent reported no organizational ties.

Hodgkin, Thomas, *Nationalism in Colonial Africa*. New York, New York University Press, 1957.

Hyman, Herbert H., and Paul Sheatsley, "'The Authoritarian Personality' — A Methodological Critique," in Richard Christie and Marie Jahoda, eds., *Studies in the Scope and Method of the Authoritarian Personality*. Glencoe, Illinois, Free Press, 1954. Comments on the relationship between membership in voluntary association and political attitudes and activity.

Jessop, R. D., "Civility and Traditionalism in English Political Culture," *British Journal of Political Science*, 1 (January 1971): 1-24.

Key, V. O., Jr., *Public Opinion and American Democracy*. New York, Alfred A. Knopf, 1964.

Kuper, Leo, *An African Bourgeoisie*. New Haven, Yale University Press, 1965. A carefully researched account of the organizational milieu of Africans in South Africa, particularly in the city of Durban. Kuper focuses on the paternalistic advisory boards, the football associations, and political organizations.

—— and M. G. Smith, eds., *Pluralism in Africa*. Berkeley and Los Angeles, University of California Press, 1969. Very little attention is given specifically to voluntary associations, but the various authors provide a good discussion of pluralism as a general political and cultural frame of analysis with particular reference to the African experience.

Kuroda, Yasumasa, "Political Role Attributions and Dynamics in a Japanese Community," *Public Opinion Quarterly*, 29 (Winter 1965): 602–613.

—— "Measurement, Correlates, and Significance of Political Participation in a Japanese Community," *Western Political Quarterly*, 20 (September 1967): 660–668.

Lane, Robert E., *Political Life*. Glencoe, Illinois, Free Press, 1959.

—— *Political Ideology*. New York, Free Press, 1962.

Laskin, Richard, and Serena Phillett, "An Integrative Analysis of Voluntary Association Leadership and Reputational Influence," *Sociological Inquiry*, 35 (Spring 1965): 176–185.

Lazarsfeld, Paul, Bernard Berelson, and Hazel Gaudet, *The People's Choice*. Second edition. New York, Columbia University Press, 1948.

Little, Kenneth, "The Role of Voluntary Associations in West-African Organizations," *American Anthropologist*, 59 (1957): 579–596.

—— "The Organization of Voluntary Associations in West-Africa," *Civilizations*, 9 (1959): 283–300.

—— *West African Urbanization*. Cambridge, Cambridge University Press, 1965.

Lorwin, Val R., "Segmental Pluralism: Ideological Cleavages and Political Cohesion in the Smaller European Democracies," *Comparative Politics*, 3 (January 1971): 141–176. A discussion of segmental pluralism or the organization of groups along lines of religious and ideological cleavages in the Netherlands, Belgium, Luxembourg, Switzerland, and Austria.

Lowry, Ritchie P., "Mediating Leadership and Community Interaction," in Alvin W. Gouldner and S. M. Miller, eds., *Applied Sociology*. New York, Free Press, Macmillan, 1965. Report on the leadership groups — locals, cosmopolitans, and mediators — in a small northern California college town; each group has a different pattern of voluntary association memberships.

Maccoby, Herbert, "The Differential Political Activity of Participants in a Voluntary Association," *American Sociological Review*, 23 (October 1958): 524–532.

McNall, Scott G., "Social Disorganization and Availability: Accounting for Radical Rightism," in Robert A. Schoenberger, ed., *The American Right Wing*. New York, Holt, Rinehart and Winston, 1969. McNall argues that the high concentration of members of the John Birch society in California is due to the society's being "*the* available organization for people who were predisposed by disorganization to join a movement." In California "there was not a series of older established groups to which people with deviant impulses could be attracted" (p. 137).

McWilliams, Robert O., "A Study of the Relationship of Political Behavior to Social Group Membership." Unpublished PhD dissertation, University of Michigan, 1953.

Matthews, Donald R., *U. S. Senators and Their World.* Chapel Hill, University of North Carolina Press, 1960.

Meillassoux, Claude, *Urbanization of an African Community.* Seattle, University of Washington Press, 1968.

Milbrath, Lester W., *The Washington Lobbyists.* Chicago, Rand McNally and Company, 1963. A political scientist examines the characteristics of lobbyists and the systems within which they operate using data gathered through lengthy structured interviews with a random sample of Washington lobbyists and with some congressmen. Although the greatest number of the respondents represented small trade associations, some of the lobbyists were agents of voluntary associations.

—— *Political Participation.* Chicago, Rand McNally, 1965.

Miller, Delbert C., "Industry and Community Power Structure: A Comparative Study of an American and English City," *American Sociological Review,* 23 (February 1958): 9–15.

Mills, C. Wright, "The Middle Classes in Middle Sized Cities," in Logan Wilson and William L. Kolb, eds., *Sociological Analysis.* New York, Harcourt, Brace, 1949.

Mulford, Charles L., "Considerations of the Instrumental and Expressive Roles of Community Differentials and Formal Organizations," *Sociology and Social Research,* 51 (January 1967): 141–147. Community power studies in Iowa showed that the most influential organizations were instrumental-expressive in character, and that high-status influential people tended to belong to them and to associate with other influential people.

Neal, Arthur G., and Melvin Seeman, "Organizations and Powerlessness: A Test of the Mediation Hypothesis," *American Sociological Review,* 29 (April 1964): 216–226. Answers to mail questionnaires sent to a sample of adult male residents of Columbus, Ohio, indicated that membership in work-based organizations (unions, business or professional organizations) is associated with a relatively strong sense of control over events.

Nelson, Joel I., "Participation and Integration: The Case of the Small Businessman," *American Sociological Review,* 33 (June 1968): 427–438. It was found that small businessmen in twenty-eight Minnesota communities tended to have an "affinity for mass behavior" if they were alienated, regardless of whether or not they participated in occupational organizations.

Nie, Norman H., G. Bingham Powell, Jr., and Kenneth Prewitt, "Social Structure and Political Participation: Developmental Relationships, I," *American Political Science Review,* 63 (June 1969): 361–378.

—— "Social Structure and Political Participation: Developmental Relationships, II," *American Political Science Review,* 63 (September 1969): 808–832.

Noel, Donald L., and Alphonso Pinkney, "Correlates of Prejudice: Some Racial

Differences and Similarities," *American Journal of Sociology,* 69 (May 1964): 609–622.

Pellegrin, Roland J., and Charles H. Coates, "Absentee-Owned Corporations and Community Power Structure," *American Journal of Sociology,* 61 (March 1956): 413–419.

Ransford, H. Edward, "Isolation, Powerlessness, and Violence: A Study of Attitudes and Participation in the Watts Riot," *American Journal of Sociology,* 73 (March 1968): 581–591.

Riggs, Fred W., "Interest and Clientele Groups," in Joseph Sutton, ed., *Problems of Politics and Administration in Thailand,* pp. 153–191. Bloomington, Indiana University Institute of Training for Public Service, 1962.

Rokkan, Stein, "Electoral Activity, Party Membership and Organizational Influence: An Initial Analysis of data from the Norwegian Election Studies, 1957," *Acta Sociologica,* 4 (1959): 25–37.

Rose, Arnold M., *The Power Structure.* New York, Oxford University Press, 1967.

Rosenau, James N., *Public Opinion and Foreign Policy: An Operational Formulation.* New York, Random House, 1961.

—— *National Leadership and Foreign Policy: A Case Study in the Mobilization of Public Support.* Princeton, Princeton University Press, 1963.

Rossi, Peter H., "Community Decision-Making," in Roland Young, ed., *Approaches to the Study of Politics.* Evanston, Northwestern University Press, 1958. Includes comments on the role of voluntary associations in the community, and on the leadership of associations as compared to local government officials.

—— "The Organizational Structure of an American Community," in Amitai Etzioni, ed., *Complex Organizations: A Sociological Reader.* New York, Holt, Rinehart and Winston, 1964.

—— and Phillips Cutright, "The Impact of Party Organization in an Industrial Setting," in Morris Janowitz, ed., *Community Political Systems.* Glencoe, Illinois, Free Press, 1961.

Rotberg, Robert, *Rise of Nationalism in Central Africa.* Cambridge, Harvard University Press, 1965. Includes material on the role of voluntary associations in Central Africa in the 1920s and 1930s.

Salisbury, Robert H., "The Urban Party Organization Member," in David W. Abbot and Edward T. Rogosky, eds., *Political Parties.* New York, Rand McNally, 1971.

Schulze, Robert O., "The Role of Economic Dominants in Community Power Structure," *American Sociological Review,* 23 (February 1958): 3–9.

—— "The Bifurcation of Power in a Satellite City," in Morris Janowitz, ed., *Community Political Systems.* Glencoe, Illinois, The Free Press, 1961.

—— and Leonard U. Blumberg, "The Determination of Local Power Elites," *American Journal of Sociology,* 63 (November 1957): 290–296.

Simpson, R. L., "Negro-Jewish Prejudice: Authoritarianism and Some Variables as Correlates," *Social Problems,* 7 (Fall 1959): 138–146. Interviews with 150 Negroes and 150 Jews randomly selected from the Negro and Jewish populations, aged twenty-one and over, in a northeastern city, indicated that in both groups people who had no close friends and belonged to no organizations were the most prejudiced. Interviews for the study were conducted by staff members of the Cornell University intergroup relations project.

Seeman, Melvin, "Alienation, Membership, and Political Knowledge: A Comparative Study," *Public Opinion Quarterly*, 30 (Fall 1966): 353–367.

Skrzypek, Stanislaw, "The Political, Cultural, and Social Views of Yugoslav Youth," *Public Opinion Quarterly*, 29 (Spring 1965): 87–106.

Sorace, Samuel J., and Melvin Seeman, "Some Correlates of Civil Rights Activism," *Social Forces*, 46 (December 1967): 197–207. Equalitarian contacts appeared to be associated with greater civil rights activism for whites and blacks in this somewhat inconclusive study.

Stouffer, Samuel A., *Communism, Conformity, and Civil Liberties*. Garden City, New York, Doubleday, 1965.

Valen, Henry, and Daniel Katz, *Political Parties in Norway: A Community Study*. Oslo, Universitets-forlaget, and London, Tavistock Publications, 1964.

Verba, Sidney, "Organizational Membership and Democratic Consensus," *Journal of Politics*, 27 (August 1965): 467–497.

Wallerstein, Immanuel, "Voluntary Associations," in James C. Coleman and Carl G. Rosberg, Jr., eds., *Political Parties and National Integration in Tropical Africa*. Berkeley, University of California Press, 1964.

White, James E., "Theory and Method for Research in Community Leadership," *American Sociological Review*, 16 (February 1950): 50–60. White interviewed heads of voluntary organizations and a sample of the population in a small rural New York community to locate formal and informal leaders. Much of the article is devoted to a discussion of methodology.

Wildavsky, Aaron, *Leadership in a Small Town*. Totowa, New Jersey, Bedminster Press, 1964. A community power study which deals minimally with voluntary associations.

Willie, Charles, Herbert Notkin, and Nicholas Rezak, "Trends in the Participation of Businessmen in Local Community Voluntary Affairs," *Sociology and Social Research*, 48 (April 1964): 289–300. A trend analysis of the participation of businessmen in voluntary health and welfare services from 1921 to 1958 in the Syracuse, New York, metropolitan area.

Wolfinger, Raymond E., Barbara K. Wolfinger, Kenneth Prewitt, and Sheilah Rosenhack, "America's Radical Right: Politics and Ideology," in Edward C. Dreyer and Walter A. Rosenbaum, eds., *Political Opinion and Electoral Behavior*. Belmont, California, Wadsworth, 1966. Interviewing by graduate students and mailed questionnaires were both employed to gain information on the political, social, and psychological characteristics of radical rightists.

Young, Ruth C., and Olaf F. Larson, "The Contribution of Voluntary Organizations to Community Structure," *American Journal of Sociology*, 71 (September 1965): 178–186.

Ziblatt, David, "High School Extracurricular Activities and Political Socialization," *Annals of the American Academy of Political and Social Science*, 361 (September 1965): 20–31.

Zimmer, Basil B., and Amos H. Hawley, "The Significance of Membership in Associations," *American Journal of Sociology*, 65 (September 1959): 196–201. The authors found that membership in formal associations was positively correlated with opposition to metropolitan government among their respondents in the Flint, Michigan, area.

Chapter Five   Surveys of Participation

In the United States the greater part of the research on voluntary associations has been the work of sociologists, who have dealt primarily with: the relationship between voluntary associations and their social environment; the place of voluntary associations in the society's power structure; the relationships between voluntary association membership and such variables as membership in other kinds of groups, class, attitudes, urban-rural location, rural location, religion, race, family roles, and neighborhood cohesion; and with the internal characteristics of associations. (See Morris in *Sociological Inquiry*, 35: 186–200.) In the next chapter the extensive literature on participation as related to social class, race, ethnicity, sex, age, and attitudes, as well as the community studies, will be considered. Here, the focus will be on survey work, and on research dealing with urbanization and neighborhood characteristics as they relate to participation.

NATIONWIDE SURVEYS

There are only a few nationwide surveys to be considered since most of the research has been conducted in limited geographical areas. In 1965 the United States Department of Labor included questions on volunteer work in its monthly labor survey involving more than 9000 persons in 4000 households. For purposes of the investigation, volunteer work was defined as "any unpaid work performed for or through an organization," excluding work for a political organization, work done as part of schooling, and volunteer work to further a hobby. Separate tabulations were made for nonreligious activity and for religious activity defined as "having to do with a church's ritual, precepts, or religious function" (p. 21).

Superficial information on the motivations of volunteers was gathered, but the data relate primarily to the number of hours individuals devoted to various types of volunteer work during a representative week in the year and during the entire year; and to the age, sex, education, occupation, and income of the volunteer. It was found that volunteers tended to be between 25 and 44 years of age, married, white, and from families in which the principal breadwinner was a white collar worker having an annual income between $5,000 and $7,500. Women in the 25-44 year old group were more likely to volunteer than men. For both women and men, education and volunteer work were positively correlated. The Bureau's statistics indicated that approximately 16 percent of the individuals over 14 years of age had contributed some labor as volunteers during 1965. The number of hours given varied: nearly half of the volunteers reported spending less than 25 hours a year; a third worked 25 to 90 hours a year. The activities also varied, although the "most popular forms of volunteer activity for the gorup as a whole were in education, social or welfare services, or services to youth." Women were more likely to work as fund raisers, as organizers or planners, youth group leaders, and teachers or teacher aides, while more men worked as organizers or planners, followed by fund raisers and youth group leaders (pp 3-8).

To our knowledge, Murray Hausknecht's *The Joiners* is the only available book-length treatment of participation in voluntary associations which is based on national surveys. Hausknecht utilized data from a National Opinion Research Corporation (NORC) survey conducted in 1955 and from another survey made by the American Institute of Public Opinion in 1954. While neither investigation was primarily concerned with the extent of voluntary association membership, both included questions dealing with the subjects' membership in organizations. Hausknecht deals with such variables as stratification and urbanization, sex, age, marital status, and social integration, in a discussion which is made doubly useful by his systematic comparisons between the results of the national surveys and those from other studies involving the same variables. The book also contains a valuable general discussion of the literature on voluntarism, including both research and theory.

In 1958 Charles Wright and Herbert Hyman published a valuable secondary analysis of the findings from two national NORC probability samples and local surveys in the New York metropolitan area, Denver, and a small city and county in Ohio. The national survey data led them to conclude that: "(1) Voluntary association membership is not characteristic of the majority of Americans . . . (2) A relatively small percentage of Americans belong to two or more voluntary associations . . . (3) Membership is more characteristic of white than Negro population . . . (4) Membership is more characteristic of Jewish than Protestant persons, and of Protestant than Catholics . . . (5) Membership is directly related to socio-economic status, as measured by level of income, occupation, home ownership, interviewer's rating of level of living, and education . . . (6) Membership is more characteristic of urban and rural nonfarm residents than of rural farm residents" (*American Sociological Review*, 23:294). The local surveys indicated that membership was not related to such situational factors as length of residence in the community or at the same address, the type of dwelling unit occupied, or the time spent commuting to work; although it was related to family status: couples with children had higher rates of participation than childless couples. Membership was also positively correlated with voting, support for local charities, and interest in public affairs.

In 1971 Hyman and Wright published another secondary analysis of national sample surveys conducted by NORC covering the years from 1955 to 1962, with some supplementary evidence from surveys conducted as recently as 1967 (*American Sociological Review*, 36: 191–206). The 1950 findings that "voluntary association membership is not characteristic of most Americans" and that a "relatively small percentage of Americans belong to two or more voluntary associations" were confirmed by these later surveys. However, there was "a small but noteworthy increase in voluntary association memberships between the mid-1950's and the early 1960's." Hyman and Wright further report that: "(4) The trend toward more membership in associations was not caused by the cohort who came of age during the period from 1955–1962, the two points in the study. (5) Membership is directly related to current socio-economic position, as measured by a variety of indicators . . . (6) The trend toward increase in associational memberships is not confined to the more well-to-do strata of the population, but occurs all along the line and especially among those of poorer economic means. (7) Current economic situation appears to have more effect on membership than does one's station or origin. (8) The trend toward increased membership applies to both Negro and white adults but is somewhat

more evident among the former thereby tending to reduce previous
subgroup differences in membership" (pp. 205–206). In neither analysis
did Wright and Hyman count union membership in scoring the number
of associations to which an individual belonged.

Wright and Hyman found that the memberships of adults were related
to the individual's adult social status rather than the status of the individual's family during his childhood. Apparently, individuals who are
socially mobile, whether the mobility is upwards or downwards, "behave like stayers in the status of their destination" (p. 200). However,
two national sample surveys, conducted by the University of Michigan
Survey Research Center, of girls between the ages of 11 and 18 and
boys between the ages of 11 and 13 offer evidence that children from
higher status families are more likely to belong to youth groups than
are children from lower status families. Wright and Hyman feel that the
seemingly contradictory findings really demonstrate a discontinuity.
"Before children have arrived at an independent status, and when they
still are under the impress of the family, their memberships reflect
those influences and circumstances. But when they are removed from
such conditions, and have arrived in a new social location, it then becomes governing and overrides the earlier influences" (p. 201).

Nicholas Babchuk and Alan Booth have questioned the validity of the
secondary analyses (and of many of the local surveys examined in the
next section) on the basis of their own interviews of a large sample of
Nebraska residents. Although their work is not national in scope, Babchuk and Booth claim that their findings are probably representative
of the national population since the respondents came from all social
strata and resided in rural farm, rural nonfarm, and metropolitan areas.
In this first longitudinal study of voluntary association membership,
Babchuk and Booth collected data from a sample of 1500 adults in
1961, and again in 1965 from a one-third random sample taken from
the original group. In further contrast to the national surveys utilized
by Wright and Hyman and by Hausknecht, the Babchuk and Booth
study was completely devoted to the examination of the correlates of
voluntary association participation and the questioning was far more
extensive.

The most striking difference between the results obtained by Babchuk
and Booth and those of a number of other researchers lies in the percentage of respondents who were found to belong to voluntary associations. More than 80 percent of the Nebraska subjects reported belonging

to at least one association, and almost half of them belonged to three or more groups. However, the much lower membership figures obtained in other studies may be due to the use of a more restrictive definition of voluntary associations. Babchuk and Booth's definition was extremely broad, including both unions and other "job-related" associations and recreational groups such as bowling leagues and card clubs. Indeed, next to membership in the PTA, affiliation with poker, bridge and card clubs and with bowling teams was the most common (*American Sociological Review*, 34: 34).

In addition to the data on membership, Babchuk and Booth also provide information on the relationships between participation and such variables as age, social class, length of residence in the community, and the size of the community; on the turnover in organizations and the factors associated with high and low turnover; and on the stability-instability in individual memberships (over 65 percent of the panel added or dropped at least one of their memberships between 1961 and 1965).

The Nebraska longitudinal study data were also used by Booth and Babchuk to analyze personal influence networks and voluntary association affiliation. They found that individuals tend to become members of formal voluntary associations as a result of personal networks and face to face contacts; that informal leaders are more influential than formal leaders when both attempt to influence the same person; and that personal influence is more likely to play a role in recruiting members for expressive organizations than for instrumental organizations. They feel these results support their theory that affiliation with a voluntary organization constitutes an "exchange" between the individual and the organization.

Aside from these American investigations, a few surveys of national scope have been conducted in other countries, although in most instances the central concern of the researchers was not with voluntary association membership and only minimal information on membership was obtained. The most important of these foreign studies — Gabriel Almond's and Sidney Verba's examination of the political cultures of Britain, Germany, Italy, Mexico, and the United States — was discussed in Chapter Four, as were the Norwegian election surveys.

Some survey research has been carried out in Canada, Denmark, Sweden, Finland, France, and West Germany. The results of a 1968 stratified, multistage, national sample in Canada in which 2767 adults

were interviewed revealed that the Canadian pattern of participation is
similar to the American in all key respects. Moreover, in both countries
the rate of affiliation for women was higher than that of women in
other highly industrialized nations and appeared to account for the
higher overall rates of affiliation since the affiliation rate for men in
both was roughly the same as that in the other nations (Curtis, *American Sociological Review*, 36:879). In Denmark a sample survey conducted in 1953–54 revealed that Danes' participation varies with socio-
economic status and that participation in voluntary associations is less
important to Danes than informal social intercourse. Although a
majority of Danes belonged to at least one association, there was also a
majority who never attended a meeting during a six-month period. However, the results of the study, which are reported (in 1957) by Kaare
Svalastoga in *Prestige, Class and Mobility*, seemed to indicate that the
overall level of participation in Denmark was at least as high as that in
the United States. According to Gunnar Heckscher, the Swedes have a
similarly high rate of participation. By the time Swedish men are 21,
no less than 10 percent have reached a position of trust in an organization, and approximately 50 percent belong to one or more organizations. In his discussion of Swedish "pluralist democracy," Heckscher
also notes that there are many organizations in Sweden, and joining is
emphasized in the culture — although the individual is expected to be
discriminating and to join the organizations of his class (*Social Research*,
15:441). A national probability sample of Finnish youth between the
ages of 10 and 29 provided data supporting the so-called "cumulativeness" hypothesis, which postulates that there is a positive correlation
among participation in all kinds of leisure activities, with, for example,
individuals who read a great deal also tending to be more active in youth
groups (See Allardt et al., *Acta Sociologica*, 3:165–172; Allardt and
Pesonen, *International Social Science Journal*, 12.1:27–39).

The results of a 1953 UNESCO-sponsored survey in West Germany as
reported by Lipset in *Political Man* (pp. 111 and 196) indicated that at
every occupational level, individuals belonging to voluntary associations
were more likely to favor a multiparty rather than a one-party system,
and that those persons who belonged to associations such as sports and
social clubs were more interested in politics, listened more often to
political radio programs, read more newspapers, and tended to vote in
greater numbers than nonjoiners. These relationships held in every social
stratum. Arnold Rose reports (in *Theory and Method in the Social
Sciences*) that a 1951 market research survey in France indicated that

only 41 percent of adult Frenchmen were members of any kind of association, including political parties, the semi-official veterans organizations, the trade unions, and other occupational associations. It also
appeared to the researchers that most of these memberships were
"casual and passive" (pp. 75–76).

LOCAL, NONRURAL SURVEYS IN THE UNITED STATES

The bulk of the research on participation in voluntary associations is
focused on a limited area such as a single city or town or several related
cities. While many of the single-city studies resemble the community
studies described in Chapter Six, the latter differ sufficiently in technique and scope to be treated separately. Typically community studies
involve extensive anthropological-type field work and are concerned
with the entire life of the community, while the research we are examining here usually depends on questionnaires and limited (if any) field
work, and is concerned with voluntary associations and participation
either exclusively or primarily. For example, one of the best and most
reliable is a sample survey of the population of Detroit conducted in
1952 by the Detroit Area Study under the direction of the University of
Michigan's Survey Research Center. The results are reported in a pamph-
let, "A Social Profile of Detroit," and in an article by Morris Axelrod
on "Urban Structure and Social Participation" in the *American Sociological Review.*

The Detroit data are based on 735 interviews conducted in 1952 with
a representative cross section of the adult population. Although membership in labor unions is included in some of the gross figures on participation, both reports also provide a detailed breakdown of the data with
separate figures being given for participation in labor unions and in each
of a variety of other organizations. It was found that, apart from
churches and labor unions, 45 percent of the population did not belong
to any organization and that two thirds of these nonmembers had never
belonged to a nonchurch organization. Moreover, approximately 14 percent of all Detroit residents had never belonged to any organization and
were part of a family in which no person had ever belonged to an organization. Most of those who did belong to an organization belonged to
only one or two, and of those belonging, only one in five were active in
organizations beyond attendance at regular meetings (Detroit Area
Study, pp. 16–19).

The reports of the survey also include data on family income, education, occupation of the family head, and informal group participation as related to formal group participation. In line with other studies, it was found that higher income, more education, and white collar occupational status were all positively correlated with formal participation. However, informal participation was "well-nigh universal," with relative or kin groupings being the most important of the informal group associations. Axelrod comments that the data provide "no substantiation of the view that formal association substitutes for informal association"; on the contrary there was some evidence of cumulativeness in that formal and informal association appeared to vary directly. Axelrod believes that if formal organizations exercise any "pervasive" influence in the urban area, it may be through the linkages between the minority who are active members and the underlying network of informal association in the entire area (p. 18).

We discovered a number of other local surveys such as John Scott's 1957 study of membership and participation patterns in the small Vermont college town of Bennington (*American Sociological Review*, 22: 315-326). Like the Detroit investigation, it is based on interviews with a random sample of the residents of the community. Although Scott is careful not to generalize from his Bennington findings to the nation as a whole, he does attempt to place his work in a broad theoretical context. Thus, he includes a review of the various hypotheses advanced to explain the proliferation of voluntary associations in the United States, noting that this proliferation has been variously ascribed to "the change of function of the family, Church, and state and the relative loss of control of these major institutions over the person"; "to the democratic and Protestant principle" of individual free choice; to the "articulation of minority groups"; to the "increased division of labor"; and to secularization (p. 318). Scott's overall findings are similar to those of the Detroit study: "At any one time, two-fifths of the population are not affiliated with voluntary associations, other than a church, and no more than half of the persons so affiliated are actively achieving the objectives established by the association or fulfilling personal objectives in the associational context. It is equally clear that control of memberships, committee memberships and official positions, and thus much of the functioning of the voluntary associations, is concentrated among relatively few persons" (p. 326).

Although Frederick Bushee's earlier article (*American Journal of Sociology*, 51:217-226) on the organization life of Boulder, Colorado (site of the University of Colorado) is based on examination of organization membership lists, rather than on a random sample survey, his coverage of the small town appears to be quite thorough. Bushee's findings were in keeping with those of other studies: 48 percent of the Boulder population either did not belong to any organized group or belonged only to a church, even though the community of 12,000 had over 240 organizations. In addition to the data on membership Bushee deals with various correlates of organizational activity; the relative attractiveness of different types of organizations; and the motives of individuals in forming and joining groups. In reference to the last topic, Bushee argues that individuals join groups out of a desire for self-improvement, individual recognition, social relations, and social and community improvement.

In Oregon both John Foskett and Walter Martin examined participation on the basis of evidence from interviews with a random sample of a community's population. Foskett worked in two cities, one a small town with few cleavages, the other a part of a growing metropolitan area with considerable internal strain and cleavage (*American Sociological Review*, 20:431-438). Despite these differences, the patterns of participation in the cities were similar. He found the usual correlations between participation and income, education, and occupation. There was some evidence that education was the most significant and age the least significant of the variables he employed in his analysis.

Martin's investigation in the rural-urban fringe of two small western Oregon communities indicated that volunteer participation in such areas is correlated with the same factors — especially socio-economic status — found significant elsewhere. It also appeared that "urban orientation," as measured by the location of the breadwinner's job and of the most frequently visited family, influences the site of organization memberships but not the overall extent of social participation (*American Sociological Review*, 17:687-694).

Further research would appear to be in order since the findings of a study conducted in Flint, Michigan, and its fringe area contradict those of Martin. Basil Zimmer and Amos Hawley (*American Journal of Sociology*, 65:196-201) report that the results of their two sample surveys indicated that 43 percent of the central city respondents belonged to formal associations while less than 25 percent of the respondents in the urban fringe held memberships. The differences were not due to "radical differences" in the demographic characteristics of the population.

While it is considerably older than the work we have discussed so far, the 1934 study of leisure time activities in the suburban area of West-chester County which George Lundberg and his associates did for the Columbia University Council for Research in the Social Sciences is still useful. Except for its concentration on leisure the work could qualify as a community study since field observation, formal interviews, question-naires, and participant diaries were all employed to produce a valuable description of the organization life of an area containing a variety of socio-economic and ethnic groups.

Lundberg found that voluntary associations were of growing im-portance, although the type of organization predominating in different communities of the county and the extent of the inhabitants' participa-tion varied. In general, the wealthier the community, the greater the tendency for individuals to participate, and to participate in leisure or pleasure oriented associations rather than in instrumental organizations providing economic and political benefits to the members. Lundberg's team also found that the poorer, more heterogeneous (both ethnically and economically) of two suburban towns had more organizations, al-though a smaller proportion of the residents in the poorer town partici-pated. The researchers suggest that the "overorganization of the poorer town" is due to its disorganization, explaining: "The heterogeneity of the population precluded agreement as to common needs, limited the range of governmental functions, and relegated many activities to separate, and at times conflicting, voluntary associations" (p. 133). The social distance between the town's various groups also necessitated a duplication of clubs serving essentially the same purposes (p. 135).

In addition, the researchers found that women predominated in the local country organizations. They argue: "Leisure not only makes pos-sible the greater organization of middle-class and upper-class women, but is, in a sense, its chief source. The non-working woman of the middle and upper classes must find outlets for the great amount of leisure which technological and economic changes have bestowed upon her and club work provides one such outlet" (p. 131).

Another early study dealing with participation in New York city which was carried out by Mirra Komarovsky, a member of the Lundberg team, was considerably less successful than the Westchester County re-search. Komarovsky had questionnaires distributed in several business concerns (chosen primarily because the management was willing to allow access to the employees). Although the number of questionnaires returned was high — over 2000 — this represented only 29 percent of those distributed. The sample was therefore obviously biased and in no sense representative of the population of the entire city. Despite these limitations, Komarovsky uses her data to generalize about the relationships between class status, ethnicity, sex, and participation of *all* city dwellers (*American Sociological Review*, 686-698).

In his study of Chicago, Herbert Goldhammer employed somewhat similar methods, but was more careful about generalizing from the data obtained (via 5500 questionnaires distributed to residents primarily through their place of business) to the Chicago population as a whole. In addition to collecting information relating to the standard variables such as age, ethnicity, and socio-economic status, Goldhammer used a scale developed by the psychologist L. L. Thurstone to obtain a measure of neuroticism. His results, combined with those from a study of married couples which was made available to him by Burgess and Cottrell and another of engaged couples by Burgess and Wallin, indicated "a distinct tendency toward an inverse relationship between neurotic score and membership frequency." Goldhammer hypothesizes that this finding may be due to the inability of the deviant personality to "find the degree of sympathy, understanding and indulgence" he desires in the "more formal framework" of the voluntary organization. Given the fact that the Thurstone Inventory tends to classify as neurotic behaviors which are "socially disesteemed and often personally distressing," the individual who scores high may well not have the desire, initiative, or capacity to utilize the formal setting of the association for the "cultivation of human relationships" (Burgess and Bogue, *Contributions to Urban Sociology*, p. 230).

While Ira De A. Reid and Emily Ehle were not primarily interested in participation, as a by-product of their 1949 study of twenty-four-block areas of Philadelphia, they discovered that 78 percent of their sample belonged to no religious organization beyond general membership in a church, 85 percent belonged to no civic or charitable associations, and 74 percent did not belong to any occupational group (*Public Opinion Quarterly*, 14:265).

Although the last of the local studies we are considering here focuses on the effect of commuting on participation, the author, Alvin Scaff, reports data on other aspects of participation in Claremont, California, as well (*American Sociological Review*, 17:215-220). Scaff gathered his information through personal interviews conducted with a sample composed of approximately 10 percent of the community's total population. He found that participation increased with education, occupational status, and length of residence in the community, but was adversely affected by commuting and decreased with an increase in commuting distance.

RURAL STUDIES

The study of rural areas has developed into a speciality within sociology with its own journal called, appropriately, *Rural Sociology*. Several articles on participation in rural environments have appeared in this journal, and a number of additional ones are scattered in other sources. For convenience and clarity, we shall deal with all of these rural studies at this point, even though some of them focus on the effect of a particular variable on participation, rather than on the locality.

Two books came out of an early but important investigation of changes in rural life between 1900 and 1936. United States census data was employed and interviews were conducted in 140 agricultural villages. Each village was studied three separate times between 1920 and 1936. Both of the books — Brunner and Kolb's *Rural Social Trends*, which deals with the period from 1920 to 1930, and Brunner and Lorge's *Rural Trends in Depression Years*, which covers the period from 1930 to 1936 — include detailed information on the social and recreational associations and the church and school subsidiary organizations in the villages and the changes that occurred in these organizations over time. Information on membership, attendance at meetings, expenditures, birth and death rates of the organizations, as well as other detail is related for each type of organization. In their report, Brunner and Kolb stress the instability of the village organizations. They attribute the short lives of the organizations to a variety of factors including poor planning and leadership, the growth of informal organizations, the competition of the organizations in combination with general conflict in the villages, and in some instances, the organization's achievement of its goals.

John Harp and Richard Gagan followed up these early studies in 1964. They compared the results they obtained from their own research in 240 population centers with the earlier results to provide a valuable longitudinal analysis. They found a continuing decline in the numbers of fraternal organizations and an increase in civic groups, but otherwise the rankings of new organizations were similar in all time periods (*Rural Sociology*, 34:80-88).

Other later studies include that of Donald Hay, who compared participation in formal and informal groups in four rural communities in the Northeast finding that participation is significantly (and positively) correlated with the occupational status and education of the male head of the household (*Rural Sociology,* 15:141–148). Hay used households rather than individuals as his units of comparison and discovered that participation for households was high, with about 90 percent involved in one or more formal organizations.

In Minnesota, Olaf Larson examined participation in seven village centers (*Social Forces,* 16:385–388). He compiled data on the average total attendance in each of nine types of organizations in the villages. He found that one individual in six did not attend any form of organized activity as frequently as an average of once a month; that a smaller proportion of farmers than of villagers participated in each type of activity; and that religious activities are more important in rural communities.

Raymond Payne compared participation in rural Mississippi, Kentucky, Ohio, Illinois, and New York, discovering greater rates of participation in religious organizations in the South, but less in other types of formal organizations in the South as compared to the North and West (*Rural Sociology.* 18:171–172).

Selz Mayo and Paul Marsh examined two rural locality groups in North Carolina (*American Journal of Sociology,* 57:243–247). One was a village center with a high degree of "group consciousness," the other an open country area with low consciousness. Residents in the area with high group consciousness were discovered to confine their participation to the locality to a greater degree than residents in the area with low group consciousness. In this study and in another Mayo conducted alone in the same region (*Rural Sociology,* 15:242–251), information was also gathered concerning the effect of age and of race on participation. Participation appeared to reach a low point between the ages of twenty and thirty and to gradually increase after thirty, peaking between fifty and sixty. There was no clear-cut pattern along the racial dimension.

In New York state, Harold Kaufman examined the participation rates of individuals in a town of 1500, finding that 35 percent of the community members did not belong to any formal organizations, while membership and leadership in both formal and informal organizations were concentrated in the "upper prestige classes" (in Bendix and Lipset *Class, Status and Power*). Ruth Young and Olaf Larson gathered data in another rural New York village and its surrounding hamlets (*American*

Sociological Review, 30:926-934). They used their results to identify subcommunities in the area, by locating clusters formed by the overlap among organization memberships. They consider two organizations to be overlapped if the larger contains at least 25 percent of the members of the smaller. They report having identified ten relatively discrete clusters in this fashion. Elsewhere in New York, David E. Holden compared the attitudes on farm-connected issues of members and nonmembers of farm organizations in two upstate school districts, finding that organization members were significantly more favorably inclined on the issues and knew more about them than the sample as a whole, but did not differ from the sample in reference to nonfarm issues (*Rural Sociology*, 30:63-74). Holden believes these results indicate that the farm organizations are reference groups for their members on farm issues but not on nonfarm issues. Other organizations were also found to serve as reference groups, affecting member opinions, on issues related to the central set of organization concerns but not on issues outside these concerns.

In a somewhat related study Neal Gross found that farmers in two Iowa rural communities were more likely to accept innovations in techniques than nonmembers (*Rural Sociology*, 14:148-156). Gross's data also support the cumulativeness hypothesis in that early adopters of innovations were better educated, younger, had higher social participation, read more general and farm periodicals and magazines, participated more fully in farm cooperatives and government farm programs, and had larger farms and higher incomes than did late- or nonadopters.

In three rural Pennsylvania communities, Emory Brown studied the relationship between an individual's actual participation, his concept of the amount of participation expected of him, and the expectations of others concerning his participation (*Rural Sociology*, 18:313-320). The three factors were generally in accord, with individuals participating as they believed they were (and in fact were) expected to. They lived up to their community roles even though in some cases they resented doing so. Similar results were obtained by W. A. Anderson when he related the self-status ratings of 344 New York farm families to their participation and to reactions of other community members (*American Sociological Review*, 11:253-258). He concluded that family social participation is the result of status reactions on the part of community members, and of the opinions families hold concerning their own position in the status system. Families appear to accept a status position for themselves and to participate in accordance with their self-judgments. Anderson used the family as his unit, having found in a previous study (also in New York State) that the social participation of an individual is to a considerable degree a function of the social participation of the family.

C. Arnold Anderson and Bruce Ryan, two sociologists at the Iowa Agricultural Experiment Station, examined participation in a prosperous Iowa farm area (*Rural Sociology*, 8.3:281–290). They were interested in the differences in participation rates of the owners and the tenants of the farms. They found a relatively small difference, although the participation of tenants who were not related to owners was considerably lower than that of tenants related to farm owners. Anderson and Ryan also collected data on the types of organizations individuals participated in and other socio-economic data on the subjects.

Finally, there have been several studies of migrants to the city from rural areas. Beers and Heflin (*Rural People in the City*), Freedman and Freedman (*Rural Sociology*, 21:50–61), and Windham (*Sociology and Social Research*, 47:201–209) all found that the migrants were less active in voluntary associations than individuals who had always lived in the urban area. However, Basil Zimmer's research indicates that while migration itself limits participation, high status tends to overcome the limiting influence of farm background (*American Journal of Sociology*, 61:470–475). Zimmer's work on farm migrants is part of a more extensive study of the participation of all migrants or newcomers to a community. The data Zimmer obtained in 1951 by interviewing a random sample of individual residents of a midwestern town of 20,000 people indicated that the effects of migration on participation in voluntary associations appears to be temporary. Although migration initially limits participation, the migrants soon approximate the participation level of the native population (*American Sociological Review*, 20:218–219).

FOREIGN STUDIES

Although most of the research on participation available to the American scholar deals with memberships and voluntary associations in the United States, some material on participation in localities outside the United States was discovered. There is a very brief reference to participation in fraternal orders in Melbourne, Australia, in a text by Oeser and Hammond. As in the United States, it was found that middle class individuals join about twice as often as working class individuals and also attend meetings more often (*Social Structure and Personality in a City*, p. 21). Another Australian study, by Hardee, indicated that status selectivity of members operates in rural organizations, but varies by the type of organization. Hardee also found that in his sample of male heads of households, only one fifth held no memberships, while two fifths belonged to at least three organizations (*Rural Sociology*, 26:240-251).

Roland Warren examined the participation of citizens in Stuttgart, Germany. His research, carried out in 1956-57, revealed that there was relatively little support for voluntary civic organizations in the city and that most of the associations in existence were either economic in nature or devoted to such recreational pursuits as sports and singing (*Social Forces*, 36:222-229).

In Guadalajara, Mexico, Floyd Dotson conducted a relatively extensive though still exploratory survey involving 415 adults in 231 households at all class levels. While Dotson discovered some participation at all income levels, in general there was a direct relationship between socio-economic status and participation similar to that in the United States. However, at all levels (with the possible exception of the highest) the degree of participation was less than that which would be expected of similar strata in the United States. While most Mexican organizations are patterned after American or European ones, the process of cultural diffusion has been selective. Secular women's clubs, for example, have not appeared, and women in general are much less active in associations than are women in the United States, a reflection of the definition of the woman's role in Mexico. Although Dotson believes that associations will make their appearance with urbanization in other countries as they have in Mexico, the Mexican experience leads him to believe that cities of similar size in different cultural areas will vary widely in the number and type of associations and in the amount of participation in them (*American Sociological Review*, 18:385-386).

We have already noted (see Chapter One) that Robert and Barbara Gallatin Anderson reached similar conclusions as a result of their excellent sociological and historical study of a Danish village. In Dragor, however, in contrast to Mexico, voluntary associations were present prior to twentieth century urbanization, and have grown more and have been used more extensively to meet a variety of social problems than is the case in Mexico. Commenting on the role of the "pliant" Danish voluntary association the Andersons write: "Easily founded, it is free to adjust with amoeba-like fluidity to a flood of problems beyond the scope or

ken of other institutions or any combination of them. Its job done, it
can go out of business without consequences beyond projects at hand.
Danish voluntary associations and forms of government share an organizational structure specially contrived to facilitate and precipitate change
by providing effective policy making leaders responsive to their electorate" (*American Journal of Sociology,* 65:272). Since the voluntary association meets the need for change by uniting people on the basis of
shared interests which often do not coincide with other social groupings,
it has the ultimate effect of causing other institutions — such as class,
neighborhood, and age groups — to lose any corporate unity, other than
that expressed in voluntary associations. In relation to government, the
Andersons found that voluntary associations "assumed functions normally beyond the concern of governmental agencies (i. e. the satisfaction
of diverse avocational interests) or not as yet of sufficient importance to
warrant active governmental intervention, or, finally, inadequately controlled by the government or by other institutions including the family
such as control and prevention of juvenile delinquency" (65:272).

In another very useful analysis the Andersons utilized eleven community studies of rural villages in various parts of Europe (England, Ireland, Wales, Denmark, the Netherlands, Belgium, France, Spain, Italy,
Yugoslavia, and Bulgaria) for information on the ways in which the village class structure is reflected indirectly in various institutions. They
found that the association is one of the structures that clearly reflect
and reinforce class distinctions. With the exception of the Yugoslavian
village in which no associations were found, each village had voluntary
organizations including at least one with a class-delimited membership.
All of the upper class associations had upper class officers, and all but
one of the lower class associations had upper class leaders. In many
cases these association leaders were also leaders in the local government.
In all of the villages with associations, the most "complete and powerful
structuring of the village social strata" occurred in the voluntary associations — they being the only institution having "the facility for providing
in one institution both a formal class leadership and a convocation of
class members in a context that permits the working out of group
opinion" (*American Anthropologist,* 64:1024).

While the Danish government has not been hostile to the development
of voluntary associations, this is apparently not the case with the French
government where the law makes organization relatively difficult. However, there is disagreement on the extent to which voluntary association

activity has been impeded. Arnold Rose used national survey data, personal observation, and the "only published systematic community study in France — that by Charles Belleheim and Suzanne Frere on Auxerre" — to bolster his contention that voluntary associations were "weak" in France (*Theory and Method*). The survey data indicate that if occupational associations and political parties are not included, only 26 percent of all Frenchmen belong to associations. (Moreover, this is probably an inflated figure since some individuals hold dual memberships and the 26 percent is derived from a table of memberships in different types of organizations.) A number of associations were discovered in Auxerre, but they appeared to be unimportant both to the individual members and to the society at large. Moreover, there were almost no associations devoted to improvement, group defense, or social welfare, all of which are quite frequent and active in the United States. These studies plus others which barely mention associations in describing the totality of life in a particular area, as well as interviews with French sociologists and "other persons apparently informed about French social life," led Rose to conclude that the social influence associations which do exist in France are largely paper organizations which do not "involve the members' interests and emotions very deeply" (pp. 75–77). Since the reasons Rose lists for the weakness of French associations are primarily political his arguments have already been discussed in Chapter Four.

Robert and Barbara Gallatin Anderson's historical and anthropological study of the French village of Wissous in which they lived for two years provides support for the Rose view of French voluntary associations. Until the latter half of the nineteenth century there were no formal voluntary associations in the village. At that time four organizations — a voluntary fire society, a hunting society, an unemployment-funeral insurance (mutuality) society, and a musical society — were established, each meeting a need that the existing institutions did not satisfy. Beginning with the second decade of the twentieth century, forty associations have been founded in Wissous. However, there is very little participation in the organizations; few meetings are held, and attendance is low (*Bus Stop for Paris*, pp. 197–226). Most of the current associations are instrumental in character and function as pressure or achievement groups. The Andersons see the voluntary associations as the constitutents of a "replicate" social structure. The organizations are based upon and devoted to the interests of the traditional units of the village society such as the church, the family, the economy, and the community itself. The associations function to "adapt indigenous groupings to the increasingly exact requirements of participation in a modern state, and they bridge the gap between local bodies and the various units of a modern political or business structure. They bureaucratize local institutions" (pp. 227-228). Thus the associations reinforce rather than destroy the traditional institutions of the village.

In contrast to the Andersons, Orvoell Gallagher has challenged the Rose thesis on French organizations on the basis of evidence from his field studies in two French communities. Gallagher found 15 associations in a small rural commune (population 800) and over 300 organizations in an urban community (population 50,000). Although these figures are not as high as those in comparable American communities, Gallagher believes they are high enough to call into question Rose's assertion that associations are not numerous in France. However, Gallagher's studies did corroborate Rose's view that there are proportionately more "expressive" associations — as compared to reform or welfare organizations — in France than there are in the United States. Moreover, like Rose, Gallagher sees the French tradition of relying on the government for action concerning matters of public health and welfare as at least partly responsible for this situation. Gallagher also believes that French associations differ from American ones in that they do not play a "mobility" or "integrative" role and are primarily oriented toward protecting special interests and preventing change (*Social Forces*, 36:159). However, Gallagher is probably underestimating the "conservative" character of many American organizations, just as Rose may have overestimated the importance American associations have for their members.

Gallagher discovered that associations were strongest among those "proletarian" and "career oriented" or "rootless bourgeoisie radicals" for whom traditional institutions had lost their appeal, while they were weakest among the propertied classes and peasantry who remained relatively oriented to the family, church, and community (p. 160). Similarly, the rural Ukrainian immigrants to France, who were studied by Robert T. and Barbara Gallatin Anderson, tended to turn to voluntary associations to fill the void left in the absence of extensive family ties in their new environment. The Andersons found that all types of associations had been established within the French Ukrainian communities and that the social life of the people had been centered around these organizations (*Anthropological Quarterly*, 35:158-168).

In Ireland, the role of voluntary association in an "underdeveloped" Western county was examined by K. O'Brien Jackson. Although several voluntary associations were found in County Galway, the organizations appeared to function primarily to reinforce the leadership activities of people who were already concerned rather than reaching those not already active. Jackson believes this is partly due to a general lack of enthusiasm for voluntary associations on the part of the Irish, who tend to be more issue oriented and crisis motivated (*International Review of Community Development*, 21:199–220).

The voluntary associations of modern Japan and their historical antecedents have been studied by Edward Norbeck. Although "common-interest" associations, as Norbeck calls them, have ancient roots in Japan, the "greatest growth of formal common-interest groups of all kinds has come in the twentieth century" (Glaser and Sills, *The Government of Associations*, p. 73). Members of the buraku, or small face-to-face communities, generally belong to fifteen to twenty-five associations depending upon their sex, age, occupation, and special interests. Almost every agricultural community in Japan has a farmers' cooperative association serving a wide range of purposes. In addition to the cooperatives, which act as powerful foci of village life, the villages are likely to have a variety of youth groups, religious associations, neighborhood groups, crime and fire preventive associations, as well as other organizations, both instrumental and expressive in character. However, at least some of these organizations are voluntary in name only, having been established under government pressure, or having obligatory membership as a result of economic and social pressures.

Norbeck believes that Japanese associations contributed to the transition from the older reliance on kinship and personal ties and that they presently function as substitutes for these ties. Much of the social and economic life of the village is conducted through the associations and "increasingly, community solidarity is expressed through identification with associations." While many of the associations are modeled after Western groups and some were even established by order of the Occupation, Norbeck is of the opinion that the range of Japanese rural associations "nevertheless follows a Japanese pattern," there having been a tradition of communal action in at least some spheres of life throughout rural Japan. In the economic sphere, associations developed rapidly once the great landowners lost their power through land reform. "The growth of the foreign-derived or foreign-influenced Janapese associations seems . . . to follow an indigenous pattern. Policy makers in the Japanese government, having an established model before them, used native and foreign models of the association to provide an effective and inexpensive channel for reaching and controlling its population" (pp. 75–76). It should be noted that the situation in Japan as described by Norbeck exhibits marked parallels to that in Denmark as the Andersons have described that country.

Although there are no significant quantitative data on participation in Japanese cities, Norbeck thinks that common-interest associations are more highly developed in Japan's rural areas than in the cities. However, this fact does not, in his view, challenge the thesis that voluntary association growth and urbanization are correlated, since Japan's rural areas are fundamentally urban or modern: "As a specialist, the rural resident may be regarded as a highly integrated part of a complex, co-operative, national economic and political scheme. The term 'peasant,' with its connotation of emotional attachment to a fixed way of life, self-sufficiency, subsistence economy, and sharp segregation from other segments of the total society, no longer seems suitable for the Japanese farmer" (pp. 77–78). Since this would also seem to be the case elsewhere, Norbeck's point would appear to have far-reaching implications.

Although there has been no single comparative study of the role of the voluntary association in modernization, there is now some basis for comparison and the initial development of a theory. In addition to the Japanese, Mexican, French, Irish, and Danish studies, valuable research has been done in Africa (see also Chapters One and Four). There is some discussion of voluntary association among the Galli people of the Shoa province in Ethiopia in the work of Herbert Lewis (in Tuden and Plotnicov, *Social Stratification in Africa*), and a more extensive consideration of voluntary association in Stanleyville (Congo) by Clement (in Forde, *Social Implications*), and in Valdo Pons's *Stanleyville*. There are chapters on ethnic groups, tribal groups, "young men's companies," and other voluntary associations in Michael Banton's detailed book on tribal life in Freetown, *West African City*. Banton sees the voluntary association in Sierra Leone as part of the modernizing, urbanizing process in which traditional institutions — such as the chiefship — decline and substitutes must be developed. In Freetown, voluntary associations provide bereavement benefits and organized entertainment. More important, the Temne young men's companies, which are the "most noteworthy of the associations," "have had the distinctive latent function of raising Temne morale and prestige. The companies take the place of the lineage or kin-group in supporting an individual and they create a new structure of recognized leaders and subordinates to combat the disorganization of tribal society in a strange city" (p. 216). Banton also examines the prestige hierarchy that appears to be developing among voluntary associations. His discussion is particularly useful because he has considered voluntary associations in the entire context of urban life and has provided survey data as well as information based on interviewing, and on such traditional sources as government documents and scholarly papers.

Claude Meillassoux deals at length with voluntary associations in Bamako, the Republic of Mali, in *Urbanization of an African Community*. Although he views voluntary associations as "marginal institutions in relation to society" and asserts that the organizations do not cover the fundamental social needs of their members, he indicates that voluntary associations do perform important social functions: "Through them the people approach such problems as social security, the need to create new social networks, to resist and break the ancient compulsions, and to solve problems of sex relationships in the modern context. Studying these associations helps pinpoint these problems and even gives a preview of what the city might become in the future" (p. 145). Meillassoux describes Bamako in detail and treats the traditional village associations and the associations in the city before and after independence. Voluntary associations flourished before independence, but the government attempted after independence to absorb all of the associations with the exception of some nonpolitical groups that were allowed to maintain a precarious existence. Meillassoux, like the students of Japan and Denmark, sees the traditional associations of the villages as having provided the basis for the creation of the modern urban voluntary association, and argues that "The discipline and rules of the association provide a general framework adaptable to new functions. In addition, the feeling that there is no proper integration into the social environment except through belonging to a cohesive and functional group is certainly strengthened when the people face the problems of a new urban milieu" (p. 57). Since the colonial administration required the registration of associations, Meillassoux is able to provide data on the numbers, rules and statutes, leaders, and meetings of associations from approximately 1940 to 1960. There were 149 registered associations of African peoples during this period, and they ranged in character from regional groups to religious, youth, and political organizations. Comparable figures are not available for the postcolonial period, but Meillassoux was able personally to study in depth about twenty-five nonofficial mutual aid, regional, youth, and entertainment associations.

Both Immanuel Wallerstein in his paper on "Voluntary Associations" in tropical Africa and Kenneth Little in his book *West African Urbanization* view voluntary associations along the same lines as Banton and Meillassoux. Wallerstein's article provides a general description of voluntary associations in modern Africa and includes some figures on membership. He asserts that a "high proportion of individuals in the cities" belong to voluntary associations and that the average individual belongs to several of them, citing a poll taken in Dakar in the early 1950s which suggests that more than two thirds of the population belonged to political parties alone and probably many more to other organizations. Wallerstein believes the voluntary associations serve a number of functions in the new urban environment. Associations help the individual to adapt to the city; teach new values and behaviors; provide the basis for a group life (to replace the declining tribal life); and have fostered nationalism in a variety of ways.

In his excellent book, which is written from an evolutionary-functionalist perspective, Little describes and analyzes in detail: the tribal associations and syncretist cults; mutual aid and recreational associations; and "modern associations" modeled after European organizations such as the Scouts, the Y's, women's clubs, literary and debating groups, and lodges and sports clubs. According to Little's analysis, the various associations foster adaptation and integration in the social system in a number of ways. The ethnic unions, to take one example, ease the process of transition for the immigrant by blending tribal duties and obligations with modern social practices. Many of the immigrants' needs which were formerly served by the kin group are served by the voluntary association in the city. The associations provide fraternity and sociability; their meetings give the migrant some stability in his contacts and help him to develop a sense of identity; and the group aids the individual in learning new manners and mores which will facilitate his adjustment to the urban environment. The groups also provide physical protection as well as both material and moral support for their members. Furthermore, by regulating the behavior of their members, voluntary associations function as mechanisms of social control. In sum, Little writes: "The voluntary association serves as an adaptive mechanism in relation to these new institutions by facilitating role segmentation. In other words, it helps to adjust the rural migrant to his fresh status as a townsman, as a member of a multi-tribal community, as a breadwinner and as a partner in a monogamous marriage. Further, since they help to establish and validate fresh norms and exercise control over the personal conduct of their own members, voluntary associations are one of the means whereby an over-all system of relationships is integrated and law and order maintained among the town's heterogeneous population" (p. 102).

Although the state of Israel is a new nation, there are, of course, significant differences between that country and the new nations of Africa. These differences are reflected in the voluntary associations of Israel and the role they play in the social system. The noted sociologist S. N. Eisenstadt has studied Israeli voluntary associations and analyzed them in several publications. His major work is not available in the United States, but there is a brief summary of his findings in the chapter he contributed to a volume of essays on *The Institutions of Advanced Societies*, edited by Arnold Rose. This material was slightly updated for inclusion in Eisenstadt's *Israeli Society*.

Eisenstadt reports that there was an extensive network of voluntary associations in the Palestine territory before Israel achieved statehood. In the prenation period, most of the groups were "closely connected with the central social and political activities of the Country." Voluntary associations were frequently part of general social movements and performed important services in the areas of defense, social welfare, and medicine. Almost all of the groups conceived of themselves as constituents of the Zionist movement, and little differentiation was made between "social, political, and cultural aspects and ideals," which were regarded as part of the Zionist effort. Individuals who did not share the Zionist pioneer value system either did not participate in voluntary activities or had their own separate groups.

Following statehood, a number of more purely social groups were established, particularly among sectors of the population that had not previously had this type of association. Other changes also took place. There was a decline in the performance of civic activities by voluntary associations, and a corresponding increase in purely philanthropic organizations. Many associations became pressure groups, directing most of their efforts toward the government. New kinds of associations, ranging from ideological discussion clubs to a national Volunteers' group which "aimed at giving new impetus to voluntary work in Israel" were established. The Volunteers' group was particularly concerned with "improving relations with the new immigrants" and with "combating various manifestations of corruption, official bureaucracy, and general apathy in public life" (Rose, *The Institutions of Advanced Societies,* pp. 435–436).

Unlike the prestate associations, the new organizations were not tied to the upper elite of the country or to any existing social movements or political parties, and were not concerned with performing civic duties. In the cultural sphere, activities have "become more and more segregated in special organizations and the participation of the general public has greatly, if not totally, decreased," while private cultural activities are on the increase.

Although Eisenstadt's chapter contains the fullest treatment of voluntary associations, there are brief (and general) references to voluntary associations in most of the other contributions to *The Institutions of Advanced Societies.* In the chapter on Brazil, Emilio Williams reports that there are only a few weak and unstable voluntary associations in that country, attributing this state of affairs to the "individualist" ethos of the Brazilian. According to Jan Szczepanski, Poland also lacks voluntary associations, in large part as a result of government suppression during most of the country's unhappy history (p. 237). The Yugoslavian contributor, Oleg Mandick, says that there are numerous cultural, educational, and sporting societies in his country, but his description indicates that the associations are semiofficial instruments of the government (pp. 237–238).

John Koty reports that there are many voluntary associations in Greece. Organizations of both expressive and instrumental character exist, and many of the latter perform welfare services that are taken care of by the government in other societies (pp. 337–338). Organizations were suppressed in Finland until the end of the First World War, but Heikki Waris notes that freedom of association is taken for granted today in that country, and there are now many voluntary and cooperative associations. The sports organizations, which are divided into two major national groups — a workingman's association and a bourgeois association — are particularly strong. Waris also observes that Finland is experiencing the trend toward bureaucratization and the professionalization of leadership in private organizations (pp. 229–230).

Australian social scientists Ronald Taft and Kenneth E. Walker believe that membership in voluntary associations in that nation is widespread but superficial or passive. In many cases individuals join large organizations, especially veterans' groups and occupational associations, because of social pressure. They also believe that men outnumber women in the total number of memberships, although women probably predominate in social improvement organizations. Most of the purely social organizations for adults are confined to one sex and are predominantly male. Youth groups, which "embrace a comparatively high percentage of young people," have members of both sexes and are almost completely social, recreational, or educational in orientation. They conclude that the strong central government in Australia and the tradition of relying on government for social welfare and improvement, have resulted in weak social influence organizations. Those social influence organizations that do exist look to the government for funds and their leaders are active lobbyists (pp. 185-186).

Much of the work on voluntary associations in Britain is reviewed, analyzed, and compared to American research in an article by Raymond Morris in *Sociological Inquiry* (35:186-200). While a number of the studies to which Morris refers are not readily available in the United States, there is some representative material in a collection of essays on *Social Mobility in Britain,* edited by David Glass. A paper on "Social Stratification in Voluntary Organizations" by Thomas Bottomore deals with his study of participation and voluntary associations in a small English country town. Bottomore was able to locate 135 organizations with a total membership of 14,649 or more than the total population of the town's adults. Bottomore describes the activities and leadership in each type of organization and analyzes the occupational status of the members in the organization. He also deals in detail, focusing on status factors, with four organizations: the Rotary chapter, a cricket club, a dramatic society, and a youth club.

In her paper in Glass's collection, Rosalind Chambers also focuses on stratification. Her in-depth examination of three organizations composed primarily of women — the Women's Institutes, the Women's Voluntary Services, and the British Red Cross Society — includes information on the history, aims, activities, and structure of the organizations themselves as well as on the social characteristics of the participants.

URBANIZATION AND NEIGHBORHOOD

Given the general assumption that urbanization and participation are correlated phenomena, it is not surprising that a number of studies have examined this relationship. For example, Scott Greer compared three Los Angeles areas of varying degrees of urbanization (as measured in terms of family structure by the Shevky-Bell typology). He found that the low urban sample "differed sharply and consistently in the direction of more participation in the local community" (*American Sociological Review*, 21:21). Moreover, urbanization proved to be associated with lower participation in voluntary associations and an increase in friendship and kinship interaction, findings which directly contradict the view that increasing urbanization means increasing importance for voluntary associations (Greer and Kube, in Sussman, *Community Structure*). A similar study by Bell and Force in San Francisco comparing participation rates in different types of urban neighborhoods indicated that individual economic and family status as well as neighborhood status affected voluntary activity (*American Sociological Review*, 21:25-34). Both the Greer and the Bell and Force studies employed random sampling techniques and elaborate statistical indexes.

In Buffalo, Eugene Litwak used information gathered from women who had recently moved into their present neighborhoods to test his hypothesis that voluntary associations function to integrate individuals into local neighborhoods. The data appeared to support the hypothesis although the findings were not conclusive. In his paper, Litwak also argues that "mature industrial bureaucracies" pressure their members to use voluntary associations as a means of controlling the local public (*American Sociological Review*, 26:261). The argument is an interesting one although Litwak does not present any systematic evidence as proof.

Mayer Zald attempted to link ecological and organizational analysis in his study of the relationships between the characteristics of urban areas and the characteristics and effectiveness of the boards of directors of YMCAs in the areas (*American Journal of Sociology*, 73:261-272). He found that the socio-economic composition of the boards and their effectiveness were correlated in a variety of ways with demographic measures of the areas each board served.

There is an excellent monograph by Nicholas Babchuk and C. Wayne Gordon on the voluntary associations in a slum area of Rochester, New York. Since the authors were interested primarily in the manner in which individuals become affiliated with associations, they chose a sample of persons who had joined one of several community groups that had been created through the efforts of an organizer who, a short time before the investigation began, had been commissioned by the

Rochester Council of Social Agencies "with the task of developing indigenous adult and children's organizations in a slum area." For comparative purposes a sample of individuals in the area who belonged to other voluntary associations (unions and churches were specifically excluded from this category) was also interviewed. Although it was found that there were, contrary to the popular view members of associations in the slum or transitional area, in general these members were not lower class individuals, but middle class persons, many of them community leaders. However, a number of lower class children were affiliated with organizations even though their parents were not members of voluntary associations. There was some evidence that either the children themselves or the parents of the lower class members aspired to higher social class status and were using the associations as avenues of upward mobility (*Voluntary Associations in the Slums*, pp. 116-119).

The Babchuk and Gordon monograph is particularly valuable because the authors provide excellent summaries of the relevant theoretical literature and findings, and discuss the theoretical implications of their own data. Furthermore, they began their work with a number of carefully formulated hypotheses, the central one being that persons enter organizations through personal influence. (They employ the definition of personal influence developed by Katz and Lazarsfeld in their book on the subject.) Babchuk and Gordon found that the Katz-Lazarsfeld hypotheses applied to the manner in which voluntary association members were recruited. In addition to providing data on children's participation and children's organizations, Babchuk and Gordon also deal with the relationships between the various stages of the life cycle and voluntary association activity, particularly as to the type of association — instrumental, expressive, or instrumental-expressive — likely to be joined in the phases considered.

The Gordon and Babchuk finding that individuals joining expressive groups were more likely to have become members through personal influence than were persons joining instrumental groups was subjected to further testing by an associate, Arthur Jacoby, who also hypothesized that there would be other social and personality differences between members of expressive and instrumental associations since the two types of organizations serve different needs and yield different types of satisfactions. In one investigation, Jacoby found that individuals living with others are more likely to join expressive associations than are individuals living alone (*The Sociological Quarterly*, 7:76-84). In another, using students at the University of Alberta, Canada, as subjects, he found that individuals who viewed their associations as performing instrumental functions were more likely to watch educational and documentary television programs; to read several newspapers and/or news magazines regularly and thoroughly; to get higher grades and be less likely to be satisfied with low grades; and were less likely to acquire traffic tickets (*Sociological Inquiry,* 35:163-175). Jacoby interprets these results to mean that individuals joining associations for their instrumental functions are in general concerned with long range goals at the expense of immediate satisfaction and with other people only as a means to their personal goals. Expressively oriented association members were found to have more friends than instrumentally oriented members had, indicating to Jacoby a greater need for and/or ability to maintain personal relationships. Expressively oriented members were also more likely to exercise personal influence in an attempt to get their friends to join the associations to which they belonged. Jacoby sees these characteristics as part of a syndrome with some persons having a general expressive orientation, which is reflected in their organization behavior.

While the Gordon and Babchuk and the Jacoby research suggest that the decision to join a voluntary association and the choice of a particular voluntary association reflect an individual's basic personality characteristics and his primary social ties, the research is too limited to permit any firm conclusions. However, the relationships among these variables continue to engage the attention of a number of researchers and some more definitive answers may be forthcoming in the near future.

BIBLIOGRAPHY

Allardt, Erik, Bentti Jartti, Faina Jyrkila, and Yrjo Littunen, "On the Cumulative Nature of Leisure Activities," *Acta Sociologica,* 3 (1958): 165-172.

Allardt, Erik, and Pertti Pesonen, "Finland," *International Social Science Journal,* 12.1 (1960): 27-39. A brief general history of voluntary associations in Finland and some figures on membership and participation in different types of organizations are given.

Almond, Gabriel A., and Sidney Verba, *The Civic Culture.* Princeton, Princeton University Press, 1963.

Anderson, C. Arnold, and Bruce Ryan, "Social Participation Differences among Tenure Classes in a Prosperous Commercialized Farming Area," *Rural Sociology,* 8.3 (1943): 281-290.

Anderson, Robert T., and Barbara Gallatin Anderson, "Voluntary Associations and Urbanization: A Diachronic Analysis," *American Journal of Sociology*, 65 (November 1959): 265–273.

Anderson, Robert T., and Barbara Gallatin Anderson, "Voluntary Associations among Ukrainians in France," *Anthropological Quarterly*, 35 (October 1962): 158–168.

Anderson, Robert T., and Barbara Gallatin Anderson, "The Indirect Social Structure of European Village Communities," *American Anthropologist*, 64 (October 1962): 1016–1027.

Anderson, Robert T., and Barbara Gallatin Anderson, *The Vanishing Village*. Seattle, University of Washington Press, 1964.

Anderson, Robert T., and Barbara Gallatin Anderson, *Bus Stop for Paris*. Garden City, New York, Doubleday, 1965.

Anderson, W. A., "Family Social Participation and Social Status Self-Ratings," *American Sociological Review*, 11 (June 1946): 253–258.

Anderson, Wilford A., and Hans H. Plambeck, *The Social Participation of Farm Families*. Mimeograph Bulletin Number 8, Department of Rural Sociology, Cornell University. Ithaca, 1943.

Arensberg, Conrad, *The Irish Countryman*. New York, Macmillan, 1936. A community study employed by Robert and Barbara Gallatin Anderson (see entry in this bibliography) in their comparative analysis of voluntary associations and village class structure.

Axelrod, Morris, "Urban Structure and Social Participation," *American Sociological Review*, 21 (February 1956): 13–19.

Babchuk, Nicholas, and Alan Booth, "Voluntary Association Membership: A Longitudinal Analysis," *American Sociological Review*, 34 (February 1969): 31–45.

Babchuk, Nicholas, and C. Wayne Gordon, *The Voluntary Association in the Slum*. Lincoln, University of Nebraska, 1962 (University of Nebraska Studies: new series no. 27).

Banfield, Edward, *The Moral Basis of a Backward Society*. New York, Free Press, 1958. Robert and Barbara Gallatin Anderson (see entry in this bibliography) have employed this study of an Italian village in their comparative analysis of voluntary associations and village class structure.

Banton, Michael, *West African City*. London, Oxford University Press, 1957.

Beal, George M., "Additional Hypotheses in Participation Research," *Rural Sociology*, 21 (September-December 1956): 249–256. Beal argues that researchers should consider dynamic variables, that is, those readily subject to change, such as membership understanding of the basic principles of the organization, as well as static or unchangeable variables such as sex. He reports findings from his own study of cooperatives in Iowa indicating positive relationships between participation and various dynamic variables.

Beers, Howard W., and Catherine P. Heflin, *Rural People in the City*. Kentucky Agricultural Experiment Station Bulletin Number 478. Lexington, 1945. Migrants to Lexington were found to be less involved in organizations than nonmigrants.

Bell, Wendell, and Maryanne T. Force, "Urban Neighborhood Types and Participation in Formal Associations," *American Sociological Review*, 21 (February

1956): 25–34. A comparison of participation in four different types of urban neighborhoods based on interviews of 700 males in San Francisco in 1953.

—— "Social Structure and Participation in Different Types of Formal Associations," *Social Forces*, 34 (May 1956): 345–350. The participation of men living in low economic status neighborhoods is compared with that of men in high status neighborhoods.

Bonser, Howard J., and Herbert W. Butt, "Selective Participation of Farmers and Their Wives in Rural Organizations." Agricultural Experimental Station Bulletin Number 257, Knoxville, Tennessee, 1957.

Booth, Alan, "Personal Influence Networks and Participation in Professional Association Activities," *Public Opinion Quarterly*, 33 (Winter 1969–70): 611–614. A study of the role of personal influence in affecting the decisions of members of professional associations to attend educational conferences sponsored by the groups.

Booth, Alan, and Nicholas Babchuk, "Personal Influence Networks and Voluntary Association Affiliation," *Sociological Inquiry*, 39 (Spring 1969): 179–188.

Bottomore, Thomas, "Social Stratification in Voluntary Organizations," in D. V. Glass, ed., *Social Mobility in Britain*. Glencoe, Illinois, Free Press, 1954.

Brown, Emory J., "The Self as Related to Formal Participation in Three Pennsylvania Rural Communities," *Rural Sociology*, 18 (December 1953): 313–320.

Brunner, Edmund de S., and J. H. Kolb, *Rural Social Trends*. New York, McGraw Hill, 1933.

Brunner, Edmund de S., and Irving Lorge, *Rural Trends in Depression Years*. New York, Columbia University Press, 1937.

Burgess, Ernest W., and Leonard S. Cottrell, Jr., *Predicting Success or Failure in Marriage*. New York, Prentice-Hall, 1939. This is of interest only for a brief report of a study made of the organizational affiliation of a sample of married couples in Illinois.

Bushee, Frederick A., "Social Organization in a Small City," *American Journal of Sociology*, 51 (November 1945): 217–226.

Chambers, Rosalind C., "A Study of Three Voluntary Organizations," in D. V. Glass, ed., *Social Mobility in Britain*. Glencoe, Illinois, Free Press, 1954.

Clement, P., "Social Patterns of Urban Life," in D. Forde, ed., *Social Implications of Industrialization and Urbanization in Africa South of the Sahara*. Unesco, Tensions and Technology Series, 1956.

Curtis, James, "Voluntary Association Joining: A Cross-National Comparative Note," *American Sociological Review*, 36 (October 1971): 872–880. Curtis compares his own findings from a Canadian survey with the data gathered by Almond and Verba for *The Civic Culture* study.

Detroit Area Study of the University of Michigan, "A Social Profile of Detroit." Ann Arbor, University of Michigan, 1952.

Dotson, Floyd, "A Note on Participation in Voluntary Associations in a Mexican City," *American Sociological Review*, 18 (1953): 380–386.

Eisenstadt, S. N., "Israel," in Arnold M. Rose, ed., *The Institutions of Advanced Societies*. Minneapolis, University of Minnesota Press, 1958.

—— *Israeli Society*. New York, Basic Books, 1967. The information on pp. 180–

183 about voluntary associations in Israel largely repeats that given in Eisenstadt's contribution to *The Institutions of Advanced Societies* edited by Arnold Rose.

Eitzen, D. Stanley, "A Study of Voluntary Association Membership among Middle-Class Women," *Rural Sociology,* 35 (March 1970): 84–91. A sample survey of women in three cities and two small towns in Kansas conducted in 1967 indicated that the small town residents had fewer memberships than the urban women. Eitzen also found that the greater the number of organization memberships held by a woman, the lower her level of anomie.

Erickson, William L., "Alienation and Participation in Rural Communities: A Path Analysis." Paper delivered at the 65th annual meeting of the American Sociological Association, September 1970.

Fallers, L. A., ed., *Immigrants and Associations.* The Hague, Mouton, 1967. Essays on immigrant associations including those of the Chinese in various parts of the world, the Lebanese in West Africa, and the Ibo tribe of Africa.

Fellin, Phillip, and Eugene Litwak, "Neighborhood Cohesion and Mobility," *American Sociological Review,* 28 (June 1963): 364–376. Includes information on membership in voluntary associations as it is related to neighborhood cohesion and mobility.

Foskett, John M., "Social Structure and Social Participation," *American Sociological Review,* 20 (August 1955): 431–438.

Frankenberg, *Village on the Border.* London, Cohen and West, 1957. A community study of a North Wales town which is employed by Robert and Barbara Gallatin Anderson in their comparative analysis of voluntary associations and village class structure (see entry in this bibliography).

Freedman, Ronald, and Deborah Freedman, "Farm-Reared Elements in the Nonfarm Population," *Rural Sociology,* 21 (March 1956): 50–61. Farm-reared individuals living in urban areas were found to be significantly less active than non-farm-reared persons in all voluntary associations, but not in churches.

Gallagher, Orvoell R., "Voluntary Associations in France," *Social Forces,* 36 (December 1957): 153–160.

Glass, David V., ed., *Social Mobility in Britain.* Glencoe, Illinois, Free Press, 1954.

Goldhammer, Herbert, "Some Factors Affecting Participation in Voluntary Associations," in Ernest W. Burgess and Donald J. Bogue, eds., *Contributions to Urban Sociology.* Chicago, University of Chicago Press, 1964.

Greer, Scott, "Urbanism Reconsidered: A Comparative Study of Local Areas in a Metropolis," *American Sociological Review,* 21 (February 1956): 19–25.

—— and Ella Kube, "Urbanism and Social Structure: A Los Angeles Study," in Marvin Sussman, ed., *Community Structure and Analysis.* New York, Thomas Y. Crowell, 1959. A report on the same Los Angeles study of three neighborhoods discussed in Greer's article "Urbanism Reconsidered: A Comparative Study of Local Areas in a Metropolis."

Gross, Neal, "The Differential Characteristics of Accepters and Non-Accepters of an Approved Agricultural Technological Practice," *Rural Sociology,* 14 (June 1949): 148–156.

Guttentag, Marcia, "Group Cohesiveness, Ethnic Organization, and Poverty,"

Journal of Socia Issues, 26 (Spring 1970): 105-132. She reports that a study of teenagers and oung adults in the Jewish communities in Poland in 1932-34 showed that almost every individual was a member of an organization and had "dominant" interest in the activities of the organizations. This interest appeared to contribute significantly to the "personal and psychological survival of many individuals." The groups served educational and collective self-help functions, and in the poverty and political danger of the times seemed to provide the "raison d'être in the lives of these adolescents" (pp. 116-117).

Halpern, Joel Martin, *A Serbian Village.* New York, Columbia University Press, 1958. A community study of a rural village in Yugoslavia which is employed by Robert and Barbara Gallatin Anderson (see entry in this bibliography) in their comparative analysis of voluntary associations and village class structure.

Hardee, J. Gilbert, "Social Structure and Participation in an Australian Community," *Rural Sociology,* 26 (September 1961): 240-251.

Harp, John, "A General Theory of Social Participation," *Rural Sociology,* 24 (September 1959): 280-284. Harp formulated a series of hypotheses drawn from general sociological theory, and tested them with research on rural cooperatives. His hypotheses involve three conceptual variables: structural cohesion, relative deprivation, and ambiguity. He found participation was positively correlated with satisfaction and with understanding of organization objectives, and that satisfaction and understanding were also positively correlated with each other.

—— and Richard J. Gagan, "Changes in Rural Social Organizations: Comparative Data from Three Studies," *Rural Sociology,* 34 (March 1969): 80-88.

Hausknecht, Murray, *The Joiners.* New York, The Bedminster Press, 1962.

Havighurst, Robert J., "The Leisure Activities of the Middle Aged," *American Journal of Sociology,* 63 (September 1957): 152-162. An elaborate study exploring the interrelations between the content and significance of leisure activities as related to age, sex, social class, and personality characteristics. Participation in formal organizations was found to be most characteristic of upper middle class women among the 234 individuals interviewed as part of the Kansas City Study of Adult Life.

Hay, Donald G., "The Social Participation of Households in Selected Rural Communities in the Northeast," *Rural Sociology,* 15 (June 1950): 141-148.

Heckscher, Gunnar, "Pluralist Democracy: The Swedish Experience," *Social Research,* 15 (December 1948): 417-461.

Henkel, Ramon, and Glenn Fuguitt, "Nonfarm Work and the Social Relations of Farmers," *Rural Sociology,* 31 (March 1966): 80-88. It was found that farmers with nonfarm work experience were more likely than other farmers to belong to nonfarm organizations located in urban centers.

Holden, David E., "Associations as Reference Groups: An Approach to the Problem," *Rural Sociology,* 30 (March 1965): 63-74.

Hollenbeck, Howard B., "Factors Influencing Citizen Participation in Survey and Planning Group Work and Recreation Services to Suburban Areas," *Social Service Review,* 33 (September 1959): 312-313. An abstract of a doctoral dissertation in social work, Washington University, St. Louis. Hollenbeck interviewed former committee members of a recreation survey to determine the effects of their membership on their subsequent activity in recreation work.

Hyman, Herbert H., and Charles Wright, "Trends in Voluntary Association Memberships of American Adults: Replication Based on Secondary Analysis of National Sample Surveys," *American Sociological Review*, 36 (April 1971): 191–206.

Jackson, K. O'Brien, "The Role of Voluntary Associations in the Development of the Rural Community," *International Review of Community Development*, 21 (December 1969): 199–220.

Jacoby, Arthur P., "Some Correlates of Instrumental and Expressive Orientation to Associational Membership," *Sociological Inquiry*, 35 (Spring 1965): 163–175.

—— "Personal Influence and Primary Relationships: Their Effect on Associational Membership," *The Sociological Quarterly*, 7 (Winter 1966): 76–84.

Janowitz, Morris, *The Community Press in an Urban Setting.* Second edition. Chicago, University of Chicago Press, 1967 (originally published in 1952). As part of his study, Janowitz surveyed samples of the population in three Chicago area communities. He found a positive association between readership of community newspapers and participation in local voluntary associations.

Jitodai, Ted T., "Urban-Rural Background and Formal Group Membership," *Rural Sociology*, 30 (March 1965): 75–83. A secondary analysis of the data from the 1954, 1955, 1957, and 1959 Detroit Area Studies conducted by the University of Michigan indicated that whether the individual's background was rural or urban was of limited importance in affecting membership.

Johnston, J. W. C., and J. Rivera, *Volunteers for Learning.* Chicago, Aldine, 1965. This study of the "educational pursuits of American adults" is based on a 1962 NORC sample survey which was later employed by Hyman and Wright in their secondary analysis of trends in voluntary association membership.

Kaltenback, John E., and David McClelland, "Achievement and Social Status in Three Small Communities," in David C. McClelland, Alfred Baldwin, Urie Bronfenbrenner, and Fred L. Strodtbeck, *Talent and Society.* Princeton, New Jersey, D. Van Nostrand, 1958. Data collected in three small towns indicated that "community activity by itself, irrespective of all other factors (income, occupational level, etc.), is the best index of perceived achievement that can be objectively obtained" (131).

Kaplan, Abraham Abbot, *Socio-Economic Circumstances and Adult Participation.* New York, Teachers College, Columbia University, 1943 (Contributions to Education, number 889). A study largely focusing on adult education which includes some data on participation in organizations. The subjects were 5001 adults in Springfield, Massachusetts.

Katz, Elihu, and Paul F. Lazarsfeld, *Personal Influence.* Glencoe, Illinois, Free Press, 1955.

Kaufman, Harold, "Prestige Classes in a New York Rural Community," in Reinhard Bendix and Seymour Martin Lipset, eds., *Class, Status and Power.* Glencoe, Illinois, Free Press, 1953.

Keur, John Y., and D. L. Keur, *The Deeply Rooted.* Monograph of the American

Ethnological Society, Number 25, 1955. A study of the Drents community in the Netherlands which is employed by Robert and Barbara Gallatin Anderson (see entry in this bibliography) in their comparative analysis of voluntary associations and village class structure.

Komarovsky, Mirra, "A Comparative Study of Voluntary Organizations of Two Suburban Communities," *Social Problems and Methods*, 27 (1933): 84–92. (Publication of the American Sociological Society.) Most of the article deals with the leisure study conducted by George Lundberg, Mary Alice McInery, and the author, although Komarovsky also makes brief references to other studies of the leisure interests of women in business, professional, and factory jobs.

——— "The Voluntary Associations of Urban Dwellers," *American Sociological Review*, 11 (1946): 686–698.

Koty, John, "Greece," in Arnold M. Rose, ed., *The Institutions of Advanced Societies*. Minneapolis, University of Minnesota Press, 1958.

Kyllonen, Tomi E., "Social Characteristics of Active Unionists," *American Journal of Sociology*, 56 (May 1951): 528–533. Includes comparisons between activity in unions and activity in other types of groups.

Larson, Olaf, "Rural Community Patterns of Social Participation," *Social Forces*, 16 (March 1938): 385–388.

Larson, Richard F., and William R. Catton, Jr., "When Does Agreement with Organizational Values Predict Behavior?" *American Catholic Sociological Review*, 22 (Summer 1961): 151–160. Using mailed questionnaires, Larson and Catton had the members and officers of an unidentified "nation-wide voluntary association" rate a list of organization goals as to their importance. It was found that there was a positive (but low) correlation between the extent to which a member agreed with the leaders' ratings and the members activity in the organization. There is a lengthy discussion of methodology and of the importance of followup studies where research results are statistically significant but unimpressive.

Laskin, Richard, *Leadership of Voluntary Organizations in a Saskatchewan Town*. Saskatoon, Canada, Center for Community Studies, 1962.

Lewis, Herbert, "Wealth, Influence, and Prestige among the Shoa Galla," in Arthur Tuden and Leonard Plotnicov, *Social Stratification in Africa*. New York, The Free Press, 1970.

Lipset, Seymour Martin, *Political Man*. Garden City, New York, Doubleday, 1960.

Little, Kenneth, *West African Urbanization*. Cambridge, England, Cambridge University Press, 1965.

Litwak, Eugene, "Voluntary Associations and Neighborhood Cohesion," *American Sociological Review*, 26 (April 1961): 258–271.

Lundberg, George, Mirra Komarovsky, and Mary Alice McInery, *Leisure: A Suburban Study*. New York: Columbia University Press, 1934.

Maas, Henry S., "The Role of Member in Clubs of Lower Class and Middle Class Adolescents," *Child Development*, 25 (December 1954): 241–251. A study of youth clubs in San Francisco and Chicago dealing primarily with the aggressiveness expressed in the club setting and the role of the adult adviser.

Mandick, Oleg, "Yugoslavia," in Arnold M. Rose, ed., *The Institutions of Advanced Societies*. Minneapolis, University of Minnesota Press, 1958.

Martin, Walter T., "A Consideration of Differences in the Extent and Location of the Formal Associational Activities of Rural Urban Fringe Residents," *American Sociological Review*, 17 (December 1952): 687-694.

Mayo, Selz C., "Age Profiles of Social Participation in Rural Areas of Wake County, North Carolina," *Rural Sociology*, 15 (September 1950): 242-251.

—— and C. Paul Marsh, "Social Participation in the Rural Community," *American Journal of Sociology*, 57 (November 1951): 243-247.

Meillassoux, Claude, *Urbanization of an African Community*. Seattle, University of Washington Press, 1968.

Mellor, H. W., "The Function of the Community Association," *The Sociological Review*, 43 (Section 9, 1951): 159-190. A study of four community centers in England indicated that only a small percentage of the population belonged to the association and that in each one a single social class tended to predominate.

Miner, Horace, ed., *The City in Modern Africa*. New York, Frederick A. Praeger, 1967. There are scattered references to associations and clubs in African urban areas.

Morris, Raymond N., "The Berinsfield Community Centre," *The Sociological Review*, 10 (November 1962): 297-312. A study of the center's contribution to community integration.

—— "British and American Research on Voluntary Associations: A Comparison," *Sociological Inquiry*, 35 (Spring 1965): 186-200.

Norbeck, Edward, "Common Interest Associations in Rural Japan," in Robert J. Smith and Richard K. Beardsley, eds., *Japanese Culture*, pp. 73-83. Chicago, Aldine, 1963.

—— "Rural Japan," in William A. Glaser and David L. Sills, eds., *The Government of Associations*. Totowa, New Jersey, The Bedminster Press, 1966.

Obenhaus, Victor, W. Wideck Schroeder, and Charles D. England, "Church Participation Related to Social Class and Type of Center," *Rural Sociology*, 23 (September 1958): 298-308. Includes data on participation in church-related voluntary associations.

Oeser, O. A., and S. B. Hammond, *Social Structure and Personality in a City*. New York, Macmillan, 1954.

Payne, Raymond, "Some Comparisons of Participation in Rural Mississippi, Kentucky, Ohio, Illinois and New York," *Rural Sociology*, 18 (June 1953): 171-172.

Pitt-Rivers, J. A., *The People of the Sierra*. London, Weidenfield and Nicholson, 1954. A community study of a Spanish rural village which is employed by Robert and Barbara Gallatin Anderson (see entry in this bibliography) in their comparative analysis of voluntary associations and village class structure.

Pons, Valdo, *Stanleyville*. London, Oxford University Press, 1969. A detailed report based on field research carried out in 1952-1953.

Reid, Ira De A., and Emily L. Ehle, "Leadership Selection in Urban Locality Areas," *Public Opinion Quarterly*, 14 (Summer 1950): 262-284.

Roper-Power, E. R., "The Social Structure of an English Town," *The Sociological Review*, old series 29 (October 1937): 391–413. While there were many associations in Hertford, they received only limited support from the populace and were valued primarily because of the opportunity they provided for socializing.

Rose, Arnold, *Theory and Method in the Social Sciences*. Minneapolis, University of Minnesota Press, 1954.

—— "Voluntary Associations under Conditions of Competition and Conflict," *Social Forces*, 34 (December 1955): 159–163. Interviews with the executive officers of ninety-one organizations in the Minneapolis–St. Paul area led Rose to conclude that conflict and competition both affect the internal structure of groups, causing the groups to be more active, cohesive, flexible, and complex in structure.

—— ed., *The Institutions of Advanced Societies*. Minneapolis, University of Minnesota Press, 1958. Guided by an outline prepared by Rose, social scientists native to the respective countries prepared essays on the social institutions of the United Kingdom, Australia, Finland, Poland, Yugoslavia, Greece, Israel, France, Brazil, and the United States. Voluntary associations are dealt with in almost all of the contributions, in most cases briefly and in a general fashion.

Rosow, Irving, "Forms and Functions of Adult Socialization," *Social Forces*, 44 (September 1965): 35–45. A general treatment of the functions of socialization (defined in terms of value commitment and behavioral conformity) in social groups.

Rothrock, Kenneth Martin, "A Study of Voluntary Association Membership." Unpublished PhD dissertation, University of Kansas, 1968. Although Rothrock presents data from his interviews with a random sample of 382 adults in Lawrence, Kansas, his work is interesting primarily for methodological reasons. He employed a variety of definitions of voluntary associations and compared the results obtained using the different criteria.

Sanders, I. T., *Balkan Village*. Lexington, University of Kentucky Press, 1949. A community study of a rural village employed by Robert and Barbara Gallatin Anderson (see entry in this bibliography) in their comparative analysis of voluntary associations and village class structure.

Scaff, Alvin H., "The Effect of Commuting on Participation in Voluntary Associations," *American Sociological Review*, 17 (April 1952): 215–220.

Scott, John C., "Membership and Participation in Voluntary Associations," *American Sociological Review*, 22 (June 1957): 315–326.

Simpson, Ida Harper, et al., eds., *Social Aspects of Aging*. Durham, Duke University Press, 1966. Chapters 12–17 by Joel Smith, Howard P. Myers, and Herman Turk report the results of a study of white aged individuals in a southern city. While most of the space is devoted to methodological considerations, there are also some statistics on participation in voluntary associations by old people as compared to a general sample of individuals in the same community.

Survey Research Center, *Adolescent Girls*. Ann Arbor, University of Michigan Survey Research Center, no date.

—— *A Study of Boys Becoming Adolescents.* Ann Arbor, University of Michigan Survey Research Center, 1960.

Svalastoga, Kaare, *Prestige, Class and Mobility.* London, William Heinemann (and the Scandinavian University Press), 1957.

Szczepanski, "Poland," in Arnold M. Rose, ed., *The Institutions of Advanced Societies.* Minneapolis, University of Minnesota Press, 1958.

Taft, Ronald, and Kenneth E. Walker, "Australia," in Arnold M. Rose, ed., *The Institutions of Advanced Societies.* Minneapolis, University of Minnesota Press, 1958.

Tanner, R. E. S., "Conflict within Small European Communities in Tanganyika," *Human Organization,* 23 (1964): 319–327.

United States Department of Labor, Manpower Administration, *Americans Volunteer.* Manpower Automation Research Monograph Number 10, April 1969.

Verba, Sidney, "Organizational Membership and Democratic Consensus," *Journal of Politics,* 27 (August 1965): 467–497.

Wallerstein, Immanuel, "Voluntary Associations," in James C. Coleman and Carl G. Rosberg, Jr., eds., *Political Parties and National Integration in Tropical Africa.* Berkeley, University of California Press, 1964.

Waris, Heikki, "Finland," in Arnold M. Rose, ed., *The Institutions of Advanced Societies.* Minneapolis, University of Minnesota Press, 1958.

Warner, W. Keith, "Attendance and Division of Labor in Voluntary Associations," *Rural Sociology,* 29 (December 1964): 396–407. An analysis of data from a sample of 191 local-level organizations.

Warner, W. Keith, and James S. Hilander, "The Relationship between Size of Organization and Member Participation," *Rural Sociology,* 29 (March 1964): 30–39. An analysis of data from the study of 191 local-level voluntary organizations in terms of the relationship between different types of participation (attendance at meetings, involvement in projects, etc.) and the size of the organization.

Warner, W. Keith, and Sidney Miller, "Organizational Problems in Two Types of Voluntary Associations," *American Journal of Sociology,* 69 (May 1964): 654–657. Data from the study of 191 local-level voluntary associations indicated that instrumental organizations had more difficulties than expressive organizations.

Warren, Roland L., "Citizens' Participation in Community Affairs in Stuttgart, Germany," *Social Forces,* 36 (May 1958): 322–329.

Whyte, William Foote, *Street Corner Society.* Chicago, University of Chicago Press, 1943 (paperback edition with some new material, 1955). A pioneering participant-observer study of the "corner boys" in Boston's Italian section. Whyte includes descriptions of the clubs formed by the slum's young men and of the relationship of these groups and of the political clubs in the area to other institutions.

Williams, Emilio, "Brazil," in Arnold M. Rose, ed., *The Institutions of Advanced Societies.* Minneapolis, University of Minnesota Press, 1958.

Williams, W. M., *Gosforth.* Glencoe, Illinois, Free Press, 1956. A study of an English village which is employed by Robert and Barbara Gallatin Anderson (see entry in this bibliography) in their comparative analysis of voluntary associations and village class structure.

Windham, G. O., "Formal Participation of Migrant Housewives in an Urban Community," *Sociology and Social Research*, 47 (January 1963): 201–209. A study of 1470 housewives in Pittsburgh, which revealed that the wives who had always lived in the city belonged to more organized groups, attended more meetings, and held more power positions in organizations than did the wives born in other cities or in rural areas.

Woodside, Alexander, "Development of Social Organizations in Vietnamese Cities in the Late Colonial Period," *Pacific Affairs*, 25 (Spring 1971): 39–64. A detailed, nonquantitative examination of the nonpolitical organizations which appeared in the 1920s and 1930s to meet the needs of the new urban classes.

Wright, Charles R., and Herbert H. Hyman, "Voluntary Association Memberships of American Adults: Evidence from National Sample Surveys," *American Sociological Review*, 23 (June 1958): 284–294.

Young, James N., and Selz C. Mayo, "Manifest and Latent Participators in a Rural Community Action Program," *Social Forces*, 38 (December 1959): 140–145. The authors argue that the attitudes of latent participators, that is, those who do not participate, create a community climate which affects the success of a voluntary enterprise. They offer some supporting evidence from a study of residents' attitudes toward a community development program in a rural North Carolina town.

Young, Ruth C., and Olaf F. Larson, "A New Approach to Community Structure," *American Sociological Review*, 30 (October 1965): 926–934.

Zald, Mayer N., "Urban Differentiation, Characteristics of Boards of Directors, and Organizational Effectiveness," *American Journal of Sociology*, 73 (November 1967): 261–272.

Zimmer, Basil, "Participation of Migrants in Urban Structures," *American Sociological Review*, 20 (April 1955): 218–224.

—— "Farm Background and Urban Participation," *American Journal of Sociology*, 61 (March 1956): 470–475.

—— and Amos H. Hawley, "The Significance of Membership in Associations," *American Journal of Sociology*, 65 (September 1959): 196–201.

SOCIAL CLASS AND PARTICIPATION

More studies of voluntary associations have focused on social class than on any other variable. According to Raymond Morris, British social scientists have been almost exclusively concerned with the relationship between class and participation in voluntary associations, while the relationship has been the "major" concern of American researchers (*Sociological Inquiry*, 35:186). All of the work on the topic has pointed in a single direction. Low socio-economic status, whether measured by education, income, occupation, a subjective judgment by an individual of his own status, or by some combination of these factors, is highly correlated in a positive direction with low rates of participation and even lower rates of holding leadership positions in organizations. There is evidence in support of this generalization in virtually every one of the studies cited in previous chapters. Further evidence is provided by the research to be discussed under various headings in this chapter. In fact, the evidence is so overwhelming that several investigators have been led to conclude that advantages "cumulate" for the advantaged, that is, those with more education and income and higher occupational status are also psychologically more confident, have greater feelings of efficacy, and participate more in both informal and formal social activities including voluntary associations; on the other hand, disadvantages "cumulate" for the disadvantaged.

A relatively early statement of this thesis can be found in a well-known 1947 article, "Portrait of the Underdog" by Genevieve Knupfer, which focuses on the cumulative disadvantages of low status. She argues that the economic restrictions of low status possibly "because of the ac-

companying lack of education and perhaps a certain adaptation to sub-
mission and failure, result in psychological restrictions which reinforce
the economic" (p. 103). While lower participation rates in the lower
class are to some extent accounted for by financial considerations such
as the cost of membership and attendance at meetings and the lack of
leisure time (particularly for lower class women who cannot afford
household help), a financial explanation is not completely adequate.
The psychological effects of low status and education appear to be at
least as important. Lower class individuals develop differential expectations of behavior and avoid activities, such as voluntary association participation, which they believe are for higher status persons. Moreover,
the economic and educational limitations accompanying low status produce a lack of interest in and lack of self-confidence in dealing with certain important areas of our culture. This in turn leads to withdrawal
from participation in these areas. Thus the lower status individual re-
stricts to his relatives his informal contacts, does not travel extensively,
reads less, is less informed on a variety of subjects, is more likely to respond "Don't Know" to a pollster's request for an opinion, and is less
likely to join formal organizations. Summarizing, Knupfer quotes Paul
Lazarsfeld's statement that: "The underprivileged youth has seen less,
read less, heard about less, has in his whole environment and experience
fewer chances than the socially privileged and he simply knows of fewer
possibilities" (p. 114).

In slightly different terms, Derek Phillips has argued that the lower
participation rates of the lower class can be explained by reference to
the concept of interaction-opportunities, or the notion that the individual's chances for social interaction are determined by his location in
the social structure. On the basis of George Homan's theories, Phillips
also contends that people with fewer opportunities for social participation will invest more in those limited opportunities, and will consequently experience greater rewards and pay higher costs. His analysis of
data from a National Opinion Research Center sample survey of six
hundred New England adults did indicate that for lower class participants in voluntary social activities including organizations, social participation was more strongly related to positive feelings (rewards) and to
negative feelings (costs), and thus to overall happiness. Phillips found
too that happiness and participation were highly related since positive
feelings were directly correlated with participation, while negative feelings were not (the difference between positive and negative feelings be-

ing a major determinant of happiness). Again using Homan's theories, Phillips argues that the correlation between positive feelings and participation is a result of the tendency of individuals to repeat activities that have been rewarding in the past. Therefore, the individual's continued participation in voluntary activities (which he is free to leave) must mean that he has found the activities rewarding; and it can be expected that participation will result in positive feelings (*American Journal of Sociology*, 72:479-488; *Sociological Quarterly*, 10:3-21).

Murray Hausknecht has attempted a fuller explanation of the factors that account for the low rates of working class joining. Like Gans and other recent observers of the working class, he sees the blue collar worker as a member of a distinctive subculture. In this culture, life is focused on the family, which also provides the model for all social relationships. These relationships are largely personal or primary and the worker is only minimally committed to the impersonal or secondary relationships of the society beyond the family. He neither understands nor trusts the larger community. His "misanthropic and intolerant perception of others," combined with a fatalistic feeling that he is powerless to change the world, result in his avoiding the voluntary association with its impersonal social relationships. When he does join, he eschews instrumental associations and tends to seek those expressive organizations which "can be structured in terms of primary relationships, and those which have roots in the immediate locality with little or no connection with the larger society" (in Shostak and Gomberg, *Blue-Collar World*, pp. 209-211).

Reviewing the evidence on working class joining, Hausknecht further notes that the blue collar individual who does join associations appears to be a marginal member of the class, who is not well integrated into his area's informal relationships either because he is mobile within the class system or is residentially mobile (p. 212).

Hausknecht also predicts that while blue collar workers reject voluntary associations, they may be attracted to mass movements. Mass movements allow for the satisfaction of expressive needs and emphasize personal loyalty to a leader rather than impersonal norms and institutionalized procedures (p. 213). Although Hausknecht is able to cite studies providing evidence in support of his other generalizations, his comments on mass movements are purely speculative. Indeed, according to Seymour Martin Lipset, the typical Nazi voter in 1932 was not the blue collar worker but the "middle-class self-employed Protestant who lived either on a farm or in a small community" (*Political Man*, p. 148).

In addition to the information provided in the general reviews of the literature which we have cited in the first chapter and the surveys discussed in chapter six, there is a useful summary of the findings of a number of older studies dealing with status variables (and all supporting the Knupfer thesis) in Leonard Reissman's article on "Class, Leisure and Social Participation." Reissman also reports on his own study in Evanston, Illinois, in which he too found that regardless of whether he used occupation, income, or education to measure class position, the higher class groups tended to show higher participation levels (p. 80).

Several social scientists have focused on the relationship between participation and one of the measures of social status. For example, William G. Mather explored "Income and Social Participation" in an Illinois "farmer's town," finding the expected correlations between high income and high participation, low income and low participation. In their research in rural North Carolina, Joel Smith and Horace D. Rawls deal with the level of formal educational attainment and participation, and with methodological questions involved in the study of this relationship (*Social Forces*, 44:57-66). Joel Gerstl analyzed the effect of occupational milieu on a group of dentists, advertising executives, and college professors (in Smigel, *Work and Leisure*). While all of the subjects shared upper middle class status, the amount and type of their participation in voluntary groups varied by occupation. Professors were significantly less active than either dentists or admen. Half of the professors in the sample denied even nominal membership in any nonprofessional organization. Dentists and admen were active in both professional and nonprofessional groups. The dentists tended to concentrate in fraternal organizations; the admen in civic work, as a result of company encouragement and the policy of allowing participation during working hours.

Richard Curtis explored the interaction between occupational mobility and membership in formal voluntary associations. In the Detroit area clubs he examined, mobility appeared not to affect participation rates (*American Sociological Review*, 24:846-848). Gresham Sykes also failed to find any significant differences in social and occupational mobility between mothers who belonged to the PTA and a matched group of mothers not belonging to the PTA in Trenton, New Jersey (unpublished dissertation, Northwestern). However, Lipset and Bendix report that two studies of adolescent boys both indicated that boys with upward mobility aspirations had higher rates of participation than boys without such aspirations (*Social Mobility*, p. 258).

There a number of studies treating the patterns of participation within a single class or group in the population. For example, Floyd Dotson interviewed fifty working class native families in New Haven, finding that the leisure time activities of the families tended to be dominated by informal association with members of their kin group. Even with labor unions included, three fifths of the men and four fifths of the women and children did not participate in any formally organized associations (*American Sociological Review*, 16:689). In another examination of blue collar workers, Bennett Berger deals with a group of Ford employees (and their families) who accompanied their plant when it was moved from a city to a suburban area. Berger discovered that the workers retained both the political and social style of their life, including minimal participation in formal associations. More than 70 percent of the respondents reported that they had no memberships, while only 8 percent reported belonging to more than one organization. Since membership was compulsory, all of the men belonged to the union, but few attended meetings. They appeared to spend most of their leisure time watching television. Like the New Haven workers, the Ford men also took part in family activities with some frequency (*Working-Class Suburb*, pp. 56–75).

F. R. Cousens examined participation in block clubs and school clubs such as the PTA in an older, predominantly Negro, blue collar area of Detroit (in Shostak and Gomberg, *Blue-Collar World*). Although almost half of his 214 respondents belonged to an organization, less than 20 percent of the parents belonged to the PTA and many of those eligible to join the block clubs were not members. In exploration of the reasons for this low rate, Cousens points to the characteristics of the class culture which we noted at the beginning of this chapter.

Students, the military, and women have also been subjects of voluntary association research. Walter Baeumler studied high school students and their parents in a small Nebraska town. He found that participation rates were high for both middle and working class students, but that middle class students were much more likely to hold office in an organization. The encouragement given by the high school administration to participation, the availability of clubs within the school, and the exclusion of high school dropouts who number one third of all those starting high school probably account for the high participation rates that were discovered (*Sociological Inquiry*, 35:236–237). In an older study of youth in Maryland, significant differences were found between the memberships of students and of nonstudents. Almost 80 percent of the nonstudents — as compared to 50 percent of the students — did not belong to any clubs. In both groups, participation was low, and three out of four of the 13,000 youngsters (aged 16 to 24 years) interviewed did not belong to any organizations. Although Howard Bell, who wrote the 1938 report for the research team of the American Youth Commission, does not break down his results according to class, he does note that participation is positively correlated with the level of education reached by the individual, which would seem to indicate that the usual class differences were present (*Youth Tell Their Story*, pp. 168-169).

Pierre de Bie of the University of Louvain in Belgium has written on the changing patterns in the participation of that institution's students (*Sociological Inquiry*, 35:201-206). Essentially, Bie found that participation reflects the changes within Belgian society which have brought more students from the lower middle classes to the university. These students, in contrast to the upper class youth who once dominated the university, are oriented toward vocational training and upward mobility rather than a "gentleman's education." Consequently, the regional clubs which appear to correspond in some ways to American fraternities and sororities have been on the decline and the vocationally oriented departmental circles have been growing in size and importance. The latter have more members from lower middle classes, while the regional associations draw their members from the traditional bourgeois and the upper middle classes and generally serve to reinforce the social ties of these groups.

A study of the American college sorority by John Finley Scott indicates that the sorority serves a similar function. Scott argues that the sororities are used by parents to maintain control of their daughters by providing them with an environment that reinforces class values and helps insure the maintenance of "class and ethnic endogamy" by "ascriptive control over mate selection" (*American Sociological Review*, 30:517-518). The sorority system is thus most highly developed in the free, open, competitive state universities where class values are most threatened. Sororities are not as likely to be found in colleges which insure a homogeneous environment through their admissions policies. Scott's article includes an excellent discussion of the techniques which the older generation uses to control the college group.

From a study done by Garbin and Laughlin of air force officers and men in Omaha, it appears that military service does not alter the usual relationship between class and participation (*Sociological Inquiry*, 35: 227-234). Data from a mailed questionnaire indicated that officers, who have higher salaries, educational levels, and status, had significantly greater numbers of memberships in voluntary associations than enlisted men had, although only a small proportion of both groups actually attended meetings with regularity.

The participation habits of women have been examined in several studies already described. We have reserved for discussion here the work of Catherine Richards and Mhyra Minnis since both deal specifically with class (and ethnic) factors. In her analysis of data from interviews with seventy-two white Cleveland women aged 25 to 55 (unpublished dissertation, Western Reserve), Richards attempted to explain the differences found in the memberships of working class and of middle class women in terms of differences in "reality," "morale," and "value" factors. Although there were "reality differences, such as the number of children and the availability of funds for dues and other membership expenses, Richards felt these were not great enough to account for the less extensive and intensive participation of the working class women. In her opinion, the greater hostility, anxiety, frustration, and anomie of working class women as compared to middle class women were more crucial factors. There were also significant differences in the amount of satisfaction with life felt by the two groups of women and in the values evidenced by the women.

Mhyra Minnis concerned herself primarily with the relationship of women's organizations to the social structure of a city (in this case, New Haven). While she reports on many aspects of women's organizations and the participation of women (such as total membership figures, the activities of the organizations, and the meaning of organizations to their members) her emphasis is on the manner in which ethnic, religious, and racial cleavages within the city are reflected in the differentiation of organizations along the same lines. Her interviews, observations of club meetings, historical research, and the results of questionnaires sent to over four hundred presidents of women's organizations led her to conclude that women's organizations are not formed according to a "simple pattern of functional differentiation and diversity of membership interest, but are born and exist in a complex pattern of interlocking strands of cleavage." While race seemed to be the "sharpest form of cleavage," religious cleavage was the most "pervasive," with ethnic differences "contributory" and social prestige a "dominant if permeable element." "To illustrate with a single summary example this complexity of organizational cleavage, with overlapping factors of race, religion,

ethnic origin, and social prestige, we may cite the existence of no less
than seven Junior Leagues in New Haven — Junior League of New
Haven (Protestant), Catholic Junior League, Junior Community League
(Negro), B'nai Brith Junior League (Jewish), Swedish Junior League,
Italian Junior League, and Polish Junior League" (*American Sociological
Review*, 18:47–53).

Corroborative data supporting Minnis' conclusions have been reported
by August Hollingshead. On the basis of information gathered by interviewing a 5 percent random sample of New Haven families, Hollingshead
argues that parallel class structures within the limits of race, ethnicity,
and religion have been developing in the city during the past fifty years,
and that the "rigidity" in the social structure is supported by the organization of the city's religious, educational, marital, and leisure time institutions (*American Sociological Review*, 17:685).

William Form has described the development of a class structure in a
"new town," Greenbelt, Maryland, in which he lived for two and a half
years as a participant observer. In planning and building Greenbelt, the
federal government made an effort to prevent the formation of stratified social classes. Limits were set on the income of residents. All of
them had similar economic resources at the time of settlement. In
addition they were all white, almost all were native born, and more than
seventy-five percent worked for the federal government. All of the
housing in the town was similar, and the plan was designed to prevent
the development of any kind of segregation of social groups. Despite
these precautions, within four years the town developed a hierarchical
structure consisting of eight main status groupings. According to Form,
stratification in Greenbelt was "based primarily on organizational participation and secondarily on occupation" (Glaser and Sills, *Government of Voluntary Associations*, p. 66). Within a few years there were
differences in occupational status and income between officers and non-
officers, although the individuals did not differ when they joined the
organization. Form interprets this finding as indicating that the "officers
were those that showed on entry larger chances of income and occupational upward mobility." Form agrees with the judgment of Glaser and
Sills, the editors of the collection containing his essay, that "The associations unintentionally became the mechanisms for differentiating
among higher and lower members of the community; the associations
made some persons leaders while others were followers; some associations became exclusive clubs for a new elite while membership in others

became a sign of lower prestige" (pp. 62–63). While there is evidence in Form's report to provide some basis for these conclusions, Form actually seems to present more evidence to the effect that occupation served as the primary basis for status differentiation. Federal government officials appeared at the top of the status hierarchy, followed by individuals having such prestigious occupations as doctor, pastor, college professor, school principal, and mayor. Religious differentiation also appeared in the status structure, with Jews being accorded less deference than Gentiles having the same occupation and income. Racial differences could not develop since Negroes were not allowed to live in the federally planned and built town (pp. 64–65).

RACE AND PARTICIPATION

Although it dates from the 1940s, Gunnar Myrdal's famous study of the Negro in *An American Dilemma* is still a basic reference. Myrdal argues that Negroes are more inclined to join associations than are whites of comparable class level, and that this extensive participation must be viewed as a compensation for the Negro's exclusion from many other aspects of organized life in America. In Myrdal's interpretation, the Negro's participation is pathological, both because it is an imitation and an exaggeration of the behavior of white Americans and because the Negro's organizations do not help him to succeed economically or politically despite the time, energy, and money he devotes to them. While Myrdal emphasizes the role that Negro organizations play in diverting the Negro and channeling his frustrations in socializing activities, he does not neglect the "improvement and reform organizations." In fact, his discussion of the post–World War I nationalist Garvey movement contains the prophetic comment that Garvey's success in gaining followers: "proves that it is possible to reach the Negro masses. It testifies to the basic unrest in the Negro community and tells of a dissatisfaction so deep it amounts to the hopelessness of ever gaining a full life in America. It suggests that the effective method of lining up the American Negroes into a mass movement is a strongly emotional race-chauvinistic protest appeal . . . [the movement also illustrates] that a Negro movement in America is doomed to ultimate dissolution and collapse if it cannot gain white support. This is a real dilemma. For white support will be denied emotional Negro chauvinism when it takes organizational and political form" (II, 749). Myrdal also foresaw that the early nonpolitical organizations might play a role in socializing the Negro for future political action. He points out that the race and improvement groups taken together "mean that Negroes have increasingly become organized in natural social groups for concerted action, have become trained in orderly cooperation, and have become accustomed to plan and work together. All of them give an institutional sanction to protests against various kinds of discrimination. When seen in perspective, they represent bases for attempts at broader organizations" (II, 79).

It might be noted that recent research on the relationships between militancy, attitudes toward violence, and participation in organizations is inconclusive. Studies among Negroes in the Watts area of Los Angeles (Ransford, *American Journal of Sociology*, 73:581-591) and the Bedford-Stuyvesant section of New York City (Feagin, *Social Problems*, 15:432-441) indicated that participation in organizations was correlated with a disavowal of violence. However, Caplan and Paige (in Kerner, *National Advisory Commission on Civil Disorders*) and Marx (*Protest and Prejudice*) found that the number of organizational memberships held was positively related to militancy (although Marx also reports that antiwhite sentiment is lower among participants; p. 190).

Black Metropolis, a detailed and fascinating study of Chicago's southside ghetto, is another early work of lasting importance. The authors, St. Clair Drake and Horace R. Cayton, discuss the organization behavior of each of the community's classes. They contend that there is almost no participation among the lower classes, which are characterized by "general disorganization," and that club activity among Negroes is associated with above average educational attainment and economic status. Participation is therefore primarily to be found in the upper and middle classes, for whom the voluntary associations perform a number of functions. Although the Negro, like the white, represents many of his activities as community services, Drake and Cayton see organization activity as largely socially oriented. They write: "Throughout the world of the (Negro) middle class 'right connections' are stressed, and this otherwise sprawling group of people with diverse incomes and occupations is given cohesiveness by an intimate and complex web of voluntary associations. These constitute the 'markets' by which individuals symbolize their aspirations and the position they have attained in the competitive struggle to get ahead. They provide occasions upon which a middle class person can display his other symbols, such as clothing and correct public behavior, among people who, like himself, prize them.

Middle class organizations put the accent on 'front,' respectability, civic responsibility of a sort and conventionalized recreation. Some of these organizations, too, become the means by which middle class people 'on the rise' come into contact 'above' them socially and by which mobile lower class individuals can rise from the class below" (p. 662). There were a few Negroes in "Bronzeville" at the time of the research who devoted themselves to "race improvement," but even these individuals gained social prestige from their activities.

Some evidence has recently been gathered which supports Myrdal's analysis of Negro organization behavior and calls into question the Drake and Cayton contention that the lower class Negro does not participate in formal associations. Nicholas Babchuk and Ralph Thompson found that Negroes of all classes in Lincoln, Nebraska, belonged to more associations than whites of the corresponding class level. Their results are particularly significant because they used random sampling techniques and carefully eliminated church and union memberships from their statistics on voluntary associations. Three fourths of the Negroes interviewed were found to be affiliated with one or more voluntary associations. Moreover, two thirds of the lower class Negroes reported a voluntary association membership. In interpreting these figures, Babchuk and Thompson argue that lower class Negroes need organizations more than lower class whites because they lack the whites' strong family ties. They agree with Myrdal that the Negro's tendency toward exaggerated affiliation and toward joining expressive rather than instrumental associations is pathological. They maintain that the voluntary associations function for Negroes of all classes "in much the same way as the church to provide the Negro not only with an opportunity for self expression and status recognition, but also with an avenue to compete for prestige, to hold office, to exercise power and control, to win applause and acclaim" (*American Sociological Review,* 27:654).

Anthony Orum analyzed data from NORC interviews of a Negro sample in Detroit, a white sample in Chicago, and a sample of blacks and whites in a Washington suburb. He discovered that at the lower class level Negroes were more likely to be affiliated with organizations than were whites; that there was a strong positive relationship between education and membership for whites but not for Negroes; and that in each socio-economic group Negroes were more likely to participate actively than whites. In contrast to Myrdal, Orum also found that "in general Negroes are more likely to participate in political organizations than whites, and second, Negroes are just as likely as whites to participate in civic organizations and tend to be somewhat more likely to participate in church associations" (*American Journal of Sociology*, 72:38). These findings, plus data pointing to similar Negro and white election turnout at comparable class levels, seem to signal a decline in "pathological" organization behavior. However, given the inadequacies of the research, it is not possible to determine if the differences between Myrdal and Orum indicate a change in Negro behavior or simply a difference in the design and interpretation of the research.

There is some evidence that the failure of Negroes in the South to participate in instrumental voluntary associations is a result of "low job support" rather than the causes Myrdal postulated. A study by J. C. Ross and Raymond Wheeler in Tampa, Florida, revealed that the more supportive his job situation, the more likely the Negro was to join militant instrumental associations. Job support also appeared to be related to membership in some expressive associations such as the Masons. In the study, "high job support" was operationally defined as working under a Negro supervisor; "moderate job support" as working with other Negroes but not having a Negro supervisor; and "low job support" as neither working with Negroes nor having a Negro supervisor (*Social Forces*, 45:584).

Marvin E. Olsen has offered another alternative or supplementary explanation to the Myrdal "compensation" thesis. Olsen acknowledges that compensatory behavior accounts for some of the black participation he found in his survey research in the Indianapolis area, but argues that feelings of identification with the ethnic community stimulated by the recent emphasis on black power and black pride have also played a role in leading many black persons to extend and intensify their participation in numerous realms of social and political life including voluntary associations. When Olsen controlled for social status and age, he found that the "adjusted participation rates for blacks were higher than for whites in every instance." He also found that there was a trend toward greater black participation in many activities since the mid-fifties (*American Sociological Review*, 35:695). Hyman and Wright, in their analysis of national survey data from the late fifties and early sixties note a similar increase in black memberships (*American Sociological Review*, 36:204). The same basic trend was found in the Detroit area in 1957 by the University of Michigan's Institute for Social Research, although it was slightly less pronounced than it was in the Indianapolis area (See Eldersveld, *Political Parties*).

The voluntary associations of Negroes are discussed in general terms by Arnold Rose — who was one of Myrdal's collaborators on *An American Dilemma* — in his book *America Divided* (written with Caroline Rose). Rose also edited a collection of articles on the Negro protest (*Annals of the American Academy of Political and Social Science,* January 1965). It includes essays on various organizations and on the changing character of the protest. Data on Negro voluntary organizations in Lexington, Kentucky, is presented in a *Phylon* article (25:27–32) by Alvin Seals and Jiri Kolaja. The authors see the organizations as constituting an incomplete social system which provides for the instrumental and expressive needs of the Negro community, but does not necessarily integrate the community into the wider social system of the area.

Oscar Handlin, a noted historian specializing in the study of immigrants, has dealt briefly with voluntary associations in the contemporary Negro and Puerto Rican communities of New York. In *The Newcomers* Handlin compares these communities with those of past immigrant groups, finding that they have not developed the "integrated pattern of voluntary organizations" which gave their predecessors a tool for understanding and dealing with the life of the city. He reports that among blacks, only the churches have "genuine vitality and influence" (p. 107).

Handlin attributes the failure of Negroes and Puerto Ricans to organize effectively to a variety of factors, including the development of the welfare state which assumed many of the tasks previously carried out by voluntary groups; the absence of a tradition of philanthropy or communal solidarity; the stigma associated with separate Negro institutions in the past, giving rise to a "rejection of any mode of action in which Negroes and Puerto Ricans were set off as groups"; the absence of creative leaders; and the growth of the mass media which provided substitutes (though inadequate ones) for some of the activities once performed by voluntary associations. Handlin, writing in the late 1950s, saw the beginnings of change and the possibility of the development of healthy ethnic communities, with their array of voluntary associations, among blacks and Puerto Ricans.

Beyond the Melting Pot by Nathan Glazer and Daniel P. Moynihan also compares New York's Negroes and Puerto Ricans with other ethnic groups — the Jews, Italians, and Irish — but concentrates less on the past than does Handlin's study. Although the authors of this study of the persistence of ethnic identification are not primarily concerned with voluntary associations, there are scattered comments on such organizations in the volume.

The Puerto Rican community of New York has been described and
analyzed by Patricia Cayo Sexton in her book *Spanish Harlem:
Anatomy of Poverty*. Mrs. Sexton agrees with Handlin that the Puerto
Rican community has lacked organization in the past. She also agrees
that local organization is a key to group progress and devotes two chapters to describing some of the recent efforts to organize the community.
She deals with the role of professional "agitators" in the Saul Alinsky
mold, and community organizers as well as volunteers who have attempted to organize self-help projects in Spanish Harlem, and describes
three projects — the community school, the study club, and cooperative
housing — which have involved the poor although they were all initiated
by professionals. She points out that "Any organization that is successful among the poor must, finally, be political in direction and tied in
with a national political movement. The 'results' the poor seek can
come only with government action — federal action in particular — to
provide economic planning for full employment, improved economic
growth rates, vastly improved educational opportunities, and decent
social legislation" (p. 162).

A further source of general information about Puerto Ricans is provided by Clarence Senior in his book *The Puerto Ricans: Strangers —
Then Neighbors*. There are brief sections on participation in civic organizations, church related activities, and community development.

ETHNICITY AND RELIGION

Mary Treudly and Helen Znaniecki Lopata both studied the role of
voluntary associations in ethnic communities, coming to somewhat di-
vergent conclusions. Treudly sees the ethnic associations in Boston's
Greek community as aids in the "Americanization" of the groups' members. She asserts that voluntary associations cushion the shock of transition to a new society; offer incentives for adapting to that society;
provide a setting in which to practice American behavior and leadership
techniques; and articulate the group concensus in regard to the choice
of culture pattern. Commenting on the last function, she writes that
the associations "record the fact that attitudes toward Greece are
ceasing to be traditional and inarticulate. Their formal discussions of the
plight of their native land help their members to think and feel as
Americans about its problems. They act in American terms petitioning
the President and Congress to adopt the policy of their preference"

(*American Sociological Review,* 14:44–53). Ironically, ethnic associations contribute to their own decline in that the Americanized individual is no longer limited to his own ethnic groups, but can, and does, enter interethnic and nonethnic organizations.

On the basis of her thorough study of Chicago's Polish community which utilized questionnaires, interviews, content analysis of newspapers, background data from the Polish-American *Who's Who,* historical analysis of "primary sources, records of meetings and speeches and secondary sources," Lopata concluded that ethnic associations slow up the rate of assimilation by helping to preserve the ethnic community as a "distinct entity." Lopata believes that Polonia's associations have come to "reflect identification with American society as a distinct subgroup" and that their primary function within the community today is as an "in-group status-sifting device." Although they sometimes act as political interest groups, the associations focus their attention "on the development of 'outgroup' recognition of the bases for such pride [in cultural and social background]. This function necessitates continued contact with the Polish national society, but of a limited type involving identification not with the present, but with the past. It also necessitates education and cultural activities directed toward the preservation not of Polish culture in toto, but only of certain positively evaluated aspects of it. It implies relations of Polish Americans not as completely assimilated individual Americans, but as a unified group" (Burgess and Bogue, *Urban Sociology,* p. 223). However, Lopata points out that the recent "geographic and economic dispersal of Polish Americans from the ecologically isolated Polonia communities" threatens the continued existence of Polish voluntary associations.

Bartolemeo Palisi has dealt with different aspects of participation among working class Italians living in an ethnic enclave in New York City (*Sociological Inquiry,* 35:219–226; *Sociological Quarterly,* 7:167–178). Palisi's research revealed that the overall rate of participation (about one third of his respondents belonged to organizations) was low, but that there was no statistically significant difference between the rates of first and of second generation individuals. He also uncovered some evidence that individuals who were most active in their immediate family circles were least active in voluntary associations, while those who were most active in the extended family circle were also most active in formal groups and had greater numbers of friends.

Herbert Gans found that the Italian American working class residents of Boston's West End had extremely low rates of participation in all community activities, including voluntary associations. Most of the "normal" person's social activity takes place in the group composed primarily of family peers or relatives of the same age and sex. The few West Enders who do participate are generally "socially marginal" or "upwardly mobile." Although there are some clubs in the area, these are mostly peer group circles which have organized as clubs only to gain access to meeting rooms or other privileges (*The Urban Villagers,* pp. 36, 107–117, 129).

Joseph Fichter, a Catholic priest and sociologist, has dealt at length with the *Social Relations in the Urban Parish,* analyzing the participation of American lay Catholics in different types of church-sponsored voluntary associations. Fichter believes that less than one half of all American lay Catholics belong to any of the categories of groups — the "parochial groups" based on residence in a parish, the "interest groups" cutting across parish lines, or the "vocational groups" in which membership depends on the role performed by the layman in the larger society (such as Catholic doctors' guilds) — and that even fewer are active in the organizations. To alter this situation, Fichter recommends that greater emphasis be placed on informal, small groupings. "Only a minority of the members of a large-scale unit like a parish are willing to serve and cooperate in any specific organization. Hence if there are only certain restricted channels of social expression for them (the several, traditional, large formal organizations), the number of active participants in these formal groupings will be few. This number of active people can be multiplied only if the number of organizations (or their subcommittees) is multiplied, and only if these are small, natural (not artificial) groupings" (p. 162).

WOMEN'S PARTICIPATION IN VOLUNTARY ASSOCIATIONS

The participation of women in voluntary associations has been given relatively little attention, although there are many studies which do report separate statistics on the participation of men and women. At least two studies compare men and women participating in similar kinds of activities along several dimensions. Babchuk, Marsey, and Gordon studied men and women in community agencies with particular reference to power and prestige factors. They found that men dominate the directing boards of most agencies, especially those that have large budgets, perform instrumental functions, and were regarded by a panel of judges as being most vital to the community. There are greater numbers of women on the boards of expressive agencies, but men remain dominant (*Anerican Sociological Review*, 25:402). Although Aileen Ross concentrates on women in her analysis of philanthropic money-raising activity (*Social Forces*, 37:124–131), she also provides some comparative data on men. Her research involved interviewing upper middle class individuals of both sexes who had taken part in a money-raising campaign in an eastern Canadian city. In general, she found that men and women differ in their approaches to fund raising with men using methods borrowed from business and women relying more on the manipulation of personal ties. Women are much more likely to draw on friendship relations, partly because they have no business connections or economic rewards at their disposal, and they are apt to employ flattery to recruit workers and obtain funds. Ross also discovered that philanthropic work functioned as a career for some women. Charitable activities were the major outlet for the women's energies and talents and a major source of satisfaction to them.

A study by Carol Slater in the late fifties suggests that the "volunteer career" is a class-linked phenomenon. Slater employed interviews with a national sample of 365 urban married women. While the upper middle class women in the sample placed a high value on membership in organizations, working class wives tended to see themselves exclusively in a narrow domestic housekeeping role and did not value participation in voluntary associations (*American Journal of Sociology*, 65:616–618).

When Arnold Rose studied university students, he found that the women expected to participate in at least two organizations following graduation, spending about ten hours a week in civic and social welfare activities alone. College men also anticipated voluntary activity although they were less likely to indicate a preference for socially oriented activities or for political and community welfare work (*Social Forces*, 30: 76–77). The highly educated women studied by a team of Columbia University researchers led by Eli Ginsburg were in fact found to be quite active in voluntary associations. However, while 79 percent of the women had some involvement in voluntary activities, the researchers felt that the "range and intensity of . . . dissatisfactions [reported] shows that . . . these activities provide only limited satisfaction for highly educated women" (*Life Styles of Educated Women*, p. 91). The 311 women in the study were all of proven high scholastic ability and had been graduate students at Columbia between 1945 and 1951. Their answers to a mail questionnaire provide the basis for a discussion of the role of voluntary activities in their lives which includes figures on the time given to voluntary activities and on the kinds of motivations and gratification reported by the women.

A study by Jean Tompkins (unpublished dissertation, State University of Iowa) indicated that the type of organization women join is dependent upon the woman's family status and the stage she occupies in the family cycle. Tompkins' findings suggested that women belong to voluntary associations for purposes of maintaining or improving their self-images in terms of the "values accorded certain role-behaviors by society" as transmitted by their reference groups. She also explored the conditions under which associations become reference groups for their members.

AGE AND PARTICIPATION

There is a long review of the literature dealing with the aged and voluntary associations — both those associations in which the aged themselves are active and those which provide services for the aged — in Arnold Rose's essay on "The Impact of Aging on Voluntary Associations." As Rose notes, most studies have indicated that participation in voluntary associations declines as people grow older, even though many of them have more leisure time in their retirement than they had when they were working. This decline appears to be partly a result of changes in "location and role at the onset of old age which often pulls the individual out of his earlier social participation" at a time when he is not as motivated or as capable of entering new relationships. Rose examines the characteristics of the aged which affect their participation as well as the characteristics of voluntary associations which affect the participation of the aged. Since he believes that older people will increasingly be drawn to voluntary associations, he considers the probable impact of elderly members on the associations as well. This essay also provides substantial information on organizations for the elderly and deals at some length with the problems of voluntary associations for the aged and the functions of such organizations. A brief section on voluntary associations for the aged outside the United States is included.

Another general discussion of the participation of the aged and of the literature on the topic can be found in Harold Wilensky's essay on "Life

Cycle, Work Situation and Participation in Formal Associations." Wilensky emphasizes the relationship between cycles of participation and cycles of family, work, and consumption. He argues that the mass of men withdraw from both work, which becomes "little more than a source of income," and the larger communal life at the age of 35 or 40 and do not reenter at retirement, since by the time the children leave and the individual has more leisure time he is fixed in a "profoundly local" leisure routine centered in family and neighborhood. Wilensky believes that secondary group ties function mainly to integrate the aged into community and society, while successful personal adjustment is more dependent upon primary group support. He is therefore worried that the failure of the aged (and of individuals at other periods of strain in the life cycle — such as adolescence) to participate in great numbers, combined with the growth in these populations, may lead to the proliferation of mass movements. He assumes, it might be noted, the truth of the Kornhauser argument that a strong associational life in a society prevents the rise of mass movements, and sees the aged, given their isolation, as a "peculiarly potent pool of extremism" (p. 239).

There is some evidence that it is not easy to activate older people to participate in the community since their very isolation places them outside the social networks through which they could be drawn into activities. A Brandeis University demonstration project carried on in the stable, upper middle class community of Newton, Massachusetts, indicated that even aged from those social groups with the highest participation rates were either unwilling or unable to volunteer their services on a steady basis to social agencies. Because of this, and the expense and difficulty the organizations encountered in attempting to utilize elderly volunteers, the authors Morris and Lambert concluded that "A steadily expanding corps of older volunteers, resulting from a rational matching of potential abilities and capacities to existing and specially created opportunities, is hardly a practical or feasible objective for most of our 18 million older people" (*New Roles for the Elderly,* p. 69). The project report contains a full description of the problems encountered in carrying out the pilot program as well as information about the attitudes of the elderly toward volunteering and the social characteristics of aged volunteers and nonvolunteers. The data were obtained through "household interviews of a sample of 297 non-institutionalized older persons, selected on a probability basis from the List of Assessed Polls prepared annually by the city of Newton" (p. 10).

ATTITUDES AND OTHER PSYCHOLOGICAL VARIABLES

The psychology of joining is a relatively unexplored topic although there have been a few investigations dealing with attitudes and other psychological variables. For example, the Babchuk and Gordon work and the Jacoby studies discussed in Chapter 5 focus on variables of this sort. Arnold Rose explored the "Attitudinal Correlates of Social Participation" in a study of migrants to the city of Minneapolis. Rose found that individuals who belonged to groups reported having more friends, held more optimistic attitudes, expressed greater satisfaction with their lives, and had more confidence in society than individuals not belonging to groups or belonging to fewer groups, but the sample bias and methodological inadequacies of the study were such that these results can be considered only suggestive. Rose believed the study provided support for his theory that participation increases the individual's opportunity to internalize the meanings and values of the culture or to become "basically socialized" (p. 206). Another study, by Derek Phillips (*American Journal of Sociology,* 72:479–488), indicated that participation in voluntary associations is positively correlated with happiness (as reported by the subjects).

An examination of the "Dimensions of Organizational Commitment" by Helen Gouldner pointed in the direction of there being various forms of organization commitment. She interviewed sixty members of the Los Angeles League of Women Voters. Officers in the League scored high on a measure of "organizational introjection" which indicated to Gouldner that the individual's self-image includes a variety of organizationally approved qualities and values. Members were more likely to score high on "cosmopolitan integration," indicating to Gouldner that the members feel a part of the League as an organization but do not try to mold themselves along the lines of perceived League norms. Gouldner uncovered another group who were "outsiders" in the sense that they were "in but not of" the organization, and regarded their membership in utilitarian, pragmatic terms.

David Horton Smith constructed a psychological model of individual participation in a formal voluntary organization, and then applied the model in gathering and interpreting data on two samples of Chileans living in Santiago. In one sample, members and a matched set of eligible nonmembers of five organizations ranging from the Red Cross and a church auxiliary to a volunteer fire company were compared. In the second sample matched groups of high and low participating members in five organizations including two of those used in the first sample were compared. Smith utilized psychological tests to obtain information on three sets of variables: (1) The subjects' personality traits such as general optimism, self-confidence, hostility; (2) those general attitudes of the subjects which were hypothesized to be relevant to formal voluntary organization membership, such as the individual's service orientation, and feelings about the value of participation; and (3) those attitudes of the subjects which Smith hypothesized to be specifically relevant to participation, such as the individual's attitudes toward particular organizations. On the basis of highly involved statistical tests, Smith concluded that "For the discrimination of members from nonmembers, the specific and general Formal Voluntary Organization – relevant attitudes should be given the most weight, while for the discrimination of active from inactive Formal Voluntary Organization members the personality variables should be given the most weight" (*American Journal of Sociology*, 72:259). Smith's data also indicated that among the personality variables, members and nonmembers differed most in their need for autonomy, with members much more likely to evidence a low need.

Urie Bronfenbrenner and his associates on the Springdale project (a community study of a small New York town) attempted to link personality variables and participation. They administered a personality inventory designed to tap nine variables – mistrust of people, static conservatism, retrogressive conservatism, rigidity, inexpressiveness, conformity, strict control, intuitiveness, individual power – to a sample of 547 adult residents of the Springdale area. All of the significant correlations "vanished" when statistical controls for social class and other factors were applied. Despite this Bronfenbrenner argues that "personality factors clearly do play a part in civic activity but they vary from individual to individual and may be as much the product as the producer of the behavior to which they relate" (*Journal of Social Issues*, 16.4:63).

Finally, in three speculative articles, the psychologists Gordon Allport (*Psychological Review*, 53:117-132; *Adult Leadership*, November 1952) and L. K. Frank (*Adult Leadership*, February 1958) contend that participation and personality are related, and each hypothesizes about the possible motives for joining organizations. For example, Allport believes people may join groups in order to conform, or for reasons of "ego defense," finding in membership safety, security, and a feeling of superiority, or for "ego-extending" reasons, membership contributing to the growth of the individual's personality (1952, p. 10).

COMMUNITY STUDIES

Although the community studies deal with many of the variables already discussed, they have been brought together for discussion in this section because they constitute a distinctive body of research. A community study is an in-depth examination, based on a variety of sociological and anthropological techniques, of the spectrum of life in a single community. Such studies provide a valuable picture of the functioning of voluntary organizations within a given social setting and of the role these organizations play in the life of the inhabitants. Unfortunately, all of them do not deal extensively with voluntary associations; here we shall confine ourselves to those which provide fairly detailed information on private organizations.

Helen and Robert Lynd's pioneering work in Muncie, Indiana, resulted in two important books — *Middletown* published in 1929 and *Middletown in Transition* published in 1937 — which together give us a picture of the associational life of the community. The Lynds' analysis, which is based on historical data from the years between 1890 and 1925 as well as their own field research, is organized around the concept of class. They make extensive comparisons between the activities and attitudes of the working or lower class and the business or upper class. In general, they found that members of the working class did not participate as much in Middletown's extensive network of organizations as did members of the business class, and that working class and business class members both tended to belong to groups composed exclusively of persons sharing their social status.

The Lynds' findings lend support to the hypothesis that voluntary associations increase in numbers with urbanization and modernization. Although Middletown had many organizations in 1890, there was a significant growth in the number of groups in the twentieth century and the organizational network was extended into the ranks of the younger citizens of the town. The quantitative increase was, in the Lynds' opinion, accompanied by a qualitative decline. By 1925 the educational work of the men's organizations had virtually disappeared, and in contrast to the 1890s when "week after week . . . baker and nailmaker sat side by side with banker and doctor, discussing such questions as 'The Ethical Life of Man'," there were only professional groups listening to specialized papers in their respective fields. The civic clubs of the 1920s and 1930s were numerous, but engaged largely in noncontroversial charitable activity. According to the Lynds they functioned primarily to further the members' business interests and to provide some escape from tension through their leisure activities. Even in the midst of the depression crisis, the civic clubs did not undertake any concerted effort to solve the city's problems. Instead, they avoided conflict among their members, who represented many different local interests, by concentrating on fellowship and on competing with other groups for prestige through the sponsorship of essay contests for high school students and other similar projects.

Class is also the organizing concept in the work of Lloyd Warner and his associates, although Warner's conceptualization of the class system is more elaborate than that of the Lynds. Warner combines "objective" measures, such as the educational level reached by an individual, with "subjective" measures, such as the rank given to an individual by other members of the community, to form indexes that enable him to locate people within a six-class stratification system. In some cases he uses the number and type of an individual's voluntary association memberships to locate his social class position in the community's status structure. Warner also developed a typology of associations by class types, and his team of researchers has utilized these measures to analyze in great and somewhat tedious detail the behavior of each class in a small Massachusetts town and another small town in Illinois.

The five-volume Yankee City series is a report on the research in Newburyport, Massachusetts, which took place between 1930 and 1935. Most of the information on voluntary groups is concentrated in *The Social Life of a Modern Community,* which focuses on the types of associations favored by members of different classes, the role of associations in integrating the larger structures of the society to the community, the relationship between organization membership and individual mobility, the differential functions of belonging for men and women, and the frequency of belonging on the part of the various classes. There are additional data on the associations of Yankee City's immigrant groups in Warner and Srole, *The Social Systems of American Ethnic Groups.* This volume also contains a model of the sequence of association development in ethnic communities from the first informal association to the "crystallized formal associational structure" which finally emerges. In his essay *American Life: Dream and Reality* Warner has drawn on all of this research for a general, speculative discussion of the functions of voluntary associations; the relationship between class and associations; and the meaning of the different types of activities observed in association meetings and work.

The research in "Jonesville" (Morris, Illinois), undertaken in the years immediately preceding and following the Second World War, was conducted under Warner's direction, but the two major chapters on associations in the final report *Democracy in Jonesville* were written by Marchia Meeker. She emphasizes the role Jonesville's numerous associations play in binding the community together: "As the activities of any association overlap those of other associations and other groups, they unify the interests and aims of discrete elements. They cut across the major divisions which exist, causing individuals from different groups and different segments of the society to meet, talk, and act together. Organizations connected with the church, school, political groups and business interests draw a large group of people into their activities and allow these institutions, with a limited role, to extend their influence throughout the community" (p. 110). On the other hand, she also observed that the ranking of associations in terms of prestige and the tendency of individuals to join associations exclusively (or largely) composed of members of their own class, resulted in the association structure mirroring the cleavages of the larger society. Her conclusion that different classes have different patterns of association behavior and that this pattern both maintains and strengthens the class structure of the community seems somewhat at odds with the view expressed in the quoted material.

A. B. Hollingshead, who studied with Warner, also conducted field research in Morris. The book that grew out of this work, *Elmtown's Youth,* is one of the best of the genre and contains valuable information on the organizational behavior of the adult and adolescent members of the five classes in the town. By focusing on the activities of high school students, Hollingshead is able to show that the class-based pattern of activity discerned in adults is established early in the individual's life. He notes that children learn very early which associations are considered "appropriate" to their class position (pp. 295–299).

Although class is considered in the study of the Canadian suburb of Crestwood Heights by John Seeley, Alexander Sim, and Elizabeth

Loosley, it is not the primary focus, in part no doubt because Crest-wood is a homogeneous upper middle class community which does not permit comparisons of behavior among different classes. The authors have devoted a good deal of attention to the psychological strains of life in Crestwood and to the struggle for status within the community. Crest-wood's numerous adult and youth clubs play their role in this struggle. "Status for the Crestwooder means psychic and social capital. Member-ships in clubs and associations which are widely recognized as being of high social status, are like negotiable securities (no less real for being psychological) which he may cash, transfer, or use as collateral in ne-gotiating a wide variety of social investments in the course of his up-ward progress" (*Crestwood Heights,* p. 296). The intimate atmosphere in some of the clubs functions too as a kind of psychological shelter for the individual, and in general, the clubs serve to relate individuals to one another and to the culture. The associations further provide an outlet for the organizing and professional skills of Crestwood's educated and somewhat frustrated women. Men, as well as women, find in the clubs an opportunity to improve a variety of skills from tennis to "making friends and influencing people," to promote themselves, and to satisfy their need for doing something constructive and worthwhile with their leisure time. As a kind of insurance for their way of life, the Crestwood adults have organized a number of children's associations to train child-ren for adult roles in the culture (p. 296).

A similar emphasis on status and anxiety can be found in other studies of suburbia such as William Whyte's examination of Park Forest, Illinois, in *The Organization Man* and Spectorsky's analysis of *The Exurbanites* — men who work in the communications industries of New York City and live in its suburbs. While Whyte and Spectorsky provide interesting insights into life in suburbia, their works are impressionistic and journal-istic in character, in contrast to the Crestwood Heights study which is a thoroughly scholarly piece of research.

Another scholar, the sociologist Herbert Gans, has examined life in Levittown, New Jersey, the prototype of the postwar suburban develop-ments. Gans employed interviews, mail questionnaires, and other field studies; in addition he lived in Levittown for the first two years of its existence and was able to observe how organization life started in the town. Within the first nine months, fourteen groups (not including churches and church-related organizations) had appeared, and by the end of two years there were seventy-seven voluntary associations. About a third of these were "external" in character, having been created by outside initiative as branches of national associations; another third were also local branches of national groups but were "internal," having been organized by Levittowners themselves; and the rest were local groups founded in response to some community or individual need ("unintended groups"). Gans describes the organizing procedure (which often involved the enlisting of friends and neighbors who joined because of these ties); the fight for group survival; the "definitional struggle" over the group's purposes, composition, and program; and the development of "interlocking directorates" and alliances among like-minded organizations.

In order to survive, Levittown's organizations had to adapt to the needs of the inhabitants. As public agencies and political groups filled "civic" and "family" needs, most of the organizations became social. "Aside from the few civic groups, which tried to intervene in municipal affairs, and the men's service clubs, which provided "community-minded" activities for the lawyers, salesmen, realtors, and politicians who needed to advertise themselves in the community, the organizations were primarily *sorting* [his italics] groups which divided and segregated people by their interests and ultimately, of course, by socio-economic, educational, and religious differences. On the block, people who shared a common space could not really express their diversity; the community sorting groups came into being for this purpose" (*The Levittowners,* p. 61). Since men are able to sort themselves in their work, while women have to rely on community activities, most of the organizations in Levittown were sexually segregated, and the "total array of women's groups offered the opportunity for extremely fine sorting."

"Springdale," a small New York State town developing into a suburb, was the subject of an intensive study conducted over a period of several years by an interdisciplinary team of researchers from Cornell University. Of the publications that grew out of the project, *Small Town in Mass Society: Class, Power and Religion in a Rural Community* by Arthur Vidich and Joseph Bensman is the most extensive. The subtitle reflects the orientation and character of the work, which the authors describe as an "attempt to explore the foundations of social life in a community which lacks the power to control the institutions that regulate and determine its existence." On the basis of observations made during their three years of residence in the town, Vidich and Bensman concluded that the "public enactment of community life and public statements of community values" bore "little relationship to the community's operating institutions and the private lives of its members" (p. x). In their attempt to explain this apparent contradiction, the authors emphasize the latent functions of voluntary associations and other community institutions. They view associations primarily as "institution connectors" between the town and the dominant mass society in which new ideas and values originate.

In addition to *Small Town and Mass Society,* an entire issue of the *Journal of Social Issues* (16.4) is devoted to reports of the findings of the Springdale research, as they relate to community participation. In the various articles, the town is described, the problems of doing research on community participation are discussed, and findings are presented on the relationships between formal and informal leadership and on neighborhood characteristics and participation in the community. There is also a general description of Springdale's organizations and a case study of a community action project initiated by the voluntary associations of the town.

There are several other monographs which provide fairly extensive information on voluntary organizations. Everett C. Hughes studied a small Quebec town in a period of transition from a French and rural orientation to an English, urban, industrial orientation. Much of Hughes's discussion is organized around the cleavage between the French and English residents. Not surprisingly, he found that there were very few voluntary associations which included members of both ethnic groups. As he observes: "Easy sociability requires a common sense of what is to be said and what is to be left unsaid; in the absence of this consensus of discretion a burden of restraint rests upon the company. Even when pursuing secular interests — for which conscious agreement is wanted — it is safer to have some consensus about basic sentiments" (*French Canada in Transition,* p. 123). Significantly, Hughes also found that immigrants from French Canadian rural areas who had not participated in voluntary institutions before migrating did join associations when they moved to urban areas where they were cut off from ties of family and village.

Like Hughes, Elin Anderson focuses on ethnic cleavages in an early study of Burlington, Vermont. In *We Americans,* Anderson provides considerable detail on the associations of the different ethnic and religious groups of the town and on the business and professional organizations as well. However, on the whole the Hughes book provides greater insight into the functions of voluntary associations.

A small midwestern farming town with a population of less than 300 persons was studied by James West (reported in *Plainville, USA*) and again by Art Gallaher (*Plainville, Fifteen Years Later*). Both scholars lived in the community for a period of time. West discovered a number of voluntary organizations in "Plainville," including lodges and their women's auxiliaries (both of which were on the decline), 4-H clubs, a women's Booster Club, and a variety of church-sponsored groups. When Gallaher observed the town fifteen years later many of these groups were still in existence. In the interim, several agricultural interest groups such as the Farm Bureau had also been established. The total number of organizations increased slightly and the functions of some of the organizations changed in the years separating the studies.

In *As You Sow*, Walter Goldschmidt reports on his observations of life in a rich farming valley of southern California. After having lived in the area for eight months, Goldschmidt concluded that rural-urban differences are disappearing in modern American society. He argues that life in "Wasco," a town of 8000 which was the focus of his study, has become "urbanized." Social ties were not close in Wasco and "invidious social distinctions" were maintained without reference to personal qualities, in voluntary associations and in other areas of life.

Finally, Edward Banfield's portrait of Montegrano, an impoverished village in southern Italy, provides a striking contrast to the American community studies. In Montegrano life has the character of a Hobbesian "war of all against all." The villagers are totally selfish and feel no obligation to anything outside their immediate family. Motivated as they are by this "amoral familism," fatalistic, suspicious, and untrusting, the villagers see no point in any form of cooperative activity. There are no organizations in Montegrano. The church and political parties represent outside forces and are not important in the lives of the people. *The Moral Basis of a Backward Society* illustrates the degree to which cultural factors and poverty are determinants of the number and character of organizations in a society.

METHODOLOGICAL LITERATURE

There are a limited number of works which present some data on participation but are primarily devoted to methodological questions. Raymond Morris' comparison of British and American research on voluntary associations (*Sociological Inquiry*, 35:186–200) contains a section on the methods used by scholars in each country which is a helpful introduction to this methodological literature. According to Morris, the British have tended to make use primarily of semistructured interview schedules, case histories, and participant observation, while the Americans have relied more on surveys of larger scale which employ more formal interviews. Morris believes that research in both nations has been deficient methodologically because investigators have failed to control variables which may have affected their results. Moreover, in neither country have researchers offered many sophisticated hypotheses or developed a cumulative research tradition.

In the study of organizations in the United States, probably the single most frequently used measuring device has been F. Stuart Chapin's rather crude "Social Participation Scale," first formulated in 1927. Recently the scale has been the subject of criticism, and its popularity among scholars appears to be declining. The scale, as published in 1937 by the University of Minnesota, is extremely simple. Chapin asked a group of social-agency executives in Minneapolis–St. Paul to rate various aspects of participation. On the basis of their judgments, he determined to score different activities as follows: a score of 1 for membership in an organization; 2 for attendance at meetings; 3 for contributions; 4 for membership on committees; and 5 for holding a position as an officer. While Chapin admits that the scale is a "rough instrument because the weights assigned are arbitrary and the continuum has not been calibrated," he argues that it appears to be "dependable as tested by reliability and validity coefficients" (*American Sociological Review*, 4:158–166). Chapin has described and defended the scale in his many articles and books and has published some tentative norms for it in his work on *Experimental Designs in Sociological Research*.

Donald Hay adapted the Chapin scale for use in rural areas by adding a number of measures of informal participation (*Rural Sociology*, 13: 285–294). William Evan also revised the scale to include measures of value commitment in order to tap the motivational dimensions of participation (*Social Forces*, 36:148–153). Evan takes issue with Chapin's isolation of only two dimensions of social participation, arguing that there are three dimensions — activity, decision-making, and commitment — which should be measured. Stuart Queen has criticized the Chapin scale, Hay's variation, and a scale developed by Atwood and Shideler (*Sociology and Social Research*, 18:436–444) which measures formal and informal participation and "derivative participation," such as attending the movies. With his colleagues at Washington University,

Queen worked out and tested a four-part scale of cultural, neighborhood, informal, and formal group participation, which includes the
Chapin scale as one of its components (*American Sociological Review*,
14:251-256).

The more recent methodological literature, such as an article on techniques for analyzing the effects of group composition on behavior, written by James L. Davis and other NORC researchers, presents increasingly
more refined methods for measuring association activity.

BIBLIOGRAPHY

Adams, B. N., and J. E. Butler, "Occupational Status and Husband Wife Social Par-
  ticipation," *Social Forces*, 45 (June 1967): 501-507. An investigation of the
  relationship between occupational status and the degree of "togetherness" exhibited by North Carolina husbands and wives in their social activities.
Allport, Gordon, "The Psychology of Participation," *Psychological Review*, 53
  (May 1945): 117-132.
—— "Why Do People Join?" *Adult Leadership*, 1 (November 1952): 10-12, 32-33.
Anderson, Elin L., *We Americans*, Cambridge, Harvard University Press, 1937.
Astin, Helen A., *The Woman Doctorate in America*. New York, Russell Sage Foundation, 1970. A survey of women receiving their doctorates in 1957 and 1958
  which deals with leisure activities as one aspect of the women's lives.
Atwood, Bartlett S., and E. H. Shideler, "Social Participation and Juvenile Delinquency," *Sociology and Social Research*, 18 (May-June 1934): 436-444. The
  authors present their own scale of social participation (the Franklin scale)
  which measures formal, informal, and derivative (such as movie-going) participation. They also report that a study comparing one hundred delinquent boys
  with one hundred nondelinquent boys revealed that the delinquents had
  higher participation rates.
Babchuk, Nicholas, and C. Wayne Gordon, *The Voluntary Association in The Slum*.
  Lincoln, University of Nebraska, 1962 (University of Nebraska Studies, new
  series no. 27).
Babchuk, Nicholas, Ruth Marsey, and C. Wayne Gordon, "Men and Women in Com-
  munity Agencies: A Note on Power and Prestige," *American Sociological Re-
  view*, 25 (June 1960): 339-403.
Babchuk, Nicholas, and Ralph V. Thompson, "The Voluntary Associations of
  Negroes," *American Sociological Review*, 27 (October 1962): 647-655.
Baeumler, Walter L., "The Correlates of Formal Participation among High School
  Students," *Sociological Inquiry*, 35 (Spring 1965): 235-240.
Banfield, Edward, *The Moral Basis of a Backward Society*. New York, Free Press,
  1958.
Bell, Howard M., *Youth Tell Their Story*. Washington, D. C., American Council on
  Education, 1938.
Berger, Bennett M., *Working-Class Suburb*. Berkeley and Los Angeles, University of
  California Press, 1960.

Bernard, Jessie, Carol Ann Hecht, Sylvia Schwartz, Sylvia Levy, and William Schiele, "The Relationship between Scores on the Bernreuter Personality Inventory and Three Indexes of Participation in a College Community," *Rural Sociology*, 15 (September 1950): 271–273. Sociological variables rather than the personality variables measured by the inventory (stability, self-sufficiency, and dominance) appeared to account for the participation rates of the subjects, who were students at Pennsylvania State College.

Bie, Pierre de, "New Patterns in the Participation of Students at the University of Louvain," *Sociological Inquiry*, 35 (Spring 1965): 201–206.

Black, Therel R., "Formal Social Participation: Method and Theory," *Rural Sociology*, 22 (March 1957): 61–65. Black revised the Chapin scale to take into account the percentage of meetings attended by the member.

Bordeau, Edwina, Ruth Dales, and Ruth Connor, "Relationship of Self-Concept to 4-H Club Leadership," *Rural Sociology*, 28 (December 1963): 413–418. Leaders were found to have a more favorable concept of self than nonleaders had.

Bradburn, Norman, and David Caplovitz, *Reports on Happiness*. Chicago, Aldine, 1965. A National Opinion Research Center study indicating that higher socio-economic status is correlated with organization involvement and higher positive feelings.

Bronfenbrenner, Urie, "Personality and Participation: The Case of the Vanishing Variables," *The Journal of Social Issues*, 16.4 (1960): 54–63.

Bruce, James M., "Intragenerational Occupational Mobility and Participation in Formal Associations," *Sociological Quarterly*, 12 (Winter 1971): 46–55. The mobile males among the 407 white respondents from Providence, Rhode Island, were no less likely to participate in organizations than the stable respondents of the same socio-economic status.

Caplan, Nathan, "The New Ghetto Man: A Review of Recent Empirical Studies," *Journal of Social Issues*, 26 (Winter 1970): 59–73.

—— and J. M. Paige, in Otto Kerner, et al., *Report on the National Advisory Commission on Civil Disorders*, pp. 127–137. New York, Bantam Press, 1968.

Chapin, F. Stuart, *Contemporary American Institutions*. New York, Harper and Brothers, 1935. In this text Chapin discusses the development of his scale for the measurement of participation. The participation scale is one of the measures he developed to provide an indication of family socio-economic status. The book also includes some brief reports of studies of the extracurricular activities of students at the University of Minnesota and a California junior college.

—— *The Social Participation Scale*. Minneapolis, University of Minnesota Press, 1937.

—— "The Effects of Slum Clearance and Rehousing on Family and Community Relationships in Minneapolis," *American Journal of Sociology*, 43 (March 1938): 744–763. A study of the effect of moving on slum families' participation and local ties.

—— "Design for Social Experiments," *American Sociological Review*, 3 (December 1938): 786–800. A report on a study comparing the participation rates of high school graduates and dropouts and on a study of the participation rates of Boy Scouts.

—— "Social Participation and Social Intelligence," *American Sociological Review*, 4 (April 1939): 157–166. Chapin describes and defends his Social Participation Scale, referring to a number of studies made by his graduate students which employed the scale.

—— *Experimental Designs in Sociological Research*. New York, Harper and Brothers, 1947.

—— "Comment," *American Journal of Sociology*, 57 (November 1951): 247–248. In the course of his comments on research by Mayo and Marsh (see entry in this bibliography), Chapin argues that his five-part Social Participation Scale can be broken down into separate measures of social acceptance and of pure participation.

Christiansen, John, and Therel R. Black, "Group Participation and Personality Adjustment," *Rural Sociology*, 19 (June 1954): 183–185. The subjects were rural Utah high school students whose personality adjustment was shown to be affected by their participation.

Cloyd, Jerry S., "Small Groups as Social Institutions," *American Sociological Review*, 30 (June 1965): 394–402. The author suggests that small groups be viewed as social institutions rather than as special phenomena whose structure is either imposed from without or emerges from the interaction of group members.

Cohen, Albert K., and Harold M. Hodges, Jr., "Characteristics of the Lower Blue Collar Class," *Social Problems*, 10 (Spring 1963): 303–334. A 1963 survey of 2600 California residents showed that more middle class individuals joined associations than did blue-collar individuals.

Cooper, Homer Chassell, "Perception of Subgroup Power and Intensity of Affiliation with a Large Organization," *American Sociological Review*, 26 (April 1961): 272–274. Although Cooper's research on the relationship between a member's perception of his subgroup's power and the strength of his feeling of identification with the group was concerned with political party members, Cooper believes the same relationships he found may also exist in voluntary associations.

Cousens, F. R., "Indigenous Leadership in Two Lower-Class Neighborhood Organizations," in Arthur B. Shostak and William Gomberg, eds., *Blue-Collar World*. Englewood Cliffs, New Jersey, Prentice-Hall, 1964.

Coyle, Grace L., "'Unaffiliated' Groups of Adolescent Youth: A Summary of Three Studies in Cleveland, Ohio," *Autonomous Groups Bulletin*, 6 (Spring 1951): 3–11. Adolescent social groups, including those in a Negro neighborhood and Jewish high school fraternities, were examined to determine their functions for the members.

Crichton, A., C. James, and J. Wakeford, "Youth and Leisure in Cardiff," *The Sociological Review*, n.s. 10 (July 1962): 203–220.

Curtis, Richard F., "Occupational Mobility and Membership in Formal Voluntary Associations: A Note on Research," *American Sociological Review*, 24 (December 1959): 846–848.

Dackawich, John S., "Voluntary Associations of Central Area Negroes," *The Pacific Sociological Review,* 9 (Fall 1966): 74–78. Comparison of white and Negro residents of the central area of Long Beach, California, indicated little difference between the two in their nonchurch related memberships. However, Dackawich failed to control for class so his results are not very meaningful.

Dalton, Melville, "Informal Factors in Career Achievement," *American Journal of Sociology,* 56 (March 1951): 407–415. A rather inconclusive study of the influence of such factors as religion, ethnicity, political beliefs, and participation in accepted organizations on the promotion chances of managers and other supervisory personnel in industry.

Davis, James L., Joe L. Spaeth, and Carolyn Huson, "A Technique for Analyzing the Effects of Group Composition," *American Sociological Review,* 26 (April 1961): 215–225.

Devereux, Edward C., Jr., "Community Participation and Leadership," *Journal of Social Issues,* 16.4 (1960): 29–45. The correlates of community participation, ranging from leadership in formal organizations and informal activities to the complete absence of community participation, are listed and discussed. This is another of the reports on the Springdale project.

—— "Neighborhood and Community Participation," *Journal of Social Issues,* 16.4 (1960): 64–84. A very detailed, closely reasoned discussion of the relationship between the character of a neighborhood and community participation in Springdale. Most of the article deals with methodological considerations, such as the development of a measure of participation deviance.

—— "Springdale and Its People," *Journal of Social Issues,* 16.4 (1960): 7–15. Devereux describes the town studied by an interdisciplinary team of Cornell researchers over a five-year period. He deals with the various groups in the population and makes some brief comments on the generally low level of participation.

—— Urie Bronfenbrenner, and John Harding, "Community Participation as a Research Problem," *Journal of Social Issues,* 16.4 (1960): 1–6. An introduction to an issue reporting on the results of an interdisciplinary research project in the small New York town of Springdale. The article describes the project and offers some general comments on community participation.

Dobriner, William M., ed., *The Suburban Community.* New York, G. P. Putnam, 1958. There are scattered comments on voluntary organizations in suburban life in some of the essays.

Dotson, Floyd, "Patterns of Voluntary Association among Urban Working-Class Families," *American Sociological Review,* 16 (October 1951): 687–693.

Drake, St. Claire, and Horace R. Cayton, *Black Metropolis.* New York, Harcourt Brace, 1945.

Dynes, Russell B., "The Consequences of Sectarianism for Social Participation," *Social Forces,* 35 (May 1957): 331–334. The analysis of returns of mailed questionnaires in Columbus, Ohio, indicated that members of Protestant sects found little need for, or satisfaction with, secular organizations since they derived a great deal of satisfaction from sect membership.

Eldersveld, Samuel J., *Political Parties.* Chicago, Rand McNally, 1964.

Evan, William Martin, "Occupation and Voluntary Associations: A Case Study," Unpublished PhD dissertation, Cornell University, 1954. Since he is concerned with consumer cooperatives, Evan's study is largely irrelevant to our concerns, despite its title. However, there are occasional references to voluntary associations.

—— "Dimensions of Participation in Voluntary Associations," *Social Forces*, 36 (December 1957): 148-153.

Feagin, J. R., "Social Sources of Support for Violence and Nonviolence in a Negro Ghetto," *Social Problems*, 15 (Spring 1968): 432-441. An analysis of data from an NORC survey in Bedford-Stuyvesant (New York City) after the 1964 riot in the area. The relationship between religious participation and organization affiliation and support for violence and nonviolence is considered.

Fichter, Joseph H., S.J., *Social Relations in the Urban Parish*. Chicago, University of Chicago Press, 1954.

Form, William H., "Status Stratification in a Planned Community," *American Sociological Review*, 10 (December 1945): 605-613.

—— "Voluntary Associations in a Planned Community," in William A. Glaser and David L. Sills, eds., *The Government of Voluntary Associations*. Totowa, New Jersey, Bedminster Press, 1966.

Fortune (the editors), *The Executive Life*. Garden City, New York, Doubleday, 1956. Includes some comments on the executives' attitudes toward participation in voluntary associations.

Frank, L. K., "What Influences People To Join Organizations?" *Adult Leadership*, 6 February 1958: 196.

Freeman, Howard, Edwin Novak, and Leo G. Reeder, "Correlates of Membership in Voluntary Associations," *American Sociological Review*, 22 (October 1957): 528-533. The authors' concerns are largely methodological. They report on a study carried out in Spokane, Washington, to determine the relative ability of different variables measuring social class to predict membership in voluntary associations. They also included measures of attitudes toward the community as an independent variable.

Friedan, Betty, *The Feminine Mystique*. New York, Norton, 1963. This angry book by a modern feminist contains some comments on volunteer work as a female activity.

Gallaher, Art, Jr., *Plainville, Fifteen Years Later*. New York, Columbia University Press, 1964.

Gans, Herbert J., *The Urban Villagers*. Glencoe, Illinois, Free Press (Macmillan), 1962.

—— *The Levittowners*. New York, Random House, 1967.

Garbin, A. P., and Vivian Lucille Laughlin, "Military Participation in Voluntary Associations," *Sociological Inquiry*, 35 (Spring 1965): 227-234.

Gerstl, Joel E., "Leisure, Taste and Occupational Milieu," in Erwin O. Smigel, ed., *Work and Leisure*. New Haven, College and University Press, 1963.

Ginsberg, Eli, with Ivar E. Berg, Carol A. Brown, John L. Herma, Alice M. Yohalem, and Sherry Gorelick, *Life Styles of Educated Women*. New York, Columbia University Press, 1966.

Glaser, William A., and David L. Sills, eds., *The Government of Associations.* Totowa, New Jersey, Bedminster Press, 1966.

Glazer, Nathan, and Daniel Patrick Moynihan, *Beyond the Melting Pot.* Cambridge, The M.I.T. Press and Harvard University Press, 1963.

Goldschmidt, Walter, *As You Sow.* Glencoe, Illinois, Free Press, 1947.

Goodchilds, Jacqueline D., and John Harding, "A Case Study of Community Participation," *Journal of Social Issues,* 16.4 (1960): 46–53. A largely descriptive account of action taken by individuals and organizations in Springdale to repair a community dam.

—— "Formal Organizations and Informal Activities," *Journal of Social Issues,* 16.4 (1960): 16–28. A discussion of the organizations in Springdale, and of the informal leisure activities of the inhabitants. Springdale's fifty-eight organizations are typed into five categories.

Gough, Harrison G., "Predicting Social Participation," *Journal of Social Psychology,* 35 (May 1962): 227–233. A largely methodological article in which Gough attempts to develop a scale for the prediction of social participation with special relevance to counseling and guidance situations.

Gouldner, Helen P., "Dimensions of Organizational Commitment," *Administrative Science Quarterly,* 4 (March 1960): 468–490.

Hagedorn, R., and S. Labovitz, "An Analysis of Community and Professional Participation among Occupations," *Social Forces,* 46 (June 1967): 482–491. An examination of the relationship between occupation and the type of associations individuals join. Study of the personnel of a large nonprofit research organization indicated that individuals who join one type of association are likely to join other types, and there are only minor differences in the types of associations joined by individuals of different occupational groups.

—— "Participation in Community Associations by Occupation: A Test of Three Theories," *American Sociological Review,* 33 (April 1968): 272–283.

—— "Occupational Characteristics and Participation in Voluntary Associations," *Social Forces,* 47 (September 1968): 16–27. Analysis of the relationship between participation and various characteristics of an occupation such as the amount of bureaucratic control, the type of leadership and the importance of formal contacts.

Hamilton, Richard F., "The Behavior and Values of Skilled Workers," in Arthur B. Shostak and William Gomberg, eds., *Blue-Collar World.* Englewood Cliffs, New Jersey, Prentice-Hall, 1964. On the basis of a secondary analysis of the same NORC survey used by Murray Hausknecht in *The Joiners,* Hamilton reports that skilled workers are closer to unskilled workers than to middle class individuals in their pattern of belonging to formal organizations.

Handlin, Oscar, *The Newcomers.* Cambridge, Harvard University Press, 1959.

Harp, John, and Richard J. Gagan, "Scaling Formal Organizations as an Element of Community Structure," *Social Forces,* 49 (March 1971): 477–482.

Harry, Joseph, "Family Localism and Social Participation," *American Journal of Sociology,* 75 (March 1970): 821–827. The author argues that marriage facilitates social participation, while the family inhibits it and encourages home localism.

Hausknecht, Murray, "The Blue-Collar Joiners," in Arthur B. Shostak and William

Gomberg, eds., *Blue-Collar World,* pp. 207–215. Englewood Cliffs, New Jersey, Prentice-Hall, 1964.

Havighurst, Robert J., "The Leisure Activities of the Middle Aged," *American Journal of Sociology,* 63 (September 1957): 152–162.

—— "Life beyond Family and Work," in E. W. Burgess, ed., *Aging in Western Societies.* Chicago, University of Chicago Press, 1960. The author describes the leisure activities and associations of the aged in Sweden, Denmark, Switzerland, West Germany, Holland, England, France, and the United States.

—— and Ruth Albrecht, *Older People.* New York, Longmans, Green, 1953. A study of the participation of older people in voluntary associations in "Prairie City," a midwestern town of 7000. The researchers found low rates of participation by the elderly, with even fewer of the aged serving as officers of associations.

Hay, Donald G., "A Scale for Measurement of Social Participation of Rural Households," *Rural Sociology,* 13 (September 1948): 285–294.

Hodge, R. W., and D. J. Treiman, "Social Participation and Social Status," *American Sociological Review,* 33 (October 1968): 722–740. Although data from a representative sample of adults in the Washington, D.C., area indicated that membership in voluntary associations was influenced as much by parents' level of participation as by the respondents' socio-economic status, other samples in the Detroit area did not produce similar results. The authors argue that ecological and structural variables have to be considered in explaining voluntary association membership rates in different areas.

Hollingshead, A. B., *Elmtown's Youth.* New York, John Wiley, 1949.

Hollingshead, August, "Trends in Social Stratification: A Case Study," *American Sociological Review,* 17 (December 1952): 679–686.

Homans, George C., *Social Behavior.* New York, Harcourt, Brace and World, 1961.

Hoyt, G. C., "The Life of the Retired in a Trailer Park," *American Journal of Sociology,* 59 (January 1954): 361–370. Hoyt found that the participation rate of the retired in the trailer park had dropped greatly after the individuals moved into the park from what it had been in their former homes.

Hughes, Everett Charrington, *French Canada in Transition.* Chicago, University of Chicago Press, 1943.

Hyman, Herbert H., and Charles R. Wright, "Trends in Voluntary Association Memberships of American Adults: Replication Based on Secondary Analysis of National Sample Surveys," *American Sociological Review,* 36 (April 1971): 191–206.

Jacoby, Arthur P., "Some Correlates of Instrumental and Expressive Orientation to Associational Membership," *Sociological Inquiry,* 35 (Spring 1965): 163–175.

—— "Personal Influence and Primary Relationships: Their Effect on Associational Membership," *The Sociological Quarterly,* 7 (Winter 1966): 76–84.

James, Bertha, "Clubs for Older People in an English Community," in Ernest W. Burgess, ed., *Aging in Western Societies,* pp. 443–445. Chicago, University of Chicago Press, 1960. A brief description of the clubs for older people sponsored by the Old People's Welfare Committee in a village on the outskirts of Greater London.

Johnson, Guion Griffis, "The Changing Status of the Southern Woman," in John C.

McKinney and Edgar T. Thompson, eds., *The South in Continuity and Change*, pp. 418-436. Durham, Duke University Press, 1965. Johnson briefly describes the organization activity of southern women, emphasizing the role of women's organizations in promoting social legislation and educating the public to the need for such legislation.

Journal of Social Issues, 16.4 (1960).

Knupfer, Genevieve, "Portrait of the Underdog," *Public Opinion Quarterly*, 11 (Spring 1947): 103-114.

Lantz, Herman, with the assistance of J. S. McCrary, *People of Coal Town*. New York, Columbia University Press, 1958. There is some limited information on voluntary associations in a small coal mining town.

Laumann, Edward, and David Sega, "Status Inconsistency and Ethnoreligious Group Membership as Determinants of Social Participation and Political Attitudes," *American Journal of Sociology*, 77 (July 1971): 36-62. The results of this analysis of data from the 1966 Detroit Area Study were inconclusive.

Lazerwitz, Bernard, "Membership in Voluntary Associations and Frequency of Church Attendance," *Journal for the Scientific Study of Religion*, 2 (Fall 1962): 74-84.

—— "National Data on Participation Rates among Residential Belts in the United States," *American Sociological Review*, 27 (October 1962): 691-696. Lazerwitz uses data from a Survey Research Center national survey to compare Protestant and Catholics living in different types of residential areas. There are tables on the organizational memberships held by both groups.

Lee, Frank F., "The Race Relations Pattern by Areas of Behavior in a Small New England Town," *American Sociological Review*, 19 (April 1954): 138-143. No hard data is presented in this somewhat ill-conceived study of Negro life and patterns of segregation in a Connecticut town. Lee's major conclusion is that segregation exists in jobs, housing, religious activity, and voluntary associations.

Lenski, Gerhard E., "Social Participation and Status Crystallization," *American Sociological Review*, 21 (August 1956): 458-464. An exploration of the hypothesis that persons whose status is poorly crystallized will tend to withdraw from or avoid social intercourse and this will be evidenced with respect to their participation in voluntary associations. The conclusions are based on data from 579 respondents in the Detroit area.

Leven, Helene, "Organizational Affiliation and Powerlessness: A Case Study of the Welfare Poor," *Social Problems*, 16 (Summer 1968): 18-32. A study of mothers receiving welfare in a northeastern city. The results indicate that members of a welfare client organization were more likely to have feelings of mastery and control than were nonmembers.

Lipset, Seymour Martin, *Political Man*. Garden City, New York, Doubleday, 1960.

—— and Reinhard Bendix, *Social Mobility in Industrial Society*. Berkeley and Los Angeles, University of California Press, 1959.

Lopata, Helen Znaniecki, "The Functions of Voluntary Associations in an Ethnic Community: 'Polonia'," in Ernest W. Burgess and Donald J. Bogue, eds., *Contributions to Urban Sociology*. Chicago, University of Chicago Press, 1964.

Lynd, Robert S., and Helen M. Lynd, *Middletown*. New York, Harcourt, Brace, 1929.
—— *Middletown in Transition*. New York, Harcourt, Brace, 1937.
Marx, Gary T., *Protest and Prejudice*. New York, Harper and Row, 1967. This report on five surveys of American urban Negro adults conducted by the NORC contains scattered information on the voluntary association memberships of the respondents.
Mather, William G., "Income and Social Participation," *American Sociological Review*, 6 (June 1941): 380-383.
Mayo, Selz C., and C. Paul Marsh, "Social Participation in the Rural Community," *American Journal of Sociology*, 57 (November 1951): 243-247.
Miller, Elizabeth W., compiler, *The Negro in America*. Second edition, revised. Cambridge, Harvard University Press, 1970. The best bibliography available on the topic.
Minnis, Mhyra S., "The Relationship of Women's Organizations to the Social Structure of a City." Unpublished PhD dissertation, Yale University, 1951.
—— "Cleavage in Women's Organizations: A Reflection of the Social Structure of a City," *American Sociological Review*, 18 (February 1953): 47-53.
Mogey, J. M., *Family and Neighborhood*. Oxford, Oxford University Press, 1956. In comparing an old working class area and a new "housing estate," Mogey found that residents of the new area were much readier to join an organization than those in the old area. The latter did not want to be identified with a particular group.
Morris, Raymond N., "British and American Research on Voluntary Associations: A Comparison," *Sociological Inquiry*, 35 (Spring 1965): 186-200.
Morris, Robert, and Camille Lambert, Jr., *New Roles for the Elderly*. Waltham, Massachusetts, Brandeis University Papers in Social Welfare (Number 10, June 1964; Issue Number 1 in the Harriet Lowenstein Goldstein Series "The Volunteer in America").
Myrdal, Gunnar, with the assistance of Richard Sterner and Arnold Rose, *An American Dilemma*. Two volumes. New York, Harper, 1944.
Nolan, Francena L., "Relationship of 'Status Groupings' to Differences in Participation," *Rural Sociology*, 21 (September-December 1956): 298-302.
Olsen, Marvin E., "Social and Political Participation of Blacks," *American Sociological Review*, 35 (August 1970): 682-697.
Orum, Anthony M., "A Reappraisal of the Social and Political Participation of Negroes," *American Journal of Sociology*, 72 (July 1966): 32-46.
Packard, Vance. *The Status Seekers*. New York, David McKay Company, 1959. A journalistic treatment of the role of club membership in status climbing and the maintenance of status lines.
Palisi, Bartolemeo J., "Ethnic Generation and Social Participation," *Sociological Inquiry*, 35 (Spring 1965); 219-226.
—— "Patterns of Social Participation in a Two-Generation Sample of Italian Americans," *The Sociological Quarterly*, 7 (Spring 1966): 167-178.
Phillips, Derek L., "Social Participation and Happiness," *American Journal of Sociology*, 72 (March 1967): 479-488.

—— "Social Class, Social Participation and Happiness: A Consideration of 'Interaction Opportunities' and 'Investment'," *Sociological Quarterly*, 10 (Winter 1969): 3-21.

Queen, Stuart A., "Social Participation in Relation to Social Disorganization," *American Sociological Review*, 14 (April 1949): 251-256.

Rainwater, Lee, R. Coleman, and G. Handel, *Workingman's Wife*. New York, Oceana Publications, 1959.

Ransford, H. Edward, "Isolation, Powerlessness, and Violence: A Study of Attitudes and Participation in the Watts Riot," *American Journal of Sociology*, 73 (March 1968): 581-591.

Reissman, Leonard, "Class, Leisure and Social Participation," *American Sociological Review*, 19 (February 1954): 76-84.

Richards, Catherine, "A Study of Class Differences in Women's Participation." Unpublished PhD dissertation, School of Applied Social Sciences, Western Reserve University, June 1958.

—— "A Study of Class Differences in Women's Participation," *Social Service Review*, 32 (September 1958): 307. An abstract of Richards' dissertation (see entry this bibliography).

Riley, Matilda White, *Aging and Society. Volume I. An Inventory of Research Findings*. New York, Russell Sage Foundation, 1968. A comprehensive summary of social science research on aging. A section on voluntary associations and the aged is included.

Rogers, David L., "Contrasts between Behavioral and Affective Involvement in Voluntary Associations: An Exploratory Analysis," *Rural Sociology*, 36 (September 1971): 340-358. Rogers' main concern is with methodology rather than with his data from interviews with Wisconsin farm operators.

Rose, Arnold, "The Adequacy of Women's Expectations for Adult Roles," *Social Forces*, 30 (October 1951): 69-77.

—— "Attitudinal Correlates of Social Participation," *Social Forces*, 37 (March 1959): 202-206.

—— "The Impact of Aging on Voluntary Associations," in Clark Tibbitts, ed., *Handbook of Social Gerontology: Societal Aspects of Aging*. Chicago, University of Chicago Press, 1960.

—— ed., "The Negro Protest," *The Annals of the American Academy of Political and Social Science*, 357 (January 1965).

Rose, Arnold, and Caroline Rose, *America Divided*. New York, Alfred A. Knopf, 1950.

Ross, Aileen D., "Control and Leadership in Women's Groups: An Analysis of Philanthropic Money Raising Activity," *Social Forces*, 37 (December 1958): 124-131.

Ross, J. C., and Raymond Wheeler, "Structural Sources of Threat to Negro Membership in Militant Voluntary Associations in a Southern City," *Social Forces*, 45 (June 1967): 583-586.

Rothe, M. L., and C. Newark, "Homemakers in Voluntary Community Activities," *Journal of Marriage and Family Living*, 20 (May 1958): 175-178.

Scott, John Finley, "The American College Sorority: Its Role in Class and Ethnic Endogamy," *American Sociological Review*, 30 (August 1965): 514-527.

Seals, Alvin M., and Jiri Kolaja, "A Study of Negro Voluntary Organizations in
Lexington, Kentucky," *Phylon*, 25 (Spring 1964): 27–32. The article is based
on Seals's more extensive work for his Master's thesis ("A Typology of Voluntary Associations: A Study of Negro Organizations in Lexington," University
of Kentucky, 1963).

Seeley, John R., Alexander R. Sim, and Elizabeth W. Loosley, *Crestwood Heights:
A Study of the Culture of Suburban Life*. New York, Basic Books, 1956.

Sexton, Patricia Cayo, *Spanish Harlem: Anatomy of Poverty*. New York, Harper
and Row, 1965.

Senior, Clarence, *The Puerto Ricans: Strangers — Then Neighbors*. Chicago, Quad-
rangle Books, 1961. Senior describes the Puerto Rican on his island and in the
United States in a book designed to dispel "myths" about the group. Senior
deals briefly with community organization. The study was sponsored by the
B'nai B'rith Anti-Defamation League.

Shibutani, Tamotsu, and Kian M. Kwan, *Ethnic Stratification*. New York, Macmillan, 1965. Textbook by two sociologists includes material on interest
groups and voluntary associations. It provides a general orientation to the role
of minorities in American life.

Slater, Carol, "Class Differences in Definition of Role and Membership in Voluntary
Associations among Urban Married Women," *American Journal of Sociology*,
65 (May 1960): 616–619.

Smith, David Horton, "A Psychological Model of Individual Participation in Formal
Voluntary Organizations: Applications to Some Chilean Data," *American
Journal of Sociology*, 72 (November 1966): 249–266.

Smith, Joel, and Horace D. Rawls, "Standardization of an Educational Variable:
The Need and Its Consequences," *Social Forces*, 44 (September 1965): 57–66.

Spectorsky, A. C., *The Exurbanites*. Philadelphia and New York, J. B. Lippincott,
1955. An impressionistic, biting, and detailed portrait of suburban life, in
particular of the men who work in New York City's communications industries. Voluntary activity is not by any means the focus, but Spectorsky does
include information on the memberships of the exurbanites.

Stein, Maurice R., *The Eclipse of Community*. Princeton, Princeton University Press,
1960. An interpretive essay which serves as a good guide to the community
studies literature.

Stodgill, R., "Leadership, Membership and Organization," *Psychological Bulletin*,
47 (January 1950): 1–14. The article reports on the position of a leader in
any group, with only scattered references to voluntary associations.

Sykes, Gresham M., "Social Mobility and Social Participation." Unpublished PhD
dissertation, Northwestern University, 1954.

Taietz, Philip, and Olaf F. Larson, "Social Participation and Old Age," *Rural Sociology*, 21 (September-December 1956): 229–238.

Teele, James E., "Measures of Social Participation," *Social Problems*, 10 (Summer
1962): 31–40.

—— "An Appraisal of Research on Social Participation," *The Sociological
Quarterly*, 6 (Summer 1965): 257–267. A very sketchy, general review of
some of the research dealing with the correlates of membership in voluntary
association and of other types of social participation.

Thrall, Robert M., and Robert C. Angell, "The Mapping of Community Organizations," *Sociometry,* 17 (August 1954): 244-271. A methodological article
dealing with the use of common memberships in organizations to measure the
relative height and spread of the organizations.

Tompkins, Jean Beattie, "Reference Groups and Status Values as Determinants of
Behavior: A Study of Women's Voluntary Association Behavior." Unpublished dissertation, State University of Iowa, 1955.

Treudly, Mary Bosworth, "Formal Organization and the Americanization Process
with Special Reference to the Greeks of Boston," *American Sociological Review,* 14 (February 1949): 44-53.

Uzzell, Odell, "Institution Membership and Class Levels," *Sociology and Social Research,* 37 (July-August 1953): 390-394. In studying YMCA members in a
southern city, Uzzell found that there was a disproportionate number of
upper and upper middle class members (in comparison to the total population
of the city).

Verwaller, Darrel J., "Social Mobility and Membership in Voluntary Associations,"
American Journal of Sociology, 75 (January 1970): 481-495. Vertical social
mobility was found to exert little or no effect on affiliations with voluntary
associations, suggesting that socialization processes operate to mediate the
individuals' response to the mobility.

Vidich, Arthur J., and Joseph Bensman, *Small Town in Mass Society: Class, Power
and Religion in a Rural Community.* Princeton, Princeton University Press,
1958.

Warner, W. Lloyd, *American Life: Dream and Reality.* Revised edition. Chicago,
University of Chicago Press, 1962 (first published 1953).

—— and Paul S. Lunt, *The Social Life of a Modern Community.* New Haven, Yale
University Press, 1941. This is one of the Yankee City volumes reporting on
extensive field research in Newburyport, Massachusetts. Data on the many
organizations in the city and on the activities of members of different classes
is presented in detail.

—— *The Status System of a Modern Community.* New Haven, Yale University
Press, 1942. This second volume in the Yankee City series contains an explanation of the way in which the researcher typed associations according to class.

Warner, William Lloyd, Marchia Meeker, and Kenneth Eells, *Social Class in America.*
Chicago, Science Research Associates, 1949. There is some material on the
characteristics of different types of associations and on the use of associational
memberships to determine an individual's status within a community in this
manual of procedure for measuring social status.

Warner, W. Lloyd, and Leo Srole, *The Social Systems of American Ethnic Groups.*
New Haven, Yale University Press, 1945. Great detail on the associational
activities in Yankee City's ethnic communities.

Warner, W. Lloyd, and associates, *Democracy in Jonesville.* New York, Harper,
1949.

Webber, Irving L., "The Organized Social Life of the Retired: Two Florida Communities," *American Journal of Sociology,* 59 (January 1954): 340-346. An
analysis of the organized life of 474 retired persons in Florida as manifested

in organization membership, attendance at secular meetings, and attendance at religious services. An area sample design was employed in the study which revealed relatively low rates of participation in nonchurch organizations.

West, James (pen name of Carl Withers), *Plainville, USA.* New York, Columbia University Press, 1945.

Whyte, William, Jr., *The Organization Man.* New York, Simon and Schuster, 1956. This journalistic account of the life of the young corporation executive includes a section on the "organization man at home" in the suburb of Park Forest, Illinois. Although informal socializing predominates, there are also formal organization activities.

Wilensky, Harold L., "Orderly Careers and Social Participation: The Impact of Work History on Social Integration in the Middle Mass," *American Sociological Review,* 26 (August 1961): 521–539. Data from a study of almost 700 white, urban, working and middle class males indicates that individuals with an orderly career have much stronger attachments to formal associations and to the community and have more stable, integrated, and wide ranging contacts with relatives, friends, and neighbors than do individuals without the experience of an orderly career.

—— "Life Cycle, Work Situation and Participation in Formal Associations" in Robert W. Kleemeier, ed., *Aging and Leisure: A Research Perspective into the Meaningful Use of Time.* New York, Oxford University Press, 1961.

Zonnevald, Robert J. van, "Clubs for Older People in the Netherlands," in Ernest W. Burgess, ed., *Aging in Western Societies,* pp. 446–447. Chicago, University of Chicago Press, 1960. A brief description of the activities of church-sponsored clubs for older people.

Chapter Seven   The Organizations

DIRECTORIES

The available statistics on voluntary organizations in the United States and elsewhere are highly unsatisfactory. No one knows with any real degree of accuracy how many or what kinds of voluntary associations there are. The United States Department of Commerce maintains some statistics, but it concentrates primarily on trade associations. In 1949 the Department published a directory of these trade associations and of selected groups of other types of organizations. The directory compiled by Jay Judkins covers 4000 organizations including 1800 manufacturers, distributors, and other trade associations; 500 associations of professional and semiprofessional members; 200 labor unions; 100 women's groups; 60 veterans' groups; and 100 sports and recreation associations. The organizations listed represent only a fraction of those in the country. The Department estimated that in 1949 there were 4000 Chambers of Commerce, 70,000 labor unions, 10,000 women's organizations, and 15,000 civic service groups, luncheon clubs, and similar organizations of business and professional men and women. It is impossible to judge the validity of these statistics however, since the Department does not indicate how they were compiled.

The *Encyclopedia of Associations,* edited by Frederick G. Ruffner, Jr., lists over 12,500 organizations, giving selected information on the officers, the number of members, staff, types of activities, and publications of each. However, the *Encyclopedia* is of limited value to social scientists since it includes trade associations, commodity exchanges, and government agencies. Moreover, it is in no sense a systematic survey of the organization scene. It appears to be based on material submitted by associations which learn of the *Encyclopedia.* Periodically, additional volumes listing new associations are published. According to the editor, these volumes will list organizations which are "new" in the sense of having been recently formed, as well as those which are simply "new" to the editor, not having come to their attention previously.

A directory of nongovernment organizations interested in international relations, *United States Citizens in World Affairs,* has been compiled by Katherine Garrigue. The listing of 434 organizations is far from complete, but some useful information is given about the associations included. The following items are listed for each organization in the directory: address, date of founding, president, number of staff members, objectives, activities, membership eligibility requirements, number of members, dues, how the organization is financed, current publications, and incorporation status. One can also find some similar date for the more than 1000 organizations listed in the *World Almanac.*

Youth organizations and "Citizen organizations" concerned with the "civic training of youth" are uncritically described in two publications that date from the 1930s. Together, *Organizations for Youth* by Elizabeth Pendry and Hugh Hartshorn and *Citizens Organizations and the Civic Training of Youth* by Bessie Pierce provide a rough guide to a portion of the organization scene at the time. Jesse Steiner's *Americans at Play,* also published in the 1930s, includes statistics on memberships and chapters on a variety of recreational associations, both rural and urban, as well as an analysis of trends in leisure organizations.

STUDIES OF INDIVIDUAL ORGANIZATIONS

There are a number of works which focus on a single organization or type of organization. David Sills's book on the National Foundation for Infantile Paralysis, *The Volunteers,* is probably the most outstanding of these. In this case study, Sills concentrates on the local members, exploring their activities in the organization, their motivation and recruitment, the rewards they experience from participation, and their perceptions of the foundation, which is the largest voluntary health organization in the United States.

Sills's book is sophisticated in theory and method. In order to achieve "replicability and explicitness," simultaneous surveys were carried out independently by the Bureau of Applied Social Research of Columbia University and the American Institute of Public Opinion. As Sills describes the work, "The Institute's research consisted of a nationwide survey of the American public and a survey of Foundation Volunteers in eighty-five counties throughout the United States while that of the Bureau took the form of one survey of the general public in four cities and another of Foundation volunteers in thirty-seven counties" (p. 15). Much of the statistical and descriptive data are presented in the text to allow the reader to judge the validity of the conclusions drawn from the findings.

Sills makes extensive use of organization theory in his work, which he describes as an "institutional analysis." Although he offers considerable descriptive material concerning the foundation's history and activities, his major concern is with the relationships between the characteristics of the organization's members and the organization's internal structure and success in achieving its goals. In the last chapter, Sills deals with the future of the foundation now that it has achieved its original goals, and with the general problem of goal succession in organizations. He attempts to draw conclusions about the process of adaptation by comparing the successful adjustment of the foundation to the adaptation of other organizations, such as the Young Men's Christian Association, the Women's Christian Temperance Union, the American National Red Cross, and the Townsend movement. On the basis of his own investigations and those of others in studying different organizations, Sills suggests that "structural constraints in the organization" and "acceptance on the part of the community" may be crucial variables in determining whether goal succession (the adoption of new goals) or goal displacement (the process in which the means become ends having value in themselves) occurs within an association (p. 198).

The YMCA and the Red Cross, like the National Foundation, were able to adapt successfully to a changing environment. In each case, the organizations were faced with having their original goals rendered irrelevant by historical changes (such as the entrance of the government into disaster relief), and in each the organizations responded by redefining their objectives.

At least two studies of the YMCA's adaptation are available, as well as a third by Seth Arsenian and Arthur Blumberg which deals with the organization after its successful adaptation. In *The Y.M.C.A. and Social Need* Owen Pence describes the increasing secularization of the YMCA in response to the increasing secularization of society. The YMCA gradually deemphasized its original goal of improving the spiritual and moral condition of young men and stressed recreational and social goals instead. Mayer N. Zald and Patricia Denton's more recent article (1963) analyzes the effect of various organization features of the YMCA on its adaptability. Partly because of such structural characteristics the YMCA was able to transform itself from an evangelical, male, Christian association to a secular organization open to all individuals regardless of age, sex, or religion. As Zald and Denton explain: "The organization's broadly stated goals and unrestricted clientele encourage a wide diversification of programs and target populations. Federated structure leads to decentralized decision making, and to control by local elites. Since YMCA professionals do not have a well-defined ideology, and since the organization is linked to an enrollment economy, the organization is highly responsive to the needs of its relatively integrated and typically middle-class clientele" (*Administrative Science Quarterly*, 8:214).

Neither the Women's Christian Temperance Union nor the Townsend organization was able to adapt successfully, and both are presently on the decline. In an excellent study of the WCTU, based on an analysis of its literature and directories and interviews with forty-six local and national leaders, Joseph Gusfield argues that the organization reacted to the "change in American drinking habits and the increased permissiveness of drinking norms" by shifting its membership while retaining its original goal of total abstinence. When the WCTU was founded, it represented a humanitarian effort on the part of the "socially-dominant" upper middle class to reform and help the lower classes, and its emphasis was not so much on drinking per se, but on the drinking problems of the poor and working classes. Temperance was viewed by the members as a means of assimilating the lower classes and immigrants into the middle class Protestant culture. At present, with temperance no longer a norm of the dominant middle class, the WCTU, by clinging to its goal, has lost prestige and middle class support. The group now draws its members from the lower middle and lower classes, and has adopted a posture of moral indignation directed at the middle class drinker. Gusfield observes: "The data suggest that temperance norms have filtered down to lower socioeconomic groups. The moral indignation of the movement is explainable by the resentment engendered by the defection of the upper middle class. These are no longer available as the models with which the religiously oriented in America can identify. The quality of 'moralizing' has ceased to be respectable . . . Today the WCTU is an organization in retreat. Contrary to the expectations of theories of institutionalization, the movement has not acted to preserve organizational values at the expense of past doctrine. In adhering to less popular positions, it has played the role of the sect and widened the gap between WCTU membership and middle class respectability" (*American Journal of Sociology*, 61:232). In a later article Gusfield described the conflict of generations within the WCTU, pinpointing the mechanisms by which the older generation has managed to retain its hold on policy determination (*Social Forces*, 35:323–330). He also deals with the organization's attempt to adapt to the changing environment by recruiting new members and leaders. So far, the adaptive process has been slow and not very successful.

The Townsend organization as analyzed by Sheldon Messinger presents a contrast to the WCTU, since it adapted by shifting its emphasis from the "impl mentation of the values of the organization is taken to represent . . . to maintaining the organizational structure as such" even though this entails a "loss of the organization's central mission" (*American Sociological Review*, 20:10). When the end of the depression and the institution of social security took the urgency from the Townsend organization's original goal of national pensions for the aged, the leaders reacted to the resulting loss of membership and financial resources by turning to the marketing of products for the aged and the creation of a recreational program to attract and retain members. However, this shift in goals did not succeed, and the organization continued to fade.

While goal succession was not a successful tactic for the WCTU, a recent study by Alvin J. Schmidt and Nicholas Babchuk suggests that it has worked for fraternal associations such as the Elks and the Eagles (in Smith et al., *Voluntary Action*). Unlike the majority of fraternal orders, which have continued to cling to outdated rituals and steadily lost membership, the Elks and Eagles have dropped the old ceremonies and reoriented their programs toward providing fun and entertainment in a club atmosphere. As a result of their adaptation, the two orders have thrived in the midst of a general "depression" for fraternal associations.

The League of Women Voters has been the subject of a detailed investigation by the Survey Research Center of the University of Michigan. The results of the study, which was undertaken at the organization's request, are reported in five volumes published in the late fifties, each dealing with a different phase of the research. The first report, entitled "The League Member Talks about the League," covers such topics as member activity; member satisfaction and dissatisfaction with

League activity and suggestions for change; member understanding of the League's purpose and procedure; and member attitudes and experiences in regard to fund raising. The report is based on interviews with a sample of 227 women in forty-four Leagues across the country who were chosen to be representative of the entire League membership.

The second report in the series concerns "Community Attitudes toward the League." To obtain the data, the researchers interviewed a sample of 509 women chosen to be representative of urban females between the ages of 25 and 64, this being the group from which the League largely draws its members. The report deals primarily with the image of the League and its members in communities which have League chapters, and the image among women whose husbands are white collar workers are compared with those among women whose husbands hold blue collar jobs.

In the third report, problems of membership, such as the difficulty the League has in attracting members from blue collar families and the inactivity of some members, are analyzed. This report draws on data from the sample of 509 urban women and from another sample of League members. Both the fourth and fifth reports are devoted to the internal operation of the League and are based on the results of a questionnaire which was mailed to representative members and to all chapter presidents and board members. In the fourth, communication within the League chapters, the relations between the leaders and members, and the amount and character of member participation are discussed. The fifth deals with the effectiveness of the local chapters. The Survey Research Center team tried to measure the effectiveness (defined for their purpose as the degree to which a chapter achieves the goals it sets for itself) of the chapters and to isolate the factors which differentiate effective from ineffective Leagues.

There are, in addition to the Michigan work, a few other articles on the League. A. S. Tannenbaum used a probability sample of League chapters to test various hypotheses concerning the relationship between the control structure of an organization and the organization's effectiveness. He found that the effectiveness of individual League chapters appeared to increase as rank and file influence and control of policy increased which may be understandable in view of the League's commitment to democratic norms. However, despite the League's democratic ideology, leaders in the average local League tended to exercise more control than the members did as a group. The Leagues differed only in the degree of "oligarchy" they exhibited; they were never without some "oligarchy" (*American Journal of Sociology*, 67:44-45).

James G. March utilized data from questionnaires returned by a small group of League members in an eastern suburban town to explore the relationship between group norms and the active minority. In general he found that the more active members tended to conform more to group norms than did the less active members (*American Sociological Review*, 19:740).

Two League members, Betsy Knapp and Mary Guyol, have described its activities, emphasizing the role of the League in political education, in an article written for the *Journal of Social Issues* (16.1:57-65). Finally, a chapter on the League employing the survey research material that appears in the University of Michigan report is contained in Rensis Likert's *New Patterns of Management*.

John R. Seeley and his associates in Community Surveys have produced an excellent book on the *Community Chest,* but the emphasis is primarily on fund raising with the research designed as a case study in philanthropy. However, there is material on volunteers scattered throughout the text, particularly in the section on manpower. Seeley and his staff lived in Indianapolis, the location of their research, and largely employed the participant observer technique.

While philanthropy is not our immediate concern here, the topic is pertinent in a discussion of voluntary associations since many of them depend on contributions for support. There are several general accounts of philanthropy such as F. Emerson Andrews' *Philanthropic Giving* and Edward C. Jenkins' *Philanthropy in America. American Philanthropy* by Robert H. Bremner is a useful short history. Bremner describes the major trends in American philanthropy and relates them to the main developments in American social history. He surveys voluntary activity in the fields of charity, religion, education, humanitarian reform, social service, war relief, and foreign aid, and discusses representative donors of money and services; promoters of moral and social reform; and various institutions and associations founded to conduct philanthropic enterprises.

Several organizations have sponsored histories or organization "biographies." These are often published privately or distributed to a limited audience, and can best be obtained by writing directly to the organizations. Those that we have seen appear to be useful to the social scientist as primary sources along with the rest of the vast outflow of written material produced by organizations, primarily for their own members.

Some controversial organizations such as the American Legion have been the subject of a polemical literature. For example, the Legion is praised by Raymond Moley, Jr., in his account of *The American Legion Story* and criticized by William Gellerman in his somewhat more scholarly work, *The American Legion as Educator.*

STUDIES OF ORGANIZATION TYPES

There are a number of studies that treat a particular type of organization as opposed to a single association. For instance, Noel Gist has written a detailed monograph on American secret societies. Although Gist employs sociological and anthropological concepts in his analysis, he concentrates on describing the rituals and activities of fraternal societies and tends to deal more with their formal structural characteristics than with their informal organization. Most of his data are drawn from interviews with officers of fraternal orders, from a variety of secondary sources, and from the literature published by the organizations. Gist views the societies as conservative institutions and writes: "Secret societies like other social institutions usually emphasize the conventional moral and ethical values of the larger social order of which they are a part. They become bulwarks of the status quo, conservers of traditional morality, transmitters of existing social values" (*Secret Societies*, p. 142). He also argues that one of the main objectives of the fraternities is the provision of security and protection in the form of insurance, mutual assistance funds, homes for the aged, and so on. Fraternities fill in the gaps left by the weakening of the family in modern society. "As a form of institutionalized cooperation, the fraternal organizations have arisen to meet the exigencies and hazards of life in a social world dominated by the impersonal forces of industrialism and commercialism" (p. 142).

In addition to his monograph, Gist has written a general article on "Fraternal Societies" which appears paired with Herbert Goldhamer's discussion of "Social Clubs" in the *Development of Collective Enterprise*, a collection of essays. On the basis of data from his study of secret societies and other material on nonsecret fraternal orders, Gist contends that "organized fraternalism with its emphasis on mutual aid and good will" is a "logical counterpart of the development of liberalism and democracy as a philosophic doctrine and way of life" (p. 72). As he sees it, the fraternal system developed in a period when the government acted primarily as a regulatory rather than a service institution, when there were fewer public sources of commercial and community recreation, and when the "channels for social intercourse" were narrower than today. In their structure and activities, fraternal organizations are essentially "collectivist" in character, although they reject the ideologies of collectivism and view themselves as adherents of the American free enterprise system (p. 80).

The Goldhamer section on "Social Clubs" draws on several sources including the author's own study of 3000 Chicago organizations and of the organization affiliations of 5000 residents. Goldhamer argues that the increase in leisure time available to some in modern society has given rise to a variety of institutions providing recreational activities, including commercial facilities and social clubs. The clubs are able to hold their own in the competition for a clientele because they provide "emotional sustenance" through the development of close personal relationships and social solidarity. Since Goldhamer, like Gist, accepts the Wirth thesis (see Chapter One), he views social clubs as "replacements" for the family, kinship, and neighborhood groups which were the source of solidarity and sustenance prior to urbanization. Social clubs also can provide social prestige, in some cases as a result of their exclusiveness, and can confer other social and economic advantages on members. Goldhamer sees the persistence of the club form despite the short lives of many individual clubs as proof that social clubs are vital institutions performing necessary functions in the modern social system.

"Fraternal Orders," one type of social club, are discussed by Frank Hankins in the first edition of the *Encyclopedia of the Social Sciences,* and are also treated, together with other types of lodges and clubs, in *Fifty Million Brothers* by Charles W. Ferguson. While Ferguson's work is written in the style of tabloid journalism, it does contain some useful information and has been cited in the social science literature. Ferguson sees clubs and lodges as "refuges from loneliness," explaining that: "From the first America has lacked a stirring nationalism — even a sense of nationality. Our heterogeneous population, our diverse and often warring interests, the very acreage of our property, our inability to feel that we are *personally* a nation — these salient characteristics of the country have made our clubs and secret orders not only plausible but imperative. The individualism one hears so much about today has been a group *individualism.* The American has not fixed his loyalties upon the state with anything approaching steady fidelity, nor has he been willing to lose his identity in the mass. His allegiance has been and remains essentially tribal" (p. 12; Ferguson's italics).

A more scholarly treatment of fraternal organizations, with special reference to ethnic or national groups, is provided by Yaroslav Chyz, who argues that "The influence of fraternal organizations reaches far beyond their actual membership. Through organizational contacts and through their press they have become leading centers of group life among many Americans of foreign origin. They publish books, subsidize historical and social research, and introduce the immigrant and his family to American life. All this is provided in addition to the material support and care which for many decades was the only 'social security' of the worker" (Brown and Roucek, *One America*, p. 399). The mutual aid functions of fraternal nationality groups are also discussed in *A Social Study of Pittsburgh* by Philip Klein and others which includes some general material on fraternal groups in the Pittsburgh area as well. The authors hypothesize that nationality groups flourish as long as "American" native organizations exclude "ethnics." When interchange between native and ethnic is blocked because of discrimination, ignorance, or some other factor, there is a tendency for nationality organizations to gain strength as compensatory devices that allow an escape from American life or as a means of exercising group pressures.

An overview of the growth and present decline of fraternal associations is provided by Alvin J. Schmidt and Nicholas Babchuk in their paper comparing those organizations that have successfully adapted to the changing social system to those that have failed (in Smith et al., *Voluntary Action*). Schmidt and Babchuk attribute the growth of lodges in the nineteenth and early twentieth centuries to their providing social integration, social prestige and status, "benevolency" in the form of charity, mutual aid, or insurance, and a form of religion for many Americans. The establishment of government and private insurance and the institution of other social service programs, urbanization, secularization, and the anonymity of contemporary life have all contributed to creating an environment in which the fraternal orders are no longer needed or have lost their capability of serving the functions they filled in the past. Groups like the Masons were once able to adapt to changes in society, but they seem unable to do so now, and are consequently losing members.

Women's organizations, which include social clubs, nationality groups, and the auxiliaries of fraternal organizations, have been analyzed in general terms by Gladys Meyerand in the early *Encyclopedia of the Social Sciences,* and in a dissertation by Mhyra Minnis (Yale, 1951) who points out that women's organizations are largely a modern phenomenon, although there are some church-connected women's groups which date from the Middle Ages. In the United States, most of the national women's organizations were founded between 1870 and 1900. However, since 1900 many of the groups have altered their goals and activities, and some new organizations, primarily of the general "service" or "social" type have also been founded.

Minnis examined the entire spectrum of women's organizations in the city of New Haven, Connecticut, focusing on the differentiation of women's clubs along ethnic, racial, religious, and class lines. She also discusses the literature of voluntarism, the internal functioning of voluntary organizations, and the meaning these organizations have for their members. Although she found that the New Haven women in her sample tended to view their organizations as service groups, Minnis felt that the groups were really social in character. She asserts that the basic purpose of the organizations is the "human need for group associations and the sharing of common experiences," and that the modern woman finds an outlet for some of her frustrations in organization activity. Minnis explains that: "The need to be on the center of stage sometime in her life, the need to be taken seriously, the desire to use talents developed in youth and now lying fallow, a strong wish to aid in a world of displacement and conflict, and a need of outlet for energies untapped at middle age — all these factors may make participation in a women's organization seem to be a stabilizing solution" (p. 20).

The women's service organization, specifically the hospital board, has been studied by Joan Moore. When she compared upper and middle class boards, she found that despite several indications of exclusiveness in upper class boards (such as restrictions on the size of the board, extremely cautious admissions procedures, and a high degree of cohesiveness and integration), the key to admission was performance. Moreover, achievement was the basis for ranking board members as well as the basis of admission. In contrast, the middle class boards were not achievement or work oriented. Moore believes differences might have been due to the upper class woman's greater commitment to her organization.

While Negro organizations fall within the various categories — women's organizations, fraternal associations, and so on — that we have already discussed, they can also be regarded as a particular type of organization. Surprisingly, there has not been much written about them aside from the journalistic accounts in the mass media. The best available guide to the literature on Negro voluntary associations (and on all other phases of Negro life in the United States) is the bibliography compiled by Elizabeth W. Miller for the American Academy of Arts and Sciences as part of the preparation for the publication of two issues of the Academy's journal *Daedalus* on the Negro in America. (The bibliography, entitled *The Negro in America,* has been separately published.) The second of the two issues, which were published in the fall of 1965 and the winter of 1966, contains a discussion of "The Civil Rights Movement: Momentum and Organization," by the black psychologist Kenneth Clark. He centers his attention on the National Association for the Advancement of Colored People, the National Urban League, the Congress of Racial Equality, the Southern Christian Leadership Conference founded by Martin Luther King, and the Student Nonviolent Coordinating Committee. Clark analyzes the characteristics, leadership, tactics, and effectiveness of the various groups in general terms. He notes that the civil rights organizations are now experiencing the kinds of problems that plague most organizations as they become more structured: "red tape, bureaucracy, hierarchical discipline restricting spontaneous and imaginative experimentation, fear of change and, therefore, of growth . . . major decisions must now reflect painstaking difficult staff work based on fact-finding intelligence, continuing critical analysis of data and strategies. Institutions tend to repress the rebel and to elevate the businessman-diplomat, yet the civil rights movement is full of rebels and its goal is independence" (p. 264). In these circumstances Clark believes that the civil rights movement may depend on sustaining such "respectable" groups as the NAACP while stimulating them to adopt new programs and "encouraging the fluid realignment of younger, more restless forces" who will provide the momentum for change.

An earlier essay on "National Organizations in the Field of Race Relations," written by Charles S. Johnson, complements Clark's survey. There are also book-length treatments of the NAACP, SNCC, and the Black Muslims, a group falling somewhere between a church and a voluntary association. Charles Flint Kellogg's account of the *NAACP* deals with the years 1909 (the founding date) to 1920. A second volume is scheduled for publication. Kellogg provides detail on the founding; the policies and internal organization of the NAACP; conflicts within the group; and the growth in chapter units and membership of the association. The book contains a thorough bibliography of works devoted to the NAACP and related material. The Kellogg volume is written from a historical rather than a sociological perspective, and Kellogg makes no attempt to test hypotheses or derive them from his data. Howard Zinn's admiring treatment of the "new abolitionists" in *SNCC* describes that organization in its early, nonviolent days. Zinn's dated 1964 book is valuable now mainly as a historical document. C. Eric Lincoln's *The Black Muslims in America* was first published in 1961, but it is a more perceptive, analytical work than Zinn's and is still useful for gaining an understanding of the movement led by Elijah Mohammed.

Finally, a 1965 issue of the *Annals of the American Academy of Political and Social Science* edited by Arnold Rose, which is devoted to "The Negro Protest" contains essays on the work of the NAACP, the Urban League, the Southern Regional Council, and the Congress of Racial Equality, as well as a general essay on "The Changing Character of the Negro Protest." Except for the last article, which was written by the sociologist James H. Laue, each of the selections was written by a top official of the organization under consideration. For example, the description of the Urban League's activities was authored by Whitney Young, the executive director, and a leading figure in the civil rights movement.

Although professional associations are in some ways similar to labor unions and trade associations, they do exhibit features of the voluntary associations. Numerous professional associations have carried out self-studies and have commissioned organization histories. Generally, reports on these are published in the respective professional journals.

The literature in political science on pressure politics also contains studies of many of these groups, with the emphasis, as might be expected, on the organization's political activities. For example, the American Medical Association was examined in a pioneering study by Oliver Garceau, *The Political Life of the American Medical Association,* and in the 1960s by the editors of the *Yale Law Journal* (in Glaser and Sills, *Government of Associations*). Semipolitical organizations which engage in pressure activities have also been examined, ranging from the John Birch Society (in a book of that title by J. Allen Broyles) on the right to the National Committee for a Sane Nuclear Policy on the left. Homer A. Jack has described the first nine years of Sane's life and outlined the problems faced by the organization (in Robertson, *Voluntary Associations*). It is significant that Sane's policy is made by a largely nonelective board despite the commitment of many of its members to democratic ideology and their demands for the democratization of the organization. Sane is typical of the organization process, too, in that it was originally conceived as a temporary group, but its life was extended and new goals adopted after the initial goal of obtaining a nuclear test-ban treaty was realized.

If organizations are classified according to their social purpose, one type that stands out is the social movement. Wendell King, the author of *Social Movements in the United States,* defines them as group ventures "extending beyond a local community or a single event and involving a systematic effort to inaugurate changes in thought, behavior and social relationships." As such, social movements combine political, religious, and voluntary association activity and encompass many of the other types of groups we have previously discussed. King's brief study covers such topics as the nature of the movements, their "careers," growth, purposes, and consequences, and utilizes illustrations drawn in the main from the histories of the Grange, the Christian Science religion, and the Ku Klux Klan. King also makes occasional references to the birth control movement which was founded by Margaret Sanger and is now centered in the Planned Parenthood Federation of America. Planned Parenthood has been studied more closely by Martin Rein who gives particular emphasis to the movement's adaptation to changing social values (in this case values concerning contraception and ideal family size) and to the problems it experienced as a result of having a charismatic leader (Sanger) uninterested in administration (in Glaser and Sills, *Government of Associations*).

The internal relations of three social movements with reference to conflict between the majority or dominant and the minority group activists is treated in a paper by Gary Marx and Michael Unseem in the *Journal of Social Issues,* 27:81:104. Although they deal specifically with the American civil rights movement, the abolitionists, and the movement to outlaw untouchability in India, they believe the recurring conflict over ideology, internal organization, and cultural differences observed in the three is typical of other movements.

THE "HOW-TO" LITERATURE FOR VOLUNTEERS

Numerous books, articles, and pamphlets have been written for the volunteer, the prospective volunteer, the leaders of voluntary associations, and those who recruit and train volunteers. Although most of this literature consists of practical advice to the individual telling him how to find and join organizations which will serve his needs, how to participate effectively, how to run a committee, and the like, a good deal of incidental information about the organizations themselves is often included. Unfortunately, since the writings are for laymen and are often by journalists rather than academics, the descriptive material is unsystematically presented (and, presumably, gathered) and usually no sources are cited for the data.

One of the best of the "how-to" books is *The Volunteer Community* by Eva Schindler-Rainman and Ronald Lippitt which was published in 1971 by the Center for a Voluntary Society of the National Training Laboratory Institute for Applied Behavioral Science. Both of the authors have doctorates and have also had considerable experience in working with organizations. Their book is addressed to organizers, consultants, the staffs of agencies using volunteers, and professors of graduate students in such professional fields as education, social work, public health, and public administration. There are chapters on the relationship between democracy, voluntarism, and personal growth and development; on the social trends that affect voluntarism; on the needs and opportunities for volunteers and new trends in the use of volunteers; on the motivation of the volunteer; on the recruitment and training of volunteers and leader-trainers; and finally a "case study of the future" describing a community in which volunteers are fully utilized for the benefit of the community and the individual. *The Volunteer Community* also contains an extensive annotated bibliography listing some of the general literature in the field and a number of works dealing with volunteer work in various settings.

In addition to *The Volunteer Community* there are several other books concerned with the general subject of volunteering. *The Citizen Volunteer* edited by Nathan Cohen, *Volunteers Today: Finding, Training and Working with Them* by Harriet Naylor, *Volunteer Training and Development: A Manual for Community Groups* by Anne K. Stenzel and Helen M. Feeney, *A Guide to Volunteer Services* by Anne K. David, and *Leadership in Voluntary Enterprise* edited by Charles Merrifield are typical examples of this genre. Other books deal with a single type of organization or volunteer work in a particular setting. For example, *Helping Hands* by Gayle Janowitz is concerned with volunteer work in education, while Henry Steeger's *You Can Remake America* focuses on volunteer work in the social services with special reference to organizations working in race relations.

Many other how-to books are aimed at specialized audiences. *The Next Step* edited by Martha S. White examines part-time voluntary opportunities for educated women in the Greater Boston area, although it contains chapters of general advice to volunteers everywhere. Barbara Dolliver's *The Intelligent Woman's Guide to Successful Organization and Club Work* is restricted to women. There are a number of books, such as Julietta K. Arthur's *Retire to Action,* George Gleason's *Horizons for Older People,* and Joseph Buckley's *The Retirement Handbook,* which focus on voluntary opportunities for the elderly, especially those who have retired and have considerable free time.

Since the how-to literature is not scholarly in character, we chose not to spend the extraordinary amount of time it would take to compile a comprehensive bibliography of the material. Much of it occurs in popular magazines, local newspapers, and the publications of various organizations and is not readily accessible. However, we did wish to call the reader's attention to the existence of this literature. We believe it constitutes a valuable, and as yet largely untouched, primary source for the social scientist interested in voluntarism.

BIBLIOGRAPHY

Akers, Ronald, and Frederick L. Campbell, "Size and Administrative Component in Occupational Associations," *Pacific Sociological Review,* 13 (Fall 1970): 241–251. Data from a study of voluntary occupational associations indicate a positive relationship between staff and membership size, but a negative association between the relative size of the staff and the membership size.

Anderson, Ellen, *Guide to Women's Organizations.* Washington, D.C., Public Affairs Press, 1950. A fairly complete list of women's organizations as of 1950.

Andrews, F. Emerson, *Philanthropic Giving.* New York, Russell Sage Foundation, 1950. The book is largely aimed at the potential philanthropist. Emerson provides detailed information on the tax laws relating to philanthropy and on the legal technicalities of foundations and trusts. He also includes some material in the history of giving, on government expansion into welfare services, on fund raising and expenditures in voluntary associations, and on the activities of voluntary associations in such fields as recreation, health, and education.

Arsenian, Seth, and Arthur Blumberg, "A Deeper Look at Volunteers," *Adult Leadership,* 9 (June 1960): 41, 65–66. A brief report on the authors' study of YMCA volunteers.

—— "Volunteers in the Y.M.C.A.," in William A. Glaser and David L. Sills, eds., *The Government of Associations,* Totowa, New Jersey, The Bedminster Press, 1966. Report on the results of a small survey of volunteers in the YMCA dealing with age, sex, religious affiliation, formal education, occupation, community activities, length of residence in the community, church activity, previous YMCA experience, and family voluntary activity as well as with some aspects of the volunteers' motivation.

Arthur, Julietta K., *Retire to Action*. Nashville, Tennessee, Abingdon Press, 1969.

Baltzell, E. Digby, *The Protestant Establishment*. New York, Random House, 1964. This critical study of the WASP includes a chapter on "The Club" as well as material on college fraternities and other organizations of this American "elite."

Birnbaum, Max, "Adult Education in General Voluntary Organizations," in Malcolm Knowles, ed., *Handbook of Adult Education in the United States*, pp. 378-392. Chicago, Adult Education Association, 1960.

Bohrnstedt, George W., "Social Mobility Aspiration and Fraternity Membership," *Sociological Quarterly*, 10 (Winter 1969): 42-52.

Bremner, Robert H., *American Philanthropy*. Chicago, University of Chicago Press, 1960.

Broyles, J. Allen, *The John Birch Society: Anatomy of a Protest*. Boston, Beacon Press, 1964. A study of the right-wing political organization which was originally a doctoral dissertation. Broyles conducted a series of interviews with leaders, members, and opponents of the society in 1962.

Buckley, Joseph C., *The Retirement Handbook*. Second revised and enlarged edition. New York, Harper and Brothers, 1962.

Carter, Richard, *The Gentle Legions*. Garden City, New York, Doubleday, 1961. A history of the major voluntary health organizations in the United States.

Chyz, Yaroslav J., "Fraternal Organizations of Nationality Groups," in Francis J. Brown and Joseph Slabey Roucek, eds., *One America*. New York, Prentice-Hall, 1946.

Clark, Kenneth B., "The Civil Rights Movement: Momentum and Organization," *Daedalus*, 95 (Winter 1966): 239-267.

Cohen, Nathan, ed., *The Citizen Volunteer*. New York, Harper, 1950. A collection of readings aimed at the prospective volunteer. Most of the articles are journalistic in character, although there are a few scholarly contributions.

David, Anne, *A Guide to Volunteer Services*. New York, Cornerstone Library, 1970. The role of the "volunteer in a changing world" and the programs of various voluntary organizations are described for the prospective volunteer.

Dewing, Rolland, "The National Education Association and Desegregation," *Phylon*, 30 (Summer 1969): 109-124. Historical account of the conflict within the association and the development of the association's policy in regard to desegregation.

Dolliver, Barbara, *The Intelligent Woman's Guide to Successful Organization and Club Work*. Philadelphia, Chilton, 1962.

Dulles, Foster Rhea, *The American Red Cross*. New York, Harper and Brothers, 1950. The formation, activities, and changes in this organization are described and analyzed in detail in this history. David Sills (see entry in this bibliography) relies completely on this book in his analysis of the Red Cross.

Feldman, Ronald A., "Interrelationships among Three Bases of Group Integration," *Sociometry*, 31 (March 1968): 30-46. A comparison of functional, interpersonal, and normative integration in children's groups. The bases of group integration appear to be related to sex composition, social milieu, and group size.

Ferguson, Charles W., *Fifty Million Brothers.* New York, Farrar and Rinehart, 1937.

Garceau, Oliver, *The Political Life of the American Medical Association.* Cambridge, Harvard University Press, 1941.

Garrigue, Katherine C., *United States Citizens in World Affairs.* New York, Foreign Policy Association, 1953. A directory listing 434 nongovernment organizations.

Gellerman, William, *The American Legion as Educator.* New York, Columbia University Teachers College, 1938.

Gerson, Walter M., "The College Sorority as a Social System," *Sociology and Social Research,* 53 (April 1969): 385-394. An analysis in terms of Parsonian categories of functional requisites.

Gist, Noel P., *Secret Societies: A Cultural Study of Fraternalism in the United States,* The University of Missouri Studies, 15 (October 1, 1940).

—— "Fraternal Societies," in Seba Eldrige and associates, *Development of Collective Enterprise.* Lawrence, University of Kansas Press, 1943.

Gleason, George, *Horizons for Older People.* New York, Macmillan, 1956. A book of advice which includes a fairly thorough bibliography and an appendix listing "selected resources for group leaders" such as government agencies, welfare councils, university-run programs, and church offices.

Goldhamer, Herbert, "Social Clubs," in Seba Eldridge and associates, *Development of Collective Enterprise.* Lawrence, University of Kansas Press, 1943.

Gusfield, Joseph R., "Social Structure and Moral Reform: A Study of the Women's Christian Temperance Union," *American Journal of Sociology,* 61 (November 1955): 221-232.

—— "The Problem of Generations in an Organizational Structure," *Social Forces,* 35 (May 1957): 323-330.

Hage, Jerald, "Organizational Structure and Communications." Paper delivered at the 65th annual meeting of the American Sociological Association, September 1970. A number of hypotheses concerning the relationship between communication and organization structure were tested in a study of sixteen health and welfare organizations.

Hall, Richard, J. Eugene Haas, and Norman J. Johnson, "Organizational Size, Complexity, and Formalization," *American Sociological Review,* 32 (December 1967): 903-912. A study of seventy-five organizations showed little relationship between size and structural characteristics.

Hall, Richard H., and Charles R. Tittle, "A Note on Bureaucracy and its 'Correlates'," *American Journal of Sociology,* 72 (November 1966): 267-272. The authors have ranked twenty-five organizations according to their degree of bureaucratization, and explored the associations between bureaucratization and the organization's relative concern with ideas or with objects.

Hankins, Frank H., "Fraternal Orders," in Edwin R. A. Seligman and Alvin Johnson, eds., *The Encyclopedia of the Social Sciences.* New York, Macmillan, 1935. Hankins gives some useful historical information on fraternal orders and discusses the contemporary growth and functions of the groups.

Hazelrigg, Lawrence E., "A Reexamination of Simmel's 'The Secret and the Secret Society': Nine Propositions," *Social Forces*, 43 (March 1969): 323-329. A theoretical analysis of Simmel's 1906 article on the characteristics of secret organizations. Most of the organizations referred to in the discussion are political or religious in nature.

Jack, Homer A., "'SANE' as a Voluntary Organization," in D. B. Robertson, ed., *Voluntary Associations: A Study of Groups in Free Societies.* Richmond, Virginia, John Knox Press, 1966.

Janowitz, Gayle, *Helping Hands.* Chicago, University of Chicago Press, 1966.

Jenkins, Edward C., *Philanthropy in America.* New York, Association Press, 1950.

Johnson, Charles S., "National Organizations in the Field of Race Relations," *The Annals of the American Academy of Political and Social Science*, 244 (March 1946): 117-127. After a general survey of seventy-five organizations dealing with race relations problems on a national basis, Johnson focuses on such well-known civil rights organizations as the NAACP and the National Urban League.

Judkins, Jay, *National Associations of the United States.* Washington, D.C., United States Department of Commerce, 1949.

Kellogg, Charles Flint, *NAACP.* Volume I. Baltimore, Johns Hopkins Press, 1967. This volume deals with the history of the National Association for the Advancement of Colored People from its establishment in 1909 to 1920.

King, C. Wendell, *Social Movements in the United States.* New York, Random House, 1956.

Klein, Philip, and collaborators, *A Social Study of Pittsburgh.* New York, Columbia University Press, 1948 (published for the Social Study of Pittsburgh and Allegheny County). In this survey of the agencies and institutions providing social and health services in the Pittsburgh area, there is some discussion of the groups formed by various ethnic communities.

Knapp, Betsy, and Mary Guyol, "Learning by Doing with the League of Women Voters," *The Journal of Social Issues*, 16.1 (1960): 57-65.

Kunz, Phillip R., "Sponsorship and Organizational Stability: Boy Scout Troops," *American Journal of Sociology*, 74 (May 1969): 666-675. Study utilizing a national probability sample of Boy Scout troops indicates that the type of sponsor has little effect on the activities of the troop. The author views sponsorship as a special case of interorganizational relations, with the organization being sponsored using other organizations to implement its program.

Levine, Sol, and Paul E. White, "Exchange as a Conceptual Framework for the Study of Inter-organizational Relationships," *Administrative Science Quarterly*, 5 (March 1961): 583-601.

Lieberson, Stanley, and Irving L. Allen, Jr., "Location of National Headquarters of Voluntary Associations," *Administrative Science Quarterly*, 8 (December 1963): 316-338. An attempt to demonstrate that the location of group head-quarters is related to the functions performed by the headquarters, the suitability of certain areas for such functions, and the distribution of the groups' membership. Nearly 60 percent of all headquarters of groups, including unions and professional and trade associations, were found to be located in New

York, Washington, and Chicago. Washington appears to be gaining as a center for association headquarters and a positive correlation was found between organizations having lobbyists and location in Washington.

Likert, Rensis, *New Patterns of Management.* New York, McGraw Hill, 1961. In Chapter 10 Likert summarizes the results of research on the effectiveness of League of Women Voters' chapters in relation to organization structure and leadership. He deals with research studies by the Institute for Social Research of the University of Michigan which are reported on in full in the Institute's five reports on the League.

Lincoln, C. Eric, *The Black Muslims in America.* Boston, Beacon Press, 1961. The first full length study (by the man who coined the descriptive phrase "Black Muslims") of a group claiming some 100,000 or more adherents. The book originated as a dissertation and is carefully researched.

McKown, Harry C., *Extracurricular Activities.* New York, Macmillan, 1927. McKown's book is addressed to school officials and is filled with descriptions of various types of school activities and of some youth organizations operating outside the schools. McKown argues that extracurricular activities are vital to the educational process since they provide opportunities for practicing the habits of good citizenship. In general, the book is superficial in character and does not reflect actual research on the operation of school activity groups.

McWorter, Gerald A., and Robert L. Crain, "Subcommunity Gladitorial Competition: Civil Rights Leadership as a Competitive Process," *Social Forces,* 46 (September 1967): 8-21. A somewhat inconclusive and sloppily done study of the factors that cause variation in the degree and kind of leadership competition in and among civil rights organizations, and the way this competition affects the success of the movement.

March, James G., "Group Norms and the Active Minority," *American Sociological Review,* 19 (December 1954): 733-741.

Marts, Armaud C., *Philanthropy's Role in Civilization.* New York, Harper and Brothers, 1953. A very general, unscholarly survey of the history of philanthropy with an emphasis on American "generosity" in support of a variety of institutions including voluntary associations. Marts describes his own experience as a professional fund raiser.

Marx, Gary T., and Michael Unseem, "Majority Involvement in Minority Movements: Civil Rights, Abolition, and Untouchability," *Journal of Social Issues,* 27.1 (1971): 81-104.

Matthews, Donald R., and James W. Prothro, *Negroes and the New Southern Politics.* New York, Harcourt, Brace and World, 1966. Although the authors' focus is on other aspects of politics, they do deal with Negro organizations insofar as these enter the political process.

Merrifield, Charles, ed., *Leadership in Voluntary Enterprise.* New York, Oceana, 1961. A collection of readings designed to be used in a training course for voluntary organization leaders. Such topics as the social context in which organizations work; the social philosophy of voluntary organizations; leadership techniques; and the character of democratic organizations are covered.

Messinger, Sheldon L., "Organizational Transformation: A Case Study of a Declining Social Movement," *American Sociological Review,* 20 (February 1955): 3-10.

Meyerand, Gladys, "Women's Organizations," in Edwin R. A. Seligman and Alvin Johnson, eds., *The Encyclopedia of the Social Sciences.* New York, Macmillan, 1935. A dated discussion of the topic which includes some useful historical data.

Milgram, Stanley, and Hans Toch, "Collective Behavior: Crowds and Social Movements," in Gardner Lindzey and Elliot Aronson, eds., *The Handbook of Social Psychology.* Second edition, volume IV, pp. 507-610. Reading, Massachusetts, Addison-Wesley, 1969. A general review of the field of social movements, of which Hans Toch is a leading practitioner.

Miller, Elizabeth W., compiler, *The Negro in America.* Second edition revised and enlarged, compiled by Mary L. Fisher. Cambridge, Harvard University Press, 1970. A bibliography.

Minnis, Mhyra S., "The Relationship of Women's Organizations to the Social Structure of a City." Unpublished PhD dissertation, Yale University, 1951.

Moley, Raymond, Jr., *The American Legion Story.* New York, Duell, Sloan and Pearce, 1966. A polemical defense of this controversial organization with a foreword by J. Edgar Hoover.

Monroe, Donald, and Keith Monroe, *How to Succeed in Community Service.* Philadelphia, J. B. Lippincott, 1962. Advice for the volunteer.

Moore, Joan M., "Exclusiveness and Ethnocentrism in a Metropolitan Upper-Class Agency," *Pacific Sociological Review,* 5 (Spring 1962): 16-20.

Motz, Anabelle Bender, Wayne C. Rohrer, and Patricia Dagilaitis, "American Sociological Regional Societies: Social Characteristics of Presidents," *Sociological Inquiry,* 35 (Spring 1965): 207-218. A discussion of the types of men — in terms of age, mobility, academic training, occupational position during presidency, and number of years in the profession — who are chosen as presidents of the sociological regional societies.

Naylor, Harriet H., *Volunteers Today: Finding, Training and Working with Them.* New York, Association Press, 1967. The book includes a bibliography of similar works on training volunteers.

Odegard, Peter, *Pressure Politics: The Story of the Anti-Saloon League.* New York, Columbia University Press, 1928. A pioneering study by a noted political scientist of activities of a highly successful voluntary association.

Pence, Owen E., *The Y.M.C.A. and Social Need.* New York, Association Press, 1939.

Pendry, Elizabeth, and Hugh Hartshorn, *Organizations for Youth.* New York, McGraw Hill, 1935. The authors have used the literature of the organizations and information gathered through questionnaires to construct capsule descriptions of youth associations as their leaders view them. The focus is on "character education."

Perrow, C., "Organizational Prestige: Some Functions and Dysfunctions," *American Journal of Sociology,* 66 (January 1961): 335-341. A theoretical discussion of organization prestige. Perrow is not primarily concerned with voluntary organizations, and uses a hospital for most of his illustrations.

—— "Organizations: Organizational Goals," in David Sills, ed., *International En-*

cyclopedia of the Social Sciences, 11:305–311. New York, Macmillan
Company and The Free Press, 1968. A general discussion with some reference
to studies of the goals of voluntary associations, particularly to the work of
David Sills in *The Volunteers.*

Pierce, Bessie, *Citizens Organizations and the Civic Training of Youth.* New York,
Charles Scribner's Sons, 1933. This report of the Commission on the Social
Studies of the American Historical Association is devoted to an examination
of a number of organizations, their programs and policies as they affect in-
struction in American public schools. There is an extensive bibliography listing
many articles from the publications of voluntary organizations as well as other
materials.

Rein, Martin, "The Transition from Social Movement to Organization," in William
A. Glaser and David L. Sills, eds., *The Government of Associations.* Totowa,
New Jersey, The Bedminster Press, 1966. This is an excerpt from a PhD dissertation tracing the growth of the birth control movement founded by Margaret
Sanger. Rein focuses on the organization characteristics of the Planned Parenthood Federation of America which was founded to carry out the movement's
goals.

Robison, Joseph B., "Organizations Promoting Civil Rights and Liberties," *Annals
of the American Academy of Political and Social Science,* 274 (May 1951):
18–26. Robison, an attorney with the American Jewish Congress at the time
of writing, describes in general terms the activities of the American Civil
Liberties Union and other groups in the field. Very superficial.

Rohrer, Wayne C., and A. B. Motz, "The Presidency in Three Learned Societies:
Social Characteristics of the Presidents and Modes of Accession to Office,"
Sociology and Social Research, 46 (April 1962): 271–281. Such characteristics as age and the number of publications before and after holding the presidency are examined.

Rose, Arnold, ed., "The Negro Protest," *The Annals of the American Academy of
Political and Social Science,* 357 (January 1965).

Ruffner, Frederick G., Jr., ed., *Encyclopedia of Associations.* Volume I, Organiza-
tions of the United States; Volume II, Geographic and Executive Index;
Volume III, New Associations. Revised fifth edition. Detroit, Gale Research
Company, 1967.

Schindler-Rainman, Eva, and Ronald Lippitt, *The Volunteer Community.* Washington, D.C., Center for a Voluntary Society, 1971.

Schmidt, Alvin J., and Nicholas Babchuk, "Formal Voluntary Groups and Change
over Time: A Study of Fraternal Associations," in David Horton Smith, Burt
R. Baldwin, and Richard I. Reddy, eds., *Voluntary Action: Theory and Research: Steps towards Synthesis.* Washington, D.C., Center for a Voluntary
Society, forthcoming.

Schnapper, M. B., *The Facts of American Life.* Washington, D.C., Public Affairs
Press, 1960. A general reference work based primarily upon information from
government agencies. Some facts concerning voluntary agencies, including
those engaged in overseas work, are included.

Seeley, John R., Buford H. Junker, Wallace R. Jones, Jr., and N. C. Jenkins, M. T.

Haugh, and I. Miller of Community Surveys, Indianapolis, *Community Chest*
Toronto, University of Toronto Press, 1957. An excellent case study of a
voluntary association. Most of the emphasis is on fund raising but there is
some material on the organization's volunteers.

Senor, James M., "Another Look at the Executive-Board Relationship," in Mayer N.
Zald, ed., *Social Welfare Institutions*. New York, John Wiley, 1965.

Shultz, James, and Marge Shultz, *An Annotated Review of the Literature on Volun
teering*. Occasional Paper Number 9, Center for a Voluntary Society, Washington, D.C., October 1970. Most of the entries deal with volunteer work in
various fields. Much of the material cited has been published by voluntary
organizations and a good deal of it is aimed at an audience of volunteers and
organization officials in charge of finding and training volunteers. The bibliography is reprinted in its entirety in *The Volunteer Community* by Eva
Schindler-Rainman and Ronald Lippitt, which is also a publication of the
Center for a Voluntary Society.

Sills, David. *The Volunteers*. Glencoe, Illinois, The Free Press, 1957.

Simpson, Robert L., and William H. Gulley, "Goals, Environmental Pressures and
Organizational Characteristics," *American Sociological Review*, 27 (June
1962): 344–350. An attempt to find relationships between pressures on
organizations and interna. communication, membership involvement, and
centralization, using questionnaires mailed to a sample of organizations listed
in the *Encyclopedia of Associations*. The validity of the results depends on
the extent to which officers and members of associations can accurately gauge
the organization's centralization and communication and membership involvement.

Smith, Clagett G., and Michael E. Brown, "Communication Structure and Control
Structure in a Voluntary Association," *Sociometry*, 27 (December 1964):
449–468. The article reworks data on the League of Women Voters which was
first presented in Tannenbaum's article on "Control and Effectiveness in a
Voluntary Association," *American Journal of Sociology*, 67 (June 1961): 33–
46.

Steeger, Henry, *You Can Remake America*. Garden City, New York, Doubleday,
1969.

Steiner, Jesse Frederick, *Americans at Play*. New York, McGraw Hill, 1933. One of
a series of monographs prepared for the President's Research Committee on
Social Trends. The two chapters dealing with associations contain statistics
on membership, chapters, growth, and so forth of various organizations and a
discussion of trends in recreational associations and of the activities of different types of organizations. The chapter on rural recreation was written by
E. W. Montgomery.

Stenzel, Anne K., and Helen M. Feeney, *Volunteer Training and Development: A
Manual for Community Groups*. New York, The Seabury Press, 1968.

Stoddard, Ellwyn R., "Organizational Structure and Victim Reaction to Disaster
Relief: A Comparative Analysis of the Salvation Army and the American Red
Cross," *Proceedings of the Southwestern Sociological Association*, 19 (1968):
29–33.

Survey Research Center, Institute for Social Research, University of Michigan, *A

Study of the League of Women Voters of the United States. Five volumes.
Ann Arbor, Michigan, Survey Research Center, 1956-1958 Report I, "The
League Member Talks about the League," October 1956. Report II, "Com-
munity Attitudes toward the League," February 1957. Report III, "Some
Problems of League Membership: Cross-sectional, Membership, and Member
Activity," August 1957. Report IV, "Organizational Phase: Factors in League
Functioning," August 1957. Report V, "Organizational Phase: Factors in
League Effectiveness," April 1958.

Swift, Henry, and Elizabeth Swift, *Community Groups and You.* New York, John
Day, 1964.

Tannenbaum, A. S., "Control and Effectiveness in a Voluntary Organization,"
American Journal of Sociology, 67 (July 1961): 33–46.

Warner, W. Keith, and David L. Rogers, "Some Correlates of Control in Voluntary
Farm Organizations," *Rural Sociology,* 36 (September 1971): 326–339.

Westin, Alan F., "The John Birch Society: Fundamentalism on the Right," in H. R.
Mahood, ed., *Pressure Groups in American Politics.* New York, Charles
Scribner's Sons, 1967. An analysis of the structure and beliefs of the John
Birch Society and its founder Robert Welch. This essay originally appeared in
Commentary magazine (32:93–104, August 1961).

Whalen, William J., *Handbook of Secret Organizations.* Milwaukee, The Bruce Pub-
lishing Company, 1966.

White, Martha, ed., *The Next Step.* Cambridge, Radcliffe College, 1964.

Willerman, Ben, and Leonard Swanson, "Group Prestige in Voluntary Organizations:
A Study of College Sororities," *Human Relations,* 6.1 (1953): 57–77.

World Almanac and Book of Facts. New York, Newspaper Enterprise Association,
1971. There is a list of associations and societies in the United States in this
annual publication. The address of the organization, year of founding, number
of members, and the name of the national secretary or executive is given. The
source of the information is the World Almanac Questionnaire.

Yale Law Journal Editors, "The American Medical Association," in William A.
Glaser and David L. Sills, eds., *The Government of Associations.* Totowa, New
Jersey, The Bedminster Press, 1966. Description of the structure of the AMA,
a discussion of the reasons for membership and nonmembership, and an analysis of the "real power structure" in the organization.

Zald, Mayer N., *Organizational Change.* Chicago, The University of Chicago Press,
1970. Zald generates a model of organization change from his study of the
Chicago YMCA as part of the international YMCA, using concepts drawn from
structural-functional and systems analysis and the exchange theories of political economists such as Buchanan and Tullock.

Zald, Mayer N., and Patricia Denton, "From Evangelism to General Service: The
Transformation of the Y.M.C.A.," *Administrative Science Quarterly,* 8 (September 1963): 214–234.

Zanden, James W. Vander, "The Klan Revival," *American Journal of Sociology,* 65
(March 1969): 456–462. An examination of the Klan revival as a resistance
organization since 1955. Zander is particularly concerned with the occupational positions of Klansmen.

Zinn, Howard, *SNCC.* Boston, Beacon Press, 1964.

Chapter Eight   Pointing to the Future

VOLUNTEERS IN GOVERNMENT SERVICE

The line between private voluntary action and the public sphere of government activity has become increasingly blurred in the second half of the twentieth century. Beginning most conspicuously with the Peace Corps, a whole new area of voluntary service, differing in at least two important ways from traditional voluntary service, has been created. In the first place, such service takes place within the institutional structure of a government bureaucracy; moreover, the work of the volunteer is full-time and salaried (although the pay is minimal, a feature which sup-posedly helps preserve the "voluntary" character of the service). How-ever, as J. Norman Parmer points out in his introduction to the May 1966 issue of *The Annals of the American Academy of Political and Social Science* which is completely devoted to the Peace Corps: "The idea of the Peace Corps is not so novel when seen in historical perspec-tive. In one sense, it represents a secularization, and perhaps a bureaucra-tization, of the volunteer tradition in American life. Peace Corps Volunteers are doing, in greater numbers and without religious connota-tions, much of the same work which church and church-inspired groups have done for many years. In an age when people look increasingly to government to provide organizational leadership and financial means, when the need abroad is so great, and when the number who might be tapped for volunteer work is so large, the appearance of the Peace Corps on the American scene is, perhaps, not so surprising" (p. ix).

Both Charles Wetzel (in his contribution to the *Annals*) and Robert Carey (in his book *The Peace Corps*) discuss the roots of the Peace Corps in the missionary work of religious groups; the peace seeking movements which first appeared in the colonial period of United States history; the American traditions of stewardship, humanitarian concern for others, and practical idealism; various government progenitors of the Peace Corps; and the activities of private organizations such as the Experiment in International Living, the International Voluntary Services, the American Friends Service Committee, and Operation Cross- roads Africa which served as an impetus to the Peace Corps and models for its operation. Carey and Wetzel also note that the United Nations and various other governments had established programs like the Peace Corps before its founding in March 1961.

Together, the Carey book, which is a straightforward journalistic history of the Peace Corps, and the essays in the *Annals* give a fairly thorough account of the founding and development of the Peace Corps; the selection and training of volunteers; the individual programs of the Corps; the characteristics of the volunteers; and the problems en- countered by the volunteers in the field and upon their return to the United States. In addition, the two works contain bibliographic informa- tion and references which should guide the reader to the rest of the literature dealing with the Peace Corps.

It is interesting to note that the Peace Corps, like many voluntary as- sociations, found it difficult to recruit minority group members and to attract a representative cross section of the population. Carey reports that in the first eight years of the Corps operation, approximately 75 percent of the volunteers and trainees were twenty-five years old or younger; 33 percent were female; 96 percent had some college educa- tion; 80 percent had at least an undergraduate degree, mostly in the liberal arts (p. 79). Though the Peace Corps was initially very successful in attracting recruits, it has experienced increasing difficulty as many of the students who formerly joined the Corps turn to its domestic counterpart VISTA (Volunteers In Service To America) and to com- munity action, under either private or government auspices. At present the Corps is placing greater emphasis on attracting volunteers with specific skills rather than liberal arts graduates without training in a vocation (Carey, p. 226).

According to Lawrence Fuchs, who directed the large Peace Corps program in the Philippines from July 1961 to June 1963, the volunteers are "usually individualistic and restless" young people dissatisfied with "institutional and organizational life" and anxious to do "something as individuals on their own." The volunteers joined the Peace Corps because it seemed to offer them the opportunity to do that something. However, they quickly discovered that they had volunteered to join a government bureaucracy which would supervise and regulate most of their lives during their two years of service. Moreover, they found themselves forced to turn to the bureaucracy for even more support and help than it had originally been prepared to give. Many volunteers experienced a good deal of psychological stress as they continued to mouth their anti-organization, individualistic rhetoric while demanding services from a government organization. The Peace Corps administration exacerbated the situation by promoting an "anti-organizational ideology through the cult of the volunteer" (*The Volunteer Aspect of Being a Peace Corps*, pp. 1–7).

In Fuch's opinion, the returning volunteers are even more individualistic, restless, and hostile to organized life in the United States than before their departure. Having experienced high status and certain freedoms abroad, they tend to be frustrated by the collapse of that status; the end of responsibility; the narrowing of their freedom; and their resulting sense of impotence in the large, impersonal, bureaucratized country that is America. Fuchs believes that the volunteers will have to learn to be effective within institutions and organizations before they can be a potent force for change in the United States (pp. 9–10).

The Peace Corps is aware of the "reentry" crises experienced by volunteers and has established programs to help the returnee adjust. So far the greatest number of returnees have gone back to school (38 percent), while 31 percent have become teachers, 29 percent have gone to work for government agencies (many filling staff positions in the Corps), 19 percent have entered business organizations, and 10 percent have joined nonprofit organizations (Carey, pp. 216–217). Many of these choices represent a change in career plans as a result of the experience abroad.

The reentry crisis of returning Peace Corps volunteers should give pause to those who are inclined to assume participation is good for both society and the individual, teaching individuals how to play within the rules of the system and insuring that they will behave as good citizens of a democracy should. In some situations the experience of importance and power as a volunteer may radicalize the individual, making him impatient with his role as a much less powerful and important person within the larger society. A priori assumptions about the effect of participation are not valid. Careful empirical investigation of the effects of different types of participatory experiences on various types of individuals in a variety of situations needs to be conducted before any assertions can be made about the consequences of the volunteer experience.

The favorable reception given to the Peace Corps was one of the factors which led to the development of domestic counterparts in the forms of the Community Action Program of the War on Poverty and VISTA, which was closely associated with CAP although not actually a part of it. Such private projects as the community organizations created by the self-styled "professional radical" Saul Alinsky and the Mobilization for Youth program to combat juvenile delinquency in New York, which was cosponsored by the Ford Foundation and several government bodies, also served as prototypes for the domestic Peace Corps. Moreover, other private voluntary groups, particularly the civil rights organizations, helped lay the basis for rapid implementation of the community participation phases of the War on Poverty (see Rubin in *The Annals of the American Academy of Political and Social Science,* 385:17).

Although the Community Action Programs, which are required by law to mobilize community resources and to be "developed, conducted and administered with the maximum feasible participation of residents of the areas and members of the groups served" (78 Statutes at Large, vol. 508, sec. 202a), have aroused a storm of controversy, VISTA has been viewed as less of a departure from the American voluntary tradition and has met with proportionately less opposition. In *The Great Society's Poor Law,* one of the most balanced assessments of the antipoverty program, Sar Levitan notes that VISTA's mission was originally defined somewhat imprecisely as that of being a "vehicle for citizen participation in the national effort to combat poverty" and a "national clearinghouse for volunteers" which would develop full-time skilled manpower to fill various "acute needs." The hope was also expressed by the founders that the volunteers would choose "to enter careers of service to the needy" (p. 216). VISTA volunteers are supposed to serve at the request of a sponsor in any public or nonprofit organization working with the poor. Each volunteer is given a minimal living allowance plus a stipend of $600. When overhead is included, the annual cost of a full-time volunteer to the government is approximately $7000 (p. 223).

In its first few years of operation, VISTA had some difficulty attracting volunteers, since many of the college students who are the major source of applicants preferred the Peace Corps. However, VISTA's appeal gradually increased as domestic affairs became more important to the students, and by 1968 VISTA had filled its quota of volunteers. In that year there were more than 5000 full-time volunteers in the field plus another 1600 students working during their summer vacations in VISTA Associates and approximately 40,000 private citizens working without pay in the Citizens' Volunteers Corps (Levitan, pp. 218–219). Both Levitan's book and the less analytic account in the Facts on File publication *War on Poverty,* edited by Louise Lander, provide descriptions of the work done by VISTA volunteers, as well as general accounts of the workings of the entire antipoverty program.

Although the volunteers are given some training, they generally bring no special skills to the job and in many cases they perform simple tasks that might better be done by the poor. There is some evidence that VISTA volunteers, only 10 percent of whom are from the ranks of the poor, have been unable to communicate with their clients and have alienated portions of the communities in which they worked. Landers reports that there are indications that the volunteers are sometimes resented by the poor, and that the poor would prefer to receive direct material benefits rather than being the object of campaigns to organize their own self-help programs (p. 131).

Given the vagueness of its goals and the impossibility of evaluating the nonmaterial benefits of the program, there is no way of assessing VISTA's real contribution to the War on Poverty. Some observers believe that its major impact has been on the middle class student volunteers instead of the poor. A study of the volunteers by David Gottleib, a sociologist affiliated with Pennsylvania State University at the time the research was conducted, does in fact show that the volunteers experienced considerable radicalization as compared with a control group of similar individuals who did not serve in the program. Almost all of the 11,000 volunteers studied by Gottleib moved to the left, while about one third became radical. About two thirds of the volunteers under 30 reported a negative response to their contacts with government and social agencies and 48 percent of these young volunteers said they were suspicious of all government-sponsored social change programs. Many of the volunteers changed their career decisions in the direction of an increased commitment to solve the social problems of the country and a lesser interest in monetary rewards (reported in the New York *Times,* May 24, 1971).

While VISTA volunteers have engaged in some of the controversial political organization of the poor which has dismayed members of the political establishment and intensified conflict in numerous communities, their activities in this area have been overshadowed by those of the Community Action Program. This is not the place to review the debate over CAP, which has alternately been praised as a great innovation and damned as a middle class professional social scientist's ill-informed and ill-formed attempt to forment rebellion. Proponents of CAP acknowledge the defects in the execution of the program but argue that in balance the idea of maximal feasible participation has, as Lillian Rubin puts it: "captured the imagination of the leaders of the poor with the force of an idea whose time has come. It has helped to validate and legitimate the aspirations of the poor and the minorities in America for self-determination" (p. 29). Sanford Kravitz and Ferne K. Kolodner, who have both been associated officially with the CAP, claim that the program has "linked low-income people to critical resources" such as education and health; "increased the accessibility of available critical services"; contributed to the creation of competent communities by developing in and among the poor the capacity for leadership, problem-solving, and participation"; and "contributed in some degree to the re-structuring of community service institutions to assure flexibility, responsiveness, respect, and true relatedness to the problems faced by the poor" (*Annals of the American Academy of Political and Social Science,* 385:39).

Opponents have leveled a variety of charges against CAP. In his book *Maximum Feasible Misunderstanding* former presidential adviser Daniel Moynihan characterizes CAP as an ill-conceived venture based on un-proven theories about the relationship between poverty and participa-tion and a confusion of purposes, since for various people community action has meant organizing the power structure, expanding it, assisting it, or confronting it (p. 168). After conceding that the CAP may have played a major role in the "formation of an urban Negro leadership echelon" (p. 129), Moynihan proceeds to thoroughly indict community action: "Over and again, the attempt by official and quasi-official agen-cies (such as the Ford Foundation) to organize poor communities led first to the radicalization of the middle-class persons who began the effort; next to a certain amount of stirring among the poor, but ac-companied by heightened racial antagonism *on the part of the poor* [his italics] if they happened to be black; next to retaliation from the larger white community; whereupon it would emerge that the community action agency, which had talked so much, been so much in the head-lines, promised so much in the way of change in the fundamentals of things, was powerless" (pp. 134–135).

Undoubtedly the Community Action Program did radicalize and in-crease hostilities in many cases, but the program also included Project Head Start and the neighborhood health centers which did provide some genuine benefits to the poor. Since CAP encompasses a mixed bag of projects ranging from recreation centers to preschool education and birth control programs, it is even more difficult to evaluate its effects than it is to analyze those of VISTA. Sar Levitan, one of the fairer, more level-headed commentators, points out that CAP is not really a program, but a "strategy for combating poverty," and notes that: "An objective evaluation of the CAA's (Community Action Agencies), and particularly of the role of the poor in these programs should compare the CAP-funded agencies with traditional welfare organizations rather than with some ideal model. On that score CAP must certainly be judged an inno-vative agency which gave the poor their first social and political role" (p. 131).

To the observer, one of the most striking aspects of the entire Office of Economic Opportunity (OEO) experience is the extent to which hy-potheses concerning the causes and cures of poverty and the importance of participation by members of a community in decision-making proved inadequate, with the result that policy makers were constantly faced with consequences they had failed to anticipate. If Moynihan is even partly right in fixing responsibility for the community action programs on the professional reformers and the social scientists who argued that a sense of community was a desperate need of alienated modern man, then certainly all those who advance the voluntary association as a uni-versal solution to the problems of the individual and society ought to have some sober second thoughts.

THE VOLUNTEER IN SOCIAL WELFARE ORGANIZATIONS

Volunteer work within the context of a government bureaucracy should be seen as an extension of an earlier movement toward the pro-fessionalization and bureaucratization of social welfare services (see Lubove, *The Professional Altruist*). Where these services were once the work of well-off volunteers engaging in charitable (and often patroni-zing) acts, they are now performed by professional social workers who are employed by private organizations or, increasingly, by the government. Volunteers still engage in social welfare, but they do so within the context of an institution which is run by a paid professional staff. It is probably fair to say that with this transition the volunteer's importance has lessened and that he or she has frequently become the instrument of the staff. In recent years, there has also been a tendency for the government to take over many of the functions previously performed by private organizations; to create agencies which work in the same fields as the private groups and which often cooperate with them in joint ventures; and to provide funds for the private organizations. As a result, it is almost impossible to tell where private action ends and government action begins. This absorption of the volunteer and the private organization into the government nexus not only places the volunteer in a setting far different from that envisaged by the classical pluralists, but also compromises the role of private organizations as buffers between the individual and the state and as checks on the state.

Various contributions in the 1965 *Encyclopedia of Social Work,* particularly those by Gordon Manser on "Voluntary Organization for Social Welfare," Violet M. Sieder on "Volunteers," Robert E. Bondy on "National Voluntary Organizations," Donald S. Howard on the "Relationships between Governmental and Voluntary Social Welfare Agencies," and Richard S. Bachman on "State, Regional, and Local Voluntary Organization," tell the story of volunteer organizations and the volunteer in social welfare activities. The Encyclopedia includes a directory of international voluntary agencies and of agencies in the United States and Canada, listing the address, director, membership, purpose, activities, and publications of each organization. There is also considerable descriptive material in *Grass Roots Private Welfare,* a 1957 collection of essays by workers in the welfare field which is edited by Alfred de Grazia.

Religious institutions have been especially active in sponsoring social welfare work. The reader can find a general description of the role of volunteers in Catholic, Protestant, and Jewish social work agencies in a monograph by the directors of such programs (Rahn, Gallagher, and Bernstein, *The Social Work Volunteer under Sectarian Auspices*). The discussion sheds some light on the religious origins of the cultural values which give support to volunteering in American society. Several of the essayists in the *Encyclopedia of Social Work* also emphasize the Judeo-Christian ethic as a significant source of voluntarism.

The network of organizations which solicit funds from the public for health or welfare activities in which they engage has grown from its origins in nineteenth century charitable activities and the American Charity Organizations Society formed in 1877 to a complex of several hundred thousand groups with a total budget of more than 10 billion (Manser, p. 825). Although no one knows precisely how many volunteers are involved in these activities, their number is probably well in the millions.

Until very recently, the volunteer leaders of the welfare councils and service organizations have almost always been white Protestant businessmen and their wives. Since these businessmen have also provided the funds for operating the organizations, it is not inaccurate to view the "traditional voluntary non-governmental service organizations as essentially the public, or community, expression of the private enterprise system" (to quote David Austin's *The Black Civic Volunteer Leaders,* a monograph on the newly emerging civic leaders from the inner city, minority groups, p. 2). According to Austin and David Westby, whom Austin cites, business leaders were attracted to volunteer civic work after the Civil War because participation in city government itself was no longer feasible. Together, the professionalization of politics with the concurrent development of political offices into full-time jobs and the electoral victories of immigrant blocs effectively drove businessmen from the party and administrative posts they had once held. As a result a "civic sphere" consisting of those "formally nonpolitical but public activities considered by the community in general as 'public-interest serving'" was established in American cities (Westby, in *Social Forces,* 45:162-163). As Austin notes: "The pattern of civic leadership which emerged had several important and persisting characteristics. Access to corporate wealth was as important as the possession of personal wealth. Both corporations and the community came to expect that part of the responsibility of corporation executives was to represent the public image of the company in civic and community service activities. Community service organizations were expected to be nonpolitical and civic leaders were often anti-political. The justification of many civic enterprises was a determination to 'keep government out,' to restrict the scope of government activities, and to keep local taxes low" (p. 6).

Aside from providing financial support and some management expertise, the businessman civic leader's main function was to legitimize the welfare organization. Although the entire boards of directors of the organizations were theoretically responsible to the public, there were no formal mechanisms to insure the accountability of the boards and the organizations to the community at large (Austin, p. 7). Under such sponsorship, the welfare organization tended to be a conservative institution, generally supporting the status quo and avoiding real innovation. Insofar as the social work profession and its organizations focused attention on alleviating the problems of particular individuals rather than promoting systematic change, and insofar as their work served to manage societal tensions thereby preventing an explosion, one might indeed regard them as rather important guardians of the established order. If this were not the case, the millions required to support them would be much more difficult to obtain.

There are a number of studies which deal with the businessman's role as a volunteer in the "civic sphere." Charles Willie analyzed the boards of directors of the Community Chest and Welfare Council in Syracuse, New York, from 1921 to 1958 (in Gouldner and Miller, *Applied Sociology*). He found that the community leaders in the voluntary health and welfare system were largely male, city dwelling business and professional persons, with the businessmen outnumbering the professionals by two to one. In general the role of the professionals was limited to the planning of services. Aileen Ross found a similar pattern in an eastern Canadian city (in Zald, *Social Welfare Institutions*). Business institutions there control the city's philanthropic activity and social welfare organizations, and sponsorship by the business elite is necessary in order to attain a high position in the voluntary civic sphere. Moreover, the business community appears to use voluntary activity as a testing ground for its executive talent, and the executive must participate to advance in his career. The firm values participation for the exposure given to both itself and the individual.

A more recent study indicated that this basic pattern remains the same, but that the establishment of "contemporary" organizations of the community action type which include representatives of the client groups may lead to some changes. Writing in the *Harvard Business Review* of April-May 1971, Dan H. Fenn, Jr., reports that a survey he conducted in conjunction with Daniel Yankelowich's polling organization for the Center for a Voluntary Society revealed that businessmen's participation is increasing. Over 83 percent of the 400 respondents reported that they were active in two or more organizations. While altruism and a concern for the problems of society played some role in generating this degree of activity, the existence of company policies encouraging and rewarding such activity was found to be crucial.

As in the past, executive volunteers tended to come primarily from larger companies and to be concerned primarily with fund raising and internal administrative problems. The businessmen did not play a direct leadership role in the on-going organization work, although the staffs told the interviewers that they wished the businessmen would do so. Older businessmen had particular difficulty in taking leadership roles in the contemporary type of organization. Fenn believes the businessman must relate to these contemporary organizations and function effectively within their heterogeneous, activist milieu; and is hopeful that the younger businessmen whom he found to be more involved in community groups will be able to adjust to the newer kind of organization.

It seems clear that the hegemony of businessmen in the civic sphere is being challenged by the new brand of activists and by the organizations they have established (Fenn's contemporary type). As David Austin points out in his monograph on the black civic leader, the rise of these leaders and organizations is intimately connected with the Community Action Programs of the War on Poverty and with the changing character of American cities. The requirement of maximum feasible participation of the poor in the Community Action Agencies resulted in diminishing the importance of the businessman civic leader on agency boards, who came to be regarded as a representative of special interests often hostile to the poor rather than a representative of the public interest as was formerly the case. The poor now have their own representatives who as members of minority groups and (frequently) of the poor differ significantly from the businessman volunteer in values, age, status in the community, occupation, income, and group identification. At the same time, in many cities a series of new voluntary organizations have been created within the black communities. Austin notes: "Some of these organizations were sparked by Community Action Agencies and received funds from them. Others have been established out of dissatisfaction with OEO programs. Others developed quite independently of anti-poverty programs. The central characteristic of all of them, however, is that formal control of the organizations rests with black volunteer civic leaders and traditional, white volunteer civic leaders have been largely excluded from any position of authority" (p. 25). With this shift in leadership, the traditional separation between the civic and political spheres is also breaking down. For the black leader who has made his reputation in protest activities, leadership in community service activities becomes inseparable from leadership in politics. The pose of disinterested altruism is not a part of the black leader's voluntarism, since his personal interests as a member of the black community and as a career activist are at stake in his civic service activities (see Austin, pp. 32–33).

Austin predicts that the increasing partisanship of the new leader will result in more open conflict and may even "lead to the collapse of voluntary, community-wide, fund-raising and planning organizations" in some communities. Competition among the new organizations combined with moves to decentralize the voluntary, nongovernment sector and establish community control may well alter the pattern of voluntarism in this country. Austin argues that: "One outcome of the competitive struggle within black communities could be the creation within the black community of a new pattern of citizen participation in civic affairs in which traditional distinctions between governmental and nongovernmental activities and between community service programs and economic activities disappear. Individuals drawn from a wide variety of economic backgrounds, age groups, and with different social philosophies would carry responsibilities as policy-makers, volunteer workers, and employed staff in programs operated for the direct benefit of community residents. If it is not possible to develop a community pattern which has both diversity and unity, the result may be a costly replication in a black ghetto of the institutional structures of the larger community, substituting an essentially middle-class black volunteer leadership for middle-class white leadership and black professionals directing programs in place of white professional administrators" (pp. 36–37).

A CONCLUDING NOTE

Although interest in voluntarism has markedly quickened in the last few years, this concern has not been matched by the formulation of realistic proposals for engaging individuals in meaningful voluntary activity nor for democratizing the voluntary association nor even, to begin with, a clear headed analysis of the characteristics and functions of volunteering and voluntary associations. There is a great deal of sloppy romantic thinking about voluntarism. With the exception of a few analysts, most of the advocates of voluntarism fail even to make the fundamental distinction between volunteering and the voluntary association. As George Pickering points out in his paper on *Voluntarism and the American Way,* the emphasis of such advocates as Richard Nixon is on volunteering rather than on the voluntary association. In the process volunteering may well be turned into another mass activity and the voluntary association may suffer. It is, says Pickering, the associations alone which can serve the functions of protecting the individual against the government and of promoting alternatives to government policy and the current social order (pp. 8-10).

Not enough attention and thought are being given to the institutionalization and bureaucratization of voluntary activities. Too frequently volunteers are used as agents of the government or other institutions; they are used to raise funds and give the stamp of legitimacy to the work of professionals, whose major concern may be in perpetuating the conditions which give them their livelihood, rather than in promoting social change or protecting the interests of the supposed beneficiaries of their ministrations. As many Peace Corps and VISTA volunteers have discovered, community development programs are frequently not a step toward restoring the dignity and importance of the individual and developing participatory democracy, but rather an attempt to coopt and emasculate genuine grassroots leaders and organizations.

Too often voluntary action is proposed as a cure-all for a variety of social ills, preventing any real effort to analyze and promote the structural, institutional changes which would be necessary to eliminate the causes of those ills. The enthusiasm of the Nixons for volunteering no doubt partly reflects the fact that volunteering as they conceive of it has the virtue of not changing or challenging the basic power structure. The individual is diverted and possibly some bandaids are applied to the structure, but that is all. Equally helpful to the "system," the individual is "socialized"; he learns to play by the rules of the game. Insofar as he does not (in VISTA, for example), the guilty agency will be eliminated.

While it is necessary to understand how voluntarism can be "routinized" and turned to the advantage of the "establishment," one must not automatically assume that voluntarism must be a conservative institution. What is needed, and is so far totally absent, are some workable solutions to the problems of oligarchy and conservatization. So far academicians have at most documented the existence of such conditions as apathy and oligarchy and bureaucratization. Clearly, one of the tasks now facing those committed to voluntary activity is to spell out how groups can be kept small enough to be meaningful and democratic, while at the same time exercising significant power in the society and performing important services in a reliable and effective way. Alternatives must be developed to the overgrown, national organizations that dominate the association scene at present. At the very least, social scientists need to break out of the current molds and conceive of alternative systems and structures rather than accepting the status quo as the only possible system. The proliferation of self-criticism within the various social sciences indicates that the time may be at hand for some constructive "utopian" thinking.

As this bibliography illustrates, there has been considerable investigation of voluntary associations, but the overall results are unsatisfying. Much of the research has been crude. Generalizations have been made on the basis of very limited samples and inadequate "measuring" instruments. Researchers have often failed to control variables, and there has been almost no attempt to develop theoretical propositions which can be operationalized and tested. All the same, some significant and exciting work has already been done. Almond and Verba's *The Civic Culture*, the Sills study of the National Foundation for Infantile Paralysis, the work of Robert and Barbara Gallatin Anderson, some of the community studies, and the African studies, especially Kenneth Little's work, come to mind. The African studies are particularly important because they shed light on the growth and functioning of organizations in the initial stages of a nation's development. The African studies also represent a contribution to the comparative study of the voluntary association. The development of such a comparative study is encouraging because it should provide the basis for more significant generalization and may help to overcome the ethnocentric character of much of the work on voluntary organizations. The establishment in 1969 of the Center for a Voluntary Society within the National Training Laboratory Institute for Applied Behavioral Science to gather and disseminate information about voluntarism and of the Association of Voluntary Action Scholars and the *Journal of Voluntary Action Research* in 1970 are other hopeful signs that the study of voluntarism may be coming of age. While a beginning has certainly been made in enlarging our understanding of voluntary associations and the volunteer, it is at present barely a beginning.

BIBLIOGRAPHY

Austin, David M., *The Black Civic Volunteer Leaders.* Waltham, Massachusetts, Brandeis University Papers in Social Welfare (Number 20, March 1970; Issue Number 5 in the Harriet Lowenstein Goldstein Series "The Volunteer in America").

Bachman, Richard S., "State, Regional, and Local Voluntary Organization," *Encyclopedia of Social Work,* fifteenth issue, pp. 779–785. New York, National Association of Social Workers, 1965.

Bolstad, Glenna, and S. T. Ginsberg, "Volunteer Services in State Mental Hospitals," *State Government,* 35 (Winter 1962): 53–56. Two professionals in the field describe the uses made of volunteer workers in 208 hospitals surveyed by the National Conference on Mental Health.

Bondy, Robert E., "National Voluntary Organization," *Encyclopedia of Social Work,* fifteenth issue, pp. 526–530. New York, National Association of Social Workers, 1965.

Brager, George, "Commitment and Conflict in a Normative Organization," *American Sociological Review,* 34 (August 1969): 482–491. This study of the Mobilization for Youth, one of the early community action programs, indicates that the relationship between the individual member's commitment to the organization and his reaction to the organization's defensive posture in a conflict is complex, and that the commitment tends to be quite fragile.

Bruyn, Severyn, *Communities in Action.* New Haven, College and University Press, 1963. A general description of community development projects and community self-studies. Of only peripheral interest to the student of voluntary associations, but Bruyn does deal with projects that employ both volunteers and voluntary associations.

Carey, Robert G., *The Peace Corps.* New York, Frederick A. Praeger, 1970.

Curtis, Russell I., Jr., and Louis A. Zurcher, Jr., "Voluntary Associations and the Social Integration of the Poor," *Social Problems,* 18 (Winter 1971): 339–357. An excellent review of the literature concerning the voluntary participation of the poor in OEO organizational bodies. Much of this literature is in mimeographed form or in reports to government agencies and is otherwise unavailable. The authors also briefly review the general literature on the participation of poorer, lower class individuals in voluntary associations.

Dare, Robert, "Involvement of the Poor in Atlanta," *Phylon,* 31 (Summer 1970): 114–128. Report on the participation of the poor in community action programs connected with the Office of Economic Opportunity.

De Grazia, Alfred, ed., *Grass Roots Private Welfare.* New York, New York University Press, 1957.

Ellis, William, *White Ethics and Black Power.* Chicago, Aldine, 1969. An analysis of a black Chicago community organization and its leaders.

Encyclopedia of Social Work. Fifteenth issue. New York, National Association of Social Workers, 1965.

Fenn, Dan H., Jr., *Techniques of Community Responsibility.* Occasional Paper Number 2, Center for a Voluntary Society, Washington, D.C., October 1970.

The author argues that businessmen on the boards of voluntary organizations should play a greater role in helping the organizations set priorities and in improving administrative procedures, particularly in fiscal matters.

—— "Executives as Community Volunteers," *Harvard Business Review*, March-April 1971, pp. 4-16, 156-157.

Ferman, Louis, ed., "Evaluating the War on Poverty," *The Annals of the American Academy of Political and Social Science*, 385 (September 1969). An evaluation by a number of experts of various phases of the poverty program at the end of its first five years.

Franklin, Ben A., "VISTA Volunteers Battle To Save Their Programs from Merger," New York *Times*, May 24, 1971, p. 24.

Freeman, Linton, Warner Bloomberg, Jr., Stephen Koff, Morris H. Sunshine, and Thomas J. Tararo, *Local Community Leadership*. Syracuse, University College of Syracuse University, 1960.

Fuchs, Lawrence A., *The Volunteer Aspect of Being a Peace Corps*. Waltham, Massachusetts, Brandeis University Papers in Social Welfare (Number 12, no date; Issue Number 2 in the Harriet Lowenstein Goldstein Series "The Volunteer in America").

Gove, Walter, and Herbert Costner, "Organizing the Poor: An Evaluation of a Strategy," *Social Science Quarterly*, 50 (December 1969): 643-656. A study of nineteen OEO-sponsored neighborhood clubs in Seattle. Participants in the clubs were found to be drawn from the relatively better-off residents of the neighborhoods.

Hoffer, Joe R., "Adult Education in Voluntary Social Welfare Organizations," in Malcolm Knowles, ed., *Handbook of Adult Education in the United States*, pp. 366-377. Chicago, Adult Education Association, 1960.

Hoopes, Roy, *The Complete Peace Corps Guide*. Fourth edition, New York, Dial Press, 1968. An uncritical treatment of the Corps aimed at prospective volunteers and written with the cooperation of Corps' officials.

Howard, Donald S., "Relationships between Governmental and Voluntary Social Welfare Agencies," *Encyclopedia of Social Work*, fifteenth issue, pp. 649-654. New York, National Association of Social Workers, 1965.

King, Clarence, *Working with People in Community Action*. New York, Association Press, 1965. An international casebook for trained community workers and volunteer community leaders in the United States and abroad. King, a former professor at the Columbia University School of Social Work, gives advice on such matters as approaching the community so as to win its confidence, discovering the needs of the community, using volunteers, and organizing committees and councils. The cases are brief selections describing how such problems were dealt with in many different parts of the world. Most of the cases were taken from the files of the United Nations or the United States International Cooperation Administration.

Kravitz, Sanford, and Ferne K. Kolodner, "Community Action: Where Has It Been? Where Will It Go?" in Louis Ferman, ed., "Evaluating the War on Poverty," *The Annals of the American Academy of Political and Social Science*, 385 (September 1969): 30-40.

Lander, Louise, ed., *War on Poverty*. New York, Facts on File, 1967. A superficial description of the legislation and programs of the War on Poverty based on material from government sources and the press.

Levens, Helene, "Organizational Affiliation and Powerlessness: A Case Study of the Welfare Poor," *Social Problems*, 16 (Summer 1968): 18–32. A comparison of welfare mothers who belonged to a Welfare Recipients League with those who did not belong. League members were found to have decreased feelings of powerlessness.

Levitan, Sar A., *The Great Society's Poor Law*. Baltimore, Johns Hopkins Press, 1969.

Levitte, Mendel, "Adult Education through Voluntary Health Agencies," in Malcolm Knowles, ed., *Handbook of Adult Education in the United States*, pp. 255–262. Chicago, Adult Education Association, 1960.

Lindeman, Eduard, *The Community*. New York, Association Press, 1921. An early work on community leadership and organization.

Lubove, Roy, *The Professional Altruist*. Cambridge, Harvard University Press, 1965. A history of the professionalization of social work covering the years 1880 through 1930.

Manser, Gordon, "Voluntary Organization for Social Welfare," *Encyclopedia of Social Work*, fifteenth issue, pp. 823–829. New York, National Association of Social Workers, 1965.

Marris, Peter, and Martin Rein, *Dilemmas of Social Reform*. New York, Atherton Press, 1967. A fundamental source on Community Action Programs.

Moynihan, Daniel P., *Maximum Feasible Misunderstanding*. New York, Free Press (Macmillan), 1969. An acerbic account of the Community Action Program by a social scientist–policy maker who played a role in the original formulation of the War on Poverty program.

Nathan, Cynthia R., *Client Involvement*. Occasional Paper Number 6, Center for a Voluntary Society, Washington, D.C., October 1970. The Director of the Office of Citizen Participation of HEW argues for the use of clients as volunteers, pointing to the benefits for both the volunteer and the agency. The client-volunteer gains self-respect and skills which may lead to a career, and the agency gains the services and advice of people with intimate knowledge and experience with the problems with which it is concerned. She also notes that agency directors are generally hostile to the use of client-volunteers, and that Congress has therefore on occasion mandated client participation.

National Social Welfare Assembly, *The Role of Voluntary Social Welfare Agencies*. New York, 1961.

New York *Times*, May 24, 1971, pp. 1 and 22, "Life in VISTA Called Radicalizing."

Parmer, J. Norman, ed., "The Peace Corps," *Annals of the American Academy of Political and Social Science*, 365 (May 1966).

Pickering, George W., *Voluntarism and the American Way*. Occasional Paper Number 7, Center for a Voluntary Society, Washington D.C., October 1970.

Pifer, Alan, "The Nongovernmental Organization at Bay," in Carnegie Corporation of New York's *Annual Report*, 1966, pp. 1–15. An analysis of the problems created for voluntary associations when government tasks are delegated to them.

Piven, Frances, "Participation of Residents in Neighborhood Community Action Programs," *Social Work*, 11 (January 1966): 73–80.

Rahn, Sheldon, Raymond J. Gallagher, and Philip Bernstein, *The Social Work Volunteer under Sectarian Auspices.* Waltham, Massachusetts, Brandeis University Papers in Social Welfare (Number 13, no date; Issue Number 3 in the Harriet Lowenstein Goldstein Series "The Volunteer in America").

Rein, Martin, and Robert Morris, "Goals, Structures, and Strategies for Community Change," in Mayer N. Zald, ed., *Social Welfare Institutions.* New York, John Wiley, 1965. A theoretical essay on the types of structures and strategies in community organizations which are appropriate to goals of change or integration. The authors distinguish between strategies of individual and cooperative rationality and between simple and federated structures.

Rezak, Nicholas, "Trends in the Participation of Businessmen in Local Voluntary Affairs," *Sociology and Social Research*, 48 (April 1964): 289–300.

Robbins, Richard, "Local Voluntarism in Race Relations Strategy: The Illinois Experience with Community Human Relations Groups," in Alvin W. Gouldner and S. M. Miller, eds., *Applied Sociology.* New York, Free Press, Macmillan, 1965. Study of local commissions and councils on human relations, all of them voluntary associations affiliated with a state commission. The effectiveness of the groups was found to be minimal to moderate.

Rooff, Madeline, *Voluntary Societies and Social Policy.* London, Routledge and Kegan Paul, 1957. A study of three voluntary services — the Royal National Institute for the Blind, The National Association for Mental Health, and the National Association for Maternity and Child Welfare — documenting the growth of cooperative government and private welfare services.

Ross, Aileen D., "Organized Philanthropy in an Urban Community," *Canadian Journal of Economics and Political Science*, 18 (November 1952): 474–486. Using her studies in "Wellsville," a Canadian city, Ross comments on the changes in philanthropy from 1909 to 1950. She emphasizes the development of organized fund raising campaigns throughout the city, the professionalization of philanthropy, and the dominance of business interests in fund raising campaigns.

—— "The Social Control of Philanthropy," *American Journal of Sociology*, 58 (March 1953): 451–460. On the basis of her interviews with men playing leading parts in the fund raising campaigns of an eastern Canadian city, Ross describes the social norms that support the campaigns. She concentrates on the feeling of obligation individuals have to help their friends and the control of philanthropy by a small group of men. She also deals with the limits of their control.

——"Philanthropic Activity and the Business Career," in Mayer N. Zald, ed., *Social Welfare Institutions.* New York, John Wiley, 1965.

Rothe, Mary Lou, and Christine Newark, "Homemakers in Voluntary Community Activities," *Marriage and Family Living*, 20 (May 1958): 175–178. Describes the participation of married women from the 1890s to the mid-1950s, emphasizing the change in women's attitudes toward volunteer work.

Rubin, Lillian B., "Maximum Feasible Participation: The Origins, Implications, and Present Status," in Louis Ferman, ed., "Evaluating the War on Poverty," *The*

Annals of the American Academy of Political and Social Science, 385 (September 1969): 14–29.

Schindler-Rainman, Eva, "The Day of the Volunteers Is Really Here!" Occasional Paper No. 8, Center for a Voluntary Society, Washington, D.C., October 1970. A superficial discussion of the impact of various societal changes on volunteering together with recommendations to voluntary association leaders for adapting to new conditions.

Sherry, Paul H., ed., "Voluntary Associations and Public Policy," *Journal of Current Social Issues,* Autumn 1971. The entire issue is devoted to a report of a conference held in May 1971.

Sieder, Violet M., "Volunteers," *Encyclopedia of Social Work,* fifteenth issue, pp. 830–837. New York, National Association of Social Workers, 1965.

Silberman, Charles E., *Crisis in Black and White.* New York, Random House, 1964. The last chapter on "The Revolt against 'Welfare Colonialism'" is devoted to a laudatory account of The Woodlawn Organization in Chicago which was created through the efforts of Saul Alinsky.

Stein, Morris I., *Volunteers for Peace.* New York, John Wiley, 1966. A study of the first group of Peace Corps volunteers — their selection, training, motivation, and effectiveness — in the Rural Community Development Program in Colombia.

Textor, Robert, ed., *Cultural Frontiers of the Peace Corps.* Cambridge, The M.I.T. Press, 1966. Fifteen social scientists analyze Peace Corps programs in thirteen different countries. Each author is an expert on the country with which he deals and each has been associated in some capacity with the Peace Corps. The emphasis is on the cultural barriers separating the volunteer from the people he is supposed to serve. There is a brief bibliography and a final summary chapter by Textor.

Westby, David, "The Civic Sphere in the American City," *Social Forces,* 45 (December 1966): 161–169.

Wetzel, Charles J., "The Peace Corps in Our Past," *Annals of the American Academy of Political and Social Science,* 365 (May 1966): 1–11.

Wilensky, Harold L., and Charles N. Lebeaux, *Industrial Society and Social Welfare.* New York, Free Press, 1965. The role of the volunteer in social welfare work in the past and present is discussed.

Willie, Charles V., "Community Leadership in the Voluntary Health and Welfare System," in Alvin W. Gouldner and S. M. Miller, eds., *Applied Sociology.* New York, The Free Press, Macmillan, 1965.

—— "Institutional Vitality and Institutional Alliances," *Sociology and Social Research,* 54 (January 1970): 249–259. Willie argues that the domination of the voluntary health and welfare system by businessmen may have weakened the system.

—— and Herbert Notkin, "Community Organization for Health: A Case Study," in E. Gantly Jaco, ed., *Patients, Physicians and Illness,* pp. 148–159. New York, Free Press, 1958.

Index